Productivity of Contemporary Economies

Productivity of Contemporary Economies:

Theory and Evidence

Edited by

Anton S. Filipenko,
Oleksandra M. Moskalenko
and Yurii K. Zaitsev

Cambridge
Scholars
Publishing

Productivity of Contemporary Economies: Theory and Evidence

Edited by Anton S. Filipenko, Oleksandra M. Moskalenko
and Yurii K. Zaitsev

This book first published 2021

Cambridge Scholars Publishing

Lady Stephenson Library, Newcastle upon Tyne, NE6 2PA, UK

British Library Cataloguing in Publication Data
A catalogue record for this book is available from the British Library

ISBN (10): 1-5275-7311-7
ISBN (13): 978-1-5275-7311-6

TABLE OF CONTENTS

LIST OF ILLUSTRATIONS

List of Tables

FOREWORD

In June 2017, the Institute of International Relations at the Taras Shevchenko National University of Kyiv held an international conference called "Productive ability of nations: Case of Ukraine."

This important event for the scientific community started a discussion on the problem of the productive capacity of countries. In particular, the researchers focused on the causes of variations in the productivity of different economies, conditions for and objectives of productivity growth in different sectors, the economic policy of governments to support national strategies for development and growth, promoting human development, and raising standards of living in modern conditions.

Obviously, the problem of productivity is familiar and relevant to the international scientific community. Economists from various scientific schools directly or indirectly study economic growth and development, multifactor productivity, labour productivity, capital productivity, the impact of IT on the economy, the effects of overflow, and much more on the productive capacity of the economy. The variety of economic research, its applied nature and the sophistication of the opinions of scientists are simply amazing. Today, we have access to big data, various databases and the latest methods of analysis, which allows scientists to conduct their research in the context of international comparisons, exchange views on the state of affairs and the state of the economy, agree or disagree with others, put forward new hypotheses, test these empirically to prove or disprove them, and select the most viable. At the same time, modern economic research focuses on an interdisciplinary approach, which greatly enriches the scientific results of these studies and their value for practice, including recommendations for governments, politicians and businesses on ways to increase productivity. It should be noted that the relevance of the interdisciplinary approach is dictated by the complexity of the problems that economists face today. The analysis of such problems with the use of an interdisciplinary approach in research allows the most viable and practice-oriented recommendations for the economy to be obtained.

In our opinion, the presented collective work on "Productivity of Contemporary Economies: Theory and Evidence" is a contribution to the development of theory and practice of productivity, and offers the results of original research in this area, which relate to associated scientific problems. Namely, these are: the strategic goals of economic policy, the role of the institution of trust, the Fourth Industrial Revolution as a motivating factor for productive capacity, noosphere-thinking in economic development, methodological capabilities of institutionalism to analyse productive capacity Moreover, the authors contribute to the analysis of the productivity in the banking system and the role of banks in productive capacity, and the role of foreign investment in the productive capacity of countries and economic growth using the examples of Central and Eastern Europe, and Ukraine in particular.

The book focuses on the current trend of slowing global productivity, which is associated with changes in the technological mode of production as a result of technological developments during the Fourth Industrial Revolution. The problem of a country's productive capacity in a globalised society is complex, which can and should be studied taking into account economic and non-economic factors. Productive ability as an economic factor is closely related to productivity, which can be measured as labour productivity and capital productivity. Non-economic factors of productivity, which are equally important to consider in the analysis of productivity, include institutional, civilisational, social and motivational aspects.

According to the authors of this book, productive capacity should be considered from different points of view and taking into account national specifics. Setting strategic goals of the government's economic policy, aimed at increasing productivity in the national economy, requires a new theory of economic policy of living standards. Richard Thaler (2015) says that we live in a world of humans who are the vast majority of people, and therefore the level of productivity in the economy determines the opportunities to improve the quality of life and review the living standards of ordinary people on an ongoing basis. Accordingly, in the global economy, there is a rethinking of the values of economic development, as it becomes more value-oriented and based on the human-centric paradigm of development.

The COVID-19 crisis, which has highlighted the problem of slowing down the rate of growth of productivity and also the need to find and implement new methods of working and management approaches, is clearly contributing to the revision of development values. In the context of the pandemic crisis, the world's economies have become more vulnerable to shocks, established value chains have been disrupted and the incomes of the vast majority of economic entities have fallen sharply. There is an urgent need to find flexible and reliable innovations that will address vulnerabilities in value chains and other bottlenecks. The international pandemic has been actively talked about as a "window of opportunity", which, acting as a shock to the economy, gives it a chance to open up new opportunities. On the agenda of developed countries, the EU in particular, was the question of the role of industry in society and the need for its restoration. "It will require an active, focused approach, a rethinking of the paradigms that underlie our understanding of how societies, economies and industries work," stated the report of the European Commission on the policy development of industry 5.0 (Breque 2021). It is important that globally politicians and opinion leaders directly or indirectly emphasise the need to revise the concepts of economic and social development towards a human-centred paradigm, and the need to combat poverty and economic inequality. At the same time, the basic model of development is a low-carbon economy, which is based on the rejection of environmentally hazardous energy sources, and sustainable development. The ideal conditions for the competitiveness of industry in the world are stability, a focus on people and sustainability, a focus on innovation, and digitalisation of all spheres of public life.

Thus, to increase productivity, a modern country must, first, formulate an economic policy that is able to create and provide favourable conditions for the preparation and implementation of innovations for the future, as well as a high level of "soft" investment in people; secondly, it should contribute to the formation of a society 5.0 that is able to meet the multifactorial challenges of the economy and society, and contribute to technological improvements and hence commensurate productivity growth. Technological improvements are an integral part of economic development. They meet the challenges, but they also pose the threat of technological substitution, which is a challenge for work and its future. Without further developing this discussion, it should be noted that in order to mitigate the challenges and threats outlined above, a necessary condition is a scientifically sound and strategically oriented government policy, an economic policy in particular, which should be conducted in the national interest and focus on productive incentives for politicians, officials, businesses and people (employees).As Tyrol noted, "by formulating goals, we will be able to find the tools to achieve them, especially if the conditions are conducive to them. As a result of the transformation, new bottlenecks are emerging. In the interests of society, new rules of competition and regulation of markets that take into account modern realities are needed" (Tirol 2020, 664).

It is important to note that we live in a world that is rapidly transforming, constantly experiencing shocks and crises, and the new socio-economic reality that is emerging before our eyes carries a key pattern: instability as a key trend. This imposes special requirements on politics and economics as social institutions and areas of interaction between different countries, nations, social groups and people. Accordingly, economists must provide relevant recommendations that can improve our lives. I strongly hope that the scientific works of the authors of this book and their recommendations will serve as a theoretical and applied guide for economists and politicians – the authors set this as a goal and were very eager to improve such a complex world of economics to make it better for ordinary people.

Oleksandra M. Moskalenko

PREFACE

The productive capacity of economic systems at national and global levels in the 21st century is defined by a brand-new complex of challenges, factors and triggers caused by the rapid growth of scientific and technological revolutions, and the emergence of new demands and contradictions, which result in a dualism of the goals and values of people, businesses and society. Economic theory and economic policy meet new (frequently opposite) and rapidly developing paradigmatic approaches to the definition of the essence and content of these goals and their implementation methods that do not always correspond to the long-term strategic interests, preservation and evolution of human civilisation on Earth, as well as the steady growth in population prosperity.

In these circumstances, the scientific analysis of the nature of the above-mentioned problems envisages the definition of the state and the level of readiness of productive powers and social economic relations of both certain countries and globalised society in general for the extremely qualitative leap to the development of the technological productive method. It also covers the transformation of its results into the new quality of welfare and self-reproduction of members of society. Moreover, this engages the research in endogenic factors slowing down the innovative advancement of productive capabilities of individual national economies, and risks resulting from the systematic application of the nanotechnological revolution and Industry 4.0. Such an approach to scientific analysis will encourage deeper understanding of the principles of building the architectonics of theoretical and practical patterns of economic policy that would be able to implement the human-centred paradigm of social development.

Therefore, the authors of this paper have focused on the investigation of core categorial and institutional forms identifying the nature and functions of the productive capacity of national economic systems, and strategies for applying the manufacturing potential in the context of constant qualitative transformations, which take place in the economy and society affected by the above-mentioned revolutionary changes in the technological method of production, and in the character and essence of social relations between key economic activity agents and all members of globalised society.

The latter aspect is quite crucial because, according to G. Hodgson, "When it comes to technology definition and transformation issues, the orthodox economic theory interprets the technology as something prescribed and lack of social content as if the technology has nothing to do with both the system of relations in manufacturing and methods for organizing labor within the firm. Technology is perceived as a natural phenomenon that should be studied as part of any social science." (Hodgson 2003, 43) At the same time, we cannot but agree with scientists who are warning nowadays: "Future is Pandora's box that, unfortunately, we cannot help but open." (Yemelin 2017, 350) Such challenges and risks for the future of humans are also confirmed by the emergence and dynamic development of dualism in the understanding of the essence of the high-priority growth paradigm in research by theorists, business views and the activities of authoritative structures in different countries. It refers to the problem of choice that is faced before society's leap into the unknown future based on new productive capabilities of economic systems – either a human-centred development paradigm, a transhumanistic development paradigm, or a dialectic harmonious combination of the two in a single conceptual system of views, prospects and routes for the evolution of human civilisation. This issue has to be, and is, the scope of research in this manuscript.

Yurii K. Zaitsev

ACKNOWLEDGEMENTS

We express our sincere gratitude to the authors of the chapters, who made great efforts to achieve the unity of the theoretical idea of this work, and who were interested in its fate and contributed greatly in every way to its publication. Furthermore, we would like to thank the young scholar Oleksandra Moskalenko, whose volunteer work and inspiration made this book possible.

INTRODUCTION

ANTON S. FILIPENKO

Productivity is a key economic indicator, which identifies a state of development on micro-, meso-, macro- and meta-economic levels. Nowadays, the economic situation around the world is characterised by the tendency for productivity growth to decrease, stipulating, on the one hand, digitalisation of economic processes and, on the other hand, the consequences of COVID-19. We now have a *sui generis* productivity paradox, according to K. Shwab (2016, 32). In as much as many goods and services have zero marginal costs via digital platforms (blockchain, IoT, big data, artificial intelligence), traditional statistics do not reflect real productivity, which is followed by lower prices. Under the conditions of COVID-19, the world's GDP in 2020 decreased by about 6% and its productive ability – particularly in terms of labour – was diminished correspondingly. The crucial task of this book is to explore productivity in contemporary economies, particularly of labour and capital and their combination in terms of total factor productivity and multifactor productivity.

Chapter One focuses on classical interpretations of productivity by A. Smith and J.S. Mill, mostly in light of the division of labour. J. Turgot, J.H. von Thünen and T. Malthus considered the problems of productivity in the narrow sense, mainly limited to the productive capacity of agriculture. Among the main measures of economic productivity, the theory of marginal utility (productivity) was stressed. In modern research, aggregate indicators such as total factor productivity (TFP) and multifactor productivity (MFP) prevail. TFP is measured by combining the effects of all the sources used in the production of goods and services (labour, capital, materials, energy, etc.) and dividing this by the output; thus, it utilises more than a single factor. MFP is the ratio of total output to a subset of inputs. A subset of inputs might consist of only labour and materials, or it could include capital. MFP is the residual contribution to output growth of an industry or economy after calculating the contribution from all its factor inputs. The OECD methodology examines key single-factor (aggregated) indicators of labour and capital productivity, considering total output and costs and, most importantly, the value added, which reflects the real increase in the welfare of the nation. The European KLEMS project (model) uses such components as energy, materials and services, in addition to labour and capital. Canadian experts offer a much wider range of indicators in the measurement of TFP.

In particular, there are intermediate costs (materials, business services, loan capital), labour costs, renewable capital costs, inventories (material values), land resources, other natural resources (fish stocks, forests, oil fields, mines), environmental improvements, working capital, cash and other financial instruments, knowledge capital (education, innovation, R&D, etc.), and infrastructure capital. A set of factors of national productivity is considered in a detailed version. Firstly, these include: the accumulation of capital by attracting domestic and foreign investment; introduction of the newest technologies capable of modernising manufacturing; and organisation of production and technological processes comparable to the best models in the world. Secondly, they are deepening the division and cooperation of labour in the system of network chains at the national and global levels at different stages of production and distribution, creating effective coordination mechanisms for prices, contracts, formal and informal agreements, communications, trust, reputation, and more. Thirdly, they relate to the development of production infrastructure (transport, energy, telecommunications) and improvement of social infrastructure, including public institutions, non-governmental organisations, and business and social networks, etc. Fourthly, this means increasing the educational level and competence of those employed in the economy, which, according to some calculations, is pivotal in increasing productivity.

Chapter Two examines the Fourth Industrial Revolution as a motivator for a great leap in a country's manufacturing capability, in particular in terms of international experience, challenges and risks in Ukraine. As Zaitsev observes, the most powerful technological revolution in the history of modern society, creating the background for meeting the entirety of critical and long-term demands of economic and social life subjects across the globe, is simultaneously providing brand-new manufacturing capabilities and tools to affect the processes of managing the life of these "human beings" and their mind, desires, emotions, etc. The rapid integration of nanotechnologies, atomistically precise manufacturing and robotic automation result in the dynamisation of qualitative changes in labour requirements, conditions to ensure the quality of human labour, etc. At the same time, there is an increasing number of external challenges, in particular technological, structural, geopolitical, technologically geopolitical, global-ecological and civilisational challenges. This is in addition to those related to: mass social mutations (glam-capitalism, downshifters, a long-term unemployed population, internal 'unemployed – principals' and 'unemployed – migrant principals' as a widespread phenomenon). Moreover, this is also related to politics and economics (aggravation of social and socio-technological competition, and the emergence of a dualistic development paradigm (human-centred or transhumanistic) of the economy and society). According to the author, the main problem in the context of scientific revolution and the digital economy is the decline, or even the loss, of the totality of such civilisational labour function, as its affordability and continuity of reproduction for a significant number of people worldwide – which will complicate human socialisation processes, and conditions for self-actualisation and creative development – turn many people into outcasts or pariahs within the operating society.

Chapter Three by A.M. Kolot and O.O. Herasymenko observes the institution of trust in the system of factors in the development of a nation's productive ability. The authors have focussed on a literature review in this area and also modern methodology. It should be noted that Ukrainian society has been in a state of political, economic and social instability for almost three decades, which is reproduced and permanently intensified not only by external global trends but also by internal crisis phenomena. The internal component of instability in Ukrainian society is closely linked to, and largely the result of, the inconsistency, uncertainty and unpredictability of domestic and foreign policies. The authors are convinced that new ways to solve the most acute socio-economic problems are connected to the potential use of non-economic factors, among which trust has a special role. In the new development trend, which is gaining momentum, there is an actualisation of the moral and spiritual non-economic component. In their recent research, the authors proceed from the fact that purely economic postulates are appearing less and less in the form of material from which to build the current and future economic lives of the country, households and each person. To conclude, trust in the economy is based on an extensive system of formal and informal norms and institutions/organisations. There is every reason to consider the institution of trust as a tool for regulating relations in the triad of "market – state – business", the formation and development of which – in the context of the interaction of participants in the coordinates of the new economy – were substantiated.

Chapter Four by I.G. Khanin is devoted to noospheric thinking as a factor in economic development. Noospheric thinking is presented here by its ontological basis in the form of the Quasi-Physical Model of Cognition (QPMC) of the noosphere. The model is convergent, since it is assumed that the noosphere includes the biosphere and the biosphere includes the physiosphere. The QPMC model includes the structure of the noosphere as a relevant scheme of the object of cognition with horizontal (interdisciplinary) connections between the spheres of phenomena (physiosphere, biosphere, noosphere). Vertical relations are established between the levels of abstraction (philosophy, methodology, mathematics, fundamental and applied knowledge, technology, practice). QPMC, at least, can serve as the basis for strategic planning, forecasting, and optimisation of economic management and cognition. The explanatory and predictive power of models and theories mentioned by the author are closely related. The explanatory power of the cognition model allows us to understand what is happening with cognition of the sphere of phenomena today. Predictive ability helps us to anticipate what events might occur during development. This should ensure that false paths and goals are avoided, as well as ensuring that the real problems are posed and addressed. The model provides the convergence of knowledge of physical and humanitarian phenomena, as well as abstract and concrete, embodied and non-embodied knowledge. At the same time, it shares practical and scientific knowledge. Practical knowledge relies on experience (analogies), guesses (heuristics) and modelling (associations). The chapter contributes to materialised forms of knowledge, which act as objects of paradigmatic and scientific knowledge. The QPMC model does not claim to be complete. The author is aware that in the process of implementation it may require changes, and looks forward to arousing interest in this topic and stimulating discussions.

Chapter Five by O.M. Moskalenko points out that strategic goals of the economic policy of the state are connected to the production ability of the national economy in a globalised society. These strategic goals are considered in the policy of raising the standard of living, and thus ensuring the institutional, economic and political conditions for economic growth and the productive capacity of the national economy. It is proved that catching-up economies, due to their low productive capacity and poor international competitiveness, will be unable to create the appropriate institutional conditions for economic growth or fit into international technological chains. Besides, the post-transformational countries (Ukraine) have implemented an outdated form of state monopoly capitalism and, thus, condemned themselves to decades of catching-up development with a faintly degrading character. It is argued that institutional inadequacy, political instability, low productivity and the immaturity of institutions in countries with a low level of economic development have led to such a situation. A globalised society is an unstable meta-system that is constantly transforming, producing qualitatively new goals and values for the development of civilisation. The political role and economic position of national economies in a globalised society is determined by the level and result of the productive capacity of a nation that is capable/incapable of producing the civilisational and cultural values (that are perceived by the majority, including other nations), innovations, effective economic results and solutions, and social stability and development.

The economic growth strategy involves organising such a set of factors that would ensure a steady growth rate over the long run, either due to the benefits created by resource availability, or due to technological superiority and high productivity, or a combination of these two components. Consequently, the productive capacity of a nation in a globalised society is determined by the economic (existing in the country and created resource-supply), technological and non-economic (related to civilisation) advantages.

V. V. Lypov in Chapter Six investigates the contemporary institutionalism and instruments of comparative analysis of the productivity of national economies. The purpose of this section is to analyse features of the tools for studying the productivity of national economies, proposed within the main areas of comparative research of institutional models of socio-economic systems, and to identify their limitations, advantages and disadvantages in the context of forming a holistic view of universal institutional mechanisms to ensure high productivity of national economies. Comparative analyses of the productivity of socio-economic systems are grounded on the concepts of the varieties of capitalism (VoC), social systems of innovation and production (SSIP), national business systems (NBS), French school of regulation (TR), institutional matrices (IM), and institutional complementarity (IC) of socio-economic systems (SES). Instruments of comparative analysis such as structural, functional, systemic, dialectical, quantitative, qualitative, historical-genetic, graphical, and ethno-metrical analysis methods of formalisation and modelling are used.

The methodological bases of comparative complementary research of institutions are qualitative (analysis of the impact of values on the nature of structural complementarity), quantitative (analysis of indicators characterising the complementarity of individual institutions and institutional areas of SES), measurement (complementarity measure). The study of structural complementarity (SC) involves the analysis of the correspondence of the elements of the institutional system to the value foundations of the national culture. The study of functional complementarity (FC) is based on the analysis of the functional unity of the elements of the institutional system. In turn, system analysis presupposes research SES in general, their individual components analysis as integral phenomena. But dialectical method focuses on dialectics of complementary relations at the level of basic SES institutions and historical-genetic – on evolution of complementary principles of production methods. The analytical apparatus of comparative studies includes graphic (figures that characterise the structural and functional relationships between institutions), econometric (measurement of institutional complementarity at the SES level), ethnometric analysis (using the results of ethnometric studies of value orientations of national cultures), and methods of constructing graphs (morphology of institutional interaction).The advantage of comparative complementary analysis is the ability to predict the qualitative characteristics of institutions inherent in certain SES models, based on knowledge of the key principle of their operation.

The analysis of the components of institutional systems is deepening. The influence of the features of the institutional structure for ensuring the growth of productivity is the centre of attention of researchers. Deductive and inductive approaches to comparative analysis of the impact of different models of economic systems and their components on productivity are being developed. Depending on the purpose and the available information base, researchers have the opportunity to choose a wide range of methods and tools of analysis.

The effects of foreign direct investment (FDI) on labour productivity are explored by O. Nosova in Chapter Seven. The paper aims to understand the effects of FDI on the labour productivity of local firms and to identify factors that will support the development of a more effective policy to encourage attractive FDI practices in Ukraine. The FDI inflows affect and promote change in labour productivity. The higher wage rates lead to increasing aggregate demand. The greater investment, with improvements in total productivity, could reinforce Ukraine's current account balance. The greater technological transparency of the information society emerging in European countries, as well as growing intra-European bilateral FDI links, have contributed to an increasing incidence of technology spillovers and external-scale economies. Foreign capital inflow increases the level of employment, the qualifications of the local labour force and the productivity of its labour, and it also improves the standard of living and purchasing power of the population. The effects of FDI on host countries' economies are mainly related to the increase in labour productivity through technological transfers, management and marketing proficiency that enables long-term technological progress and economic growth. The author proves that the development of performance management skills according to the standards imposed by the major leading corporate systems, an increase in the population's training level and its capacity to adapt to the technological developments can contribute to the increase in the quality of labour resources.

The authors of Chapter Eight, S. Tsyganov and N. Tsyganova, have studied banks and their role in the system of resource provision for the productivity of countries. The banking system of Ukraine, according to the authors, has passed the initial stage of its formation, but it shows a significant backlog in terms of the economy's needs: increased sensitivity to external shocks, structural imbalances, and limited resource opportunities for the real sector lending, especially of medium- and long-term credits.

The role of banks in the system of resource provision for the countries' productive capacity is determined by the quantitative and qualitative parameters of the resources according to the business needs and general macroeconomic parameters. The capacity of national financial markets determines the number of resources that are redistributed on the basis of the market mechanisms such as free market pricing, voluntary exchanges and competition.

This means that a change in the number of banks ambiguously affects their role in the resource provision system for the productive capacity of countries. Resource capabilities of individual banks depend on the number of banking institutions and the level of consolidation of the banking sector.

In the current context, the chapter concludes, consolidating the capital in the banking sector is essential for the formation of the resource provision system for the productive capacity of national economies, which is based on a number of objective and subjective factors, among them being a prominent place occupied by technological changes in production that require large amounts of funding.

Chapter Nine by O.A. Chugaiev is about foreign investments and business regulation in small and large economies. This chapter reviews the results of research on the effect of economy size on international investments. But it is also necessary to verify the robustness of previous findings by using more recent data. Thus, analysis of variance (ANOVA) was applied to the data after the economic crisis of 2008–2009. Also, unlike the traditional classification of countries, medium-sized economies are distinguished in the current study. Most of the analysed indicators do not have a proven optimal range of values in order to maximise economic growth, or at least the differences are not statistically significant (these indicators are: inflows of FDI, portfolio investments in bonds, real interest rate, tax rates, corruption incidence, simplicity to register business start-ups, obtaining electricity, enforcing contracts and resolving insolvency, legal rights of borrowers and lenders, transparency in the public sector, bank capital to assets ratio). The author concludes that in recent years the attractiveness of Ukraine for foreign investments was negatively affected by the existing economic dynamics but also positively affected by the low value of assets. Also, despite Ukraine having a wide range of industries, its economy is not large enough to provide efficiency for some of the branches. This is also related to the investment options being limited by other criteria (riskiness, payback period, shadow economy etc.) i.e. the country does not possess all the types of assets in order to satisfy the needs of investors (those who prefer specific industries, long-term investments, or avoiding risks or corruption). The high volatility of production in Ukraine also makes it similar to small economies and curbs foreign investments.

The productive efficiency and economic growth in the countries of Central and Eastern Europe are the subjects of Chapter Ten by Bilenko. After many decades of experience in post-socialist countries, the economic development in a market economy allows research on the models of productive efficiency and economic growth, and their correspondence with classical exogenous and new endogenous theories of economic growth, to determine the dominant factors of the trajectory of development of countries in different institutional environments. This study tries to measure the efficiency of the economic performance of Central and Eastern European countries in a period of economic reforms and transition to a market economy, and to explain what factors play an important role in the economic performance changing. For the analysis, a group of 10 countries of Central and Eastern Europe that have joined the European Union (Bulgaria, Romania, Poland, Hungary, Czech Republic, Slovakia, Slovenia, Estonia, Lithuania and Latvia), as well as four post-Soviet European countries (Ukraine, Belarus, Russia and Moldova) and Albania, were selected. In the sample, for efficiency estimation the most productive countries in the world, USA and Germany, were also included. Research was conducted over the period 1991–2013 (390 observations). Results of the research confirm Parente and Prescott's (2000; 2005) theory of country-specific TFP, which they refer to as a theory of relative efficiency which is based on policy differences. More specifically, they show how various policies that constrain choices of technology and work practices at the level of the production unit determine the aggregate efficiency at which a country uses its resources in production.

LIST OF ABBREVIATIONS

AR	Average revenue
ATM	Automated teller machine
CA	Comparative analysis
CAI	Comparative analysis of institutions
CCA	Consciousness, cognitive-creative activity
CIA	Comparative institutional analysis
CIS	Commonwealth of Independent States
ESA	Enterprise and systems architecture
ES	Economic systems
EU	European Union
FC	Functional complementarity
FDI	Foreign direct investment
GMM	Generalised method of moments
GUF	German–Ukrainian Fund
GDP	Gross domestic product
GNI	Gross national income
GVC	Global value chain
IMF	International Monetary Fund
IC	Institutional complementarity
IM	Institutional matrices
IT	Information technology
LP	Labour productivity
KFW	German Reconstruction Credit Institute
M&A	Mergers and acquisitions
MFIs	Microfinance institutions
MFP	Multifactor productivity
MPP	Marginal physical productivity
MNEs	Multinational enterprises
OOAD	Object-oriented analysis and design
PIDev	Paradigmatic innovative development
PPP	Parity of purchasing power
QPMC	Quasi-Physical Model of Cognition
RT	Regulation Theory

SES	Socio-economic systems
SME	Small and Medium-sized Enterprises
SC	Structural complementarity
SOVS	Social orientations of value systems
ST	Semantic technologies
TFP	Total factor productivity
TNCs	Transnational corporations
TPP	Total physical productivity
TPBP	Theory and practice of business processes
UNCTAD	United Nations Conference on Trade and Development
UNESCO	United Nations Educational, Scientific and Cultural
VAT	Value-added tax
VMP	Value (cost) of marginal productivity
VIPK	Vertical integration and the parabola of knowledge
VoC	Varieties of capitalism
WGI	Worldwide governance indicators

CHAPTER ONE

PRODUCTIVE ABILITY OF THE ECONOMY: THEORY AND METHODOLOGY

ANTON S. FILIPENKO

1. Classical interpretations of productivity

The common notion of productivity is defined as the ratio of output to resources expended. The productive capacity of the economy, or the productive capacity of nations, is a much broader multidimensional process. It reflects the general state of the economy, the efficiency of use of all resources, the nature and level of the institutional environment, the quality of human and social capital, and so on.

The forefathers of economics paid great attention to the problems of the creation and distribution of wealth, and the welfare of nations, determining the causes, nature and factors influencing these processes. Particular attention was paid to the efficient use of land, labour and capital. Among the main prerequisites for the economic capacity of a nation were the natural and geographical environment, the level of development of material and spiritual culture, the division of labour, international trade, and others. At the same time, A. Smith (2001, 11), in particular, stressed that "the greatest improvement in the productive powers of labour, and the greater part of the skill, dexterity, and judgement with which it is anywhere directed, or applied, seem to have been the effects of the division of labour." Smith mainly considered the firm (factory, manufacturer) from the point of view of the division of labour (organic and heterogeneous manufacturing) as the main factor in productivity growth. J.S. Mill analysed productivity through the prism of property relations and the cooperative nature of the social institution, dividing the productivity of the worker and the manager depending on their ownership of the means of production (Witztum 2012, 342-343). Mill distinguished simple cooperation, when workers carried out joint activities in the process of producing one product (vertical relations), and complex cooperation, when different products are produced for exchange (horizontal relations). According to Mill, the scale, size and limits (boundaries) of a firm are determined by the following components: technological conditions, the impact of distribution relations on productivity, the transnational nature of competition and the evolution of human nature (ethology). J.M. Keynes (2007, 43) critically evaluated the category of wealth, its dynamics and structure in the definitions of classical economists, in particular noting the descriptive nature of their interpretations.

J. Turgot, J.H. von Thünen and T. Malthus considered the problems of productivity in a narrow sense, mainly limited to the productive capacity of agriculture. The law of declining productivity of the agricultural sector (soil) was formulated. G. Hegel and F. Engels divided different nationalities into "historic" and "non-historic" in terms of their ability to yield economic and cultural development. While the historic nationalities created states and were entitled to exist, the non-historic nationalities were doomed to extinction. The fallacy of this statement is obvious, because in the historical process, state and civilisation structures were created, destroyed and restored (Toynbee 1995, 252-254).

2. The main measures of economic productivity

2.1. Theory of marginal utility (productivity)

Over time, the issue of wealth was transformed into a standard category of gross domestic product, while the issues of its generation were localised by the competitiveness of nations (Porter 1990) and by the study of the productivity of two main factors: labour and capital. In fact, during the second half of the 20th century and at the beginning of the 21st century, the productive capacity of a nation has been grounded mainly upon models of total factor productivity (TFP) or multifactor productivity (MFP).

To better understand these complex categories, let us consider the basic principles and concepts with reference to the theory of marginal utility (productivity) in the context of the marginalism paradigm that led to the second revolution in economics. Measuring marginal productivity is carried out gradually in several steps. First, the general formula of marginal physical productivity is determined:

$$MPP_n = TPP_n - TPP_{n-1} \quad (1)$$

where MPP_n is the marginal physical productivity of the n-th unit of labour;

TPP_n is the total physical productivity of the n-th number of workers;

TPP_{n-1} is the total physical productivity of the n-1 unit of workers.

Marginal physical productivity means an increase in output caused by one factor of productivity while the other remaining factors are unchanged. An illustration is provided as follows. Six workers produce 120 quintals of wheat (120 quintals / 6 workers = 20 quintals per worker). If another (seventh) worker is involved in production, the wheat harvest should total 140 quintals. In this case, the maximum physical productivity of an additional employee is 20 quintals (140 − 120 = 20). At the same time, there may be situations when the seventh employee may have lower productivity (lack of additional equipment, lack of experience, physical capabilities, etc.), then the question arises whether it is feasible or not to attract an additional unit of labour in the context of marginal utility theory.

Marginal revenue productivity is defined as the increase in total revenue due to the attraction of a unit of additional factor upon the invariability of other factors. Suppose that one worker produces wheat resulting in revenue of $50. Another worker is hired and as a result the revenue increases to $60. In this case, the marginal revenue productivity of the second worker equals $10 ($60 − $50 = $10).

The value (cost) of marginal productivity is equal to the product of marginal physical productivity and the market price of the product:

$$VMP = MPP \text{ x } AR \quad (2)$$

where VMP is the value of marginal productivity;

MPP is the marginal physical productivity;

AR is the average revenue (market price of the product).

If the market price of one quintal of wheat is $10 and the marginal physical productivity of the first additional worker is 20 quintals of wheat, then the marginal productivity of the additional worker will be equal to $200 (20 x $10 = $200).

2.2. Total factor productivity and multifactor productivity

Measuring productivity is a complex process that has its own history, initiated, as noted above, by the forefathers of economics (Malthus, Smith, Marshall, etc.). In modern research, aggregate indicators such as TFP and

MFP prevail. TFP is measured by combining the effects of all the resources used in the production of goods and services (labour, capital, materials, energy, etc.) and dividing it by the output; thus, it utilises more than a single factor. MFP is the ratio of total output to a subset of inputs. A subset of inputs might consist of only labour and materials, or it could include capital. MFP is the residual contribution to output growth of an industry or economy after calculating the contribution from all its factor inputs.

The OECD provides a tabular version for measuring the performance of essential elements of the economic system (see Table 1-1).

Table 1-1. Measuring the productivity of the economic system

Type of output	**Type of input measure**			
	Labour	Capital	Capital and labour	Capital, labour and intermediate inputs (energy, materials, services)
Gross output	Labour productivity (based on gross output)	Capital productivity (based on gross output)	Capital-labour MFP (based on gross output)	KLEMS* - MFP
Value added	Labour productivity (based on value added)	Capital productivity (based on value added)	Capital-labour MFP (based on value added)	
	Single factor productivity measures		MFP measures	

* The model has resulted from the work of a consortium of 16 research, analytical and statistical organisations from different EU countries established in 2003 (the project has been titled EU-KLEMS).

Source: OECD 2001. "Measuring productivity. Measurement of aggregate and industry-level productivity growth," Paris p. 12.

The OECD methodology examines key single-factor (aggregated) indicators of labour and capital productivity, considering total output and costs and, most importantly, the value added, which reflects the real increase in the welfare of the nation. This creates the possibility of a separate analysis of productivity of both labour and capital, to carry out their synthesis based on multifactoriality and finally to take into account the full range of factors based on the KLEMS model. A database of comparable statistics at the industry level is being developed to analyse the relationship between skills growth, technological progress and innovation, on the one hand, and productivity, on the other. An important unit of measurement of the productivity of a nation (country, national economy) is also the TFP. It is grounded on the Cobb–Douglas production function, with its parameters reflecting the contribution of two main factors – labour and capital – to the country's GDP growth:

$$\ln TFP = \ln Y - \alpha \ln L - (1 - \alpha) \ln K \tag{3}$$

where Y is the output of GDP;
α is the labour (wages) share in the GDP;
$1 - \alpha$ is the capital share in the GDP;
L is the labour;
K is the capital.

The dynamic aspect involves determining the rate of the TFP growth defined as:

$$p_t = dY_t / dt - \alpha dL_t / dt - (1 - \alpha)\, dK_t / dt \tag{4}$$

where p_t is the rate of TFP growth;
Y_t is output (GDP);
dY_t / dt is the rate of output growth;
L is the labour input;
K is the capital input;
α is the share of wages in the national GDP;
t is the time required for economic measurements.

The logarithmic version of TFP growth (*dynamics*) is described as follows:

$$p_t = d\ln Y_t / dt - \alpha d\ln L_t / dt - (1 - \alpha)\, d\ln K_t / dt \tag{5}$$

(Wolff 2014, 134, 137)

In addition to this basic formula, there are a number of methods for determining TFP, such as empirically based quantitative indices, in particular, the hyperbolic Diewert index, econometric methods, stochastic boundary element methods, operating environment analysis and so on. Exploring the TFP, Kim and Loayza (2019, 6-10) also take into account such factors as innovation, education, market efficiency, infrastructure and institutions.

In the framework of European cohesion policy, it is important to equalise productivity levels between different regions, divided into four categories: frontier regions, catching-up regions, keeping-pace regions and diverging regions. Frontier regions are those with the highest level of productivity in each country and where the population of the region amounts to 10% of the total population. Catching-up regions have reduced the gap in productivity levels vis-à-vis frontier regions during the period in question. Keeping-pace regions have maintained the productivity-level gap of (+-5%) vis-à-vis frontier regions. Diverging regions have increased the productivity gap vis-à-vis frontier regions (see Table 1-2).

Table 1-2. Contributions of the different regional productivity patterns to aggregate EU GDP and employment growth, 2000–2014

	Contribution to EU GDP growth	**Share of EU GDP 2000**	**Share of EU GDP 2014**	**Share of EU employment 2000**	**Share of EU employment 2014**
Frontier regions	32%	22%	24%	18%	19%
Catching-up regions	24%	18%	19%	23%	22%
Keeping-pace regions	30%	40%	38%	38%	39%
Diverging regions	15%	21%	20%	21%	21%

Source: Bachtler 2019, 23.

As can be seen from Table 1-2, almost two thirds of the EU GDP and its employment was in keeping-pace and diverging regions in 2014. At the same time, these regions contributed only 45% to the EU's economic growth during 2000–2014, while frontier regions – representing 19% of employment – provided 32% of the EU's economic growth and 24% of the EU's GDP in 2014. Catching-up regions showed slow progress with a slight increase over the period in their contribution to the EU's GDP and a slight decrease in employment. Regions are also differentiated as mostly urban, intermediate and mostly rural. Thus, rural regions make up almost half (48%) within diverging regions, while they account for 42% within catching-up regions. At the same time, the share of mostly urban regions is 25% in diverging regions and 40% in keeping-pace regions.

In research, it is essential to compare the TFP of different countries, to identify trends in the convergence or divergence of productivity levels. There are β and σ convergences (Wolff 2014, 61-62). β-convergence is based on the fundamental principles of neoclassical growth theory and it mainly characterises the convergence of indicators of less developed countries with industrialised ones in terms of economic development (new global convergence). At the same time, countries with a lower initial level of capital accumulation and a lower level of income accumulate capital faster than the average rate, while countries where the initial capital accumulation exceeded the average level slow down the rate of capital accumulation.

σ-convergence means reducing inequalities in productivity and per capita income between the richest and poorest countries (Wolff 2014, 61-62).

The first and second indicators may differ. The country may be approaching the growth rate of developed countries and even be ahead of it. However, the gap in GDP per capita may still increase.

The main indicators are the volume of GDP per capita, the human development index, indices and indicators of sustainable development, etc. If a number of countries have the same initial conditions and show close convergence rates, this process is called club or group convergence. A clear example of such convergence is the economic development of the so-called Asian tigers in the 1970s (Singapore, Republic of Korea, Hong Kong, Taiwan) and the 1980s (Malaysia, Thailand, Indonesia, India).

Productivity is measured, as noted, based on TFP or MFP models. The starting points are economic growth models with an emphasis on the Solow balance and the Cobb–Douglas production function. Thus, productivity is a relative indicator, the basis of which in the narrow sense is the analysis of the contribution of two key factors – labour and capital – in the generation of national wealth. Thus, the Bank of England's model for determining TFP uses the same two main factors: labour and capital. In a broad sense, the TFP and MFP models – not being fundamentally any different to each other – use a much wider set of criteria and indicators. For example, the European KLEMS project (model) uses such components as energy, materials and services, in addition to labour and capital. Canadian experts offer a much wider range of indicators in the measurement of TFP. In particular, we are talking about intermediate costs (materials, business services, loan capital), labour costs, renewable capital costs, inventories (material values), land resources, other natural resources (fish stocks, forests, oil fields, mines), environmental improvements, working capital, cash and other financial instruments, knowledge capital (education, innovation, R&D, etc.), and infrastructure capital (Koszerek et al. 2007, 1).

Some studies use the methodology of differentiation of productivity into three approaches: labour productivity, MFP, and public productivity or productivity of social services (see Table 1-3).

Table 1-3. Three approaches to measuring productivity

	Labour productivity	**MFP**	**Public productivity**
Costs	Labour – hours of work, number of jobs, number of employees	The quality of labour in the context of the volume of production from labour	Labour – the equivalent of full employment or the estimated amount of labour
		Capital – capital services index	Capital – consumption of fixed capital
			Intermediate – the cost of intermediate goods and services
Output	Total value added	Total value added	Output measured as a value-based activity with a qualitative assessment
Scope	The whole economy, market sector	Market sector, industry	General public services broken down according to the classification of government services

Source: Office for National Statistics 2021, https://www.ons.gov.uk.

Table 1-2 allows us to conclude that labour productivity is measured by the volume of production compared with the number of employees or the final indicator of total value added. The multifactor indicator consists of the total value added formed by the volume of production by labour, the volume of production by capital and the balance of Solow. Productivity of public services is measured by the total output, where intermediate services are added to the multifactor indicator. This methodology allows carrying out economic and statistical observations of the dynamics of the main indicators of productivity of different hierarchical levels. An option of comparing the cost–output by V. Leontief is introduced for a more detailed analysis, which complements the theory and methodology of productivity study (Leontief 2006, 85-87).

3. Productive capacity of the nation

The productive capacity of a nation is a much broader concept than the productivity of an economy or its individual units. This concept resonates in some way with the concept of "competitive advantage of nations" introduced by M. Porter (1990). Many factors that distinguish competitiveness, especially at the macro level, are directly linked to productive capacity. However, in the analysis of productive capacity, the focus is not so much on the current state of affairs, on the one hand, that is crucial for the initial stage of the study. The term 'ability' contains the potential for diversification and growth, and has a certain mobilising, perspectival orientation. In particular, A. Toynbee (1995, 20) focuses on the positive sources of "new creative capacity". On the other hand, the purely economic and technological (according to Porter) components are supplemented by nation-building ones, such as anthropological, psychological, mental, socio-cultural and institutional components, etc. Therefore, the theoretical foundations of the nation's productive capacity are based on a wide range of factors and processes that result in its economic potential, and reveal the mechanisms and tools of its effective use.

A set of factors of national productivity is considered in a detailed version. Firstly, these include: the accumulation of capital by attracting domestic and foreign investment; introduction of the newest technologies capable of modernising manufacturing; and organisation of production and technological processes comparable to the best models in the world. Secondly, they are deepening the division and cooperation of labour in the system of network chains at the national and global levels at different stages of production and distribution, creating effective coordination mechanisms for prices, contracts, formal and informal agreements, communications, trust, reputation, and more. Thirdly, they relate to the development of production infrastructure (transport, energy, telecommunications) and improvement of social infrastructure, including public institutions, non-governmental organisations, and business and social networks, etc. Fourthly, this means increasing the educational level and competence of those employed in the economy, which, according to some calculations, is pivotal in increasing productivity (Nelson 2006).

Indirect productivity factors include: support of civil liberties; openness to foreigners; positive relationships with subordinates; self-esteem and a sense of personal competence; participation in public and national affairs; interpersonal trust; and satisfaction with one's own life.

Experts also take into account the mental model of the nation, consisting of definite and specific beliefs, preferences, conclusions and goals. This is a kind of mental map of the nation. There is a set of institutions, beliefs and guidelines that are either pro-innovative and create conditions for productivity and prosperity, or anti-innovative and inhibit progress and development. Thus, F. Hayek noted that the Anglo-Saxon legal system created better preconditions, and a wider corridor of freedom for economic development and entrepreneurship than the continental one. Similarly, according to M. Weber and other researchers, Protestant ethics gave a huge impetus to undermining the feudal foundations and the rapid development of capitalist relations, productivity growth, capital, economy and the nation as a whole (Weber 1994, 56-57). In analysing the productive capacity of the Ukrainian nation, as well as other communities, an important component is consideration of the business culture of the people. To this end, three groups of business cultures are distinguished: monoactive, polyactive and reactive. Ukrainian business culture tends to be polyactive, characterised by: general planning, multitasking, flexibility in terms of working hours, non-punctuality, unpredictability of schedules and rapid changes of plans according to the significance of an event, overlapping between a project, loose interpretation of facts, dominant collectivism, a large power distance (distance between leader and subordinate), and a strong desire to avoid uncertainty.

According to the calculations of the Federal Bank of St. Louis, the total productivity of factors of production in Ukraine was 0.48 in 1990 compared with the United States, and only 0.176 in 1999, which was primarily due to the transformation crisis after the collapse of the Soviet Union. Positive dynamics of overall performance were observed from 2000 to 2011, but the level of 1990 was still never reached (0.35 compared with the United States in 2011) (Federal Reserve Bank St. Louis 2020).

These indicators illustrate, firstly, the low level of productivity of Ukraine's economy, especially given the key indicators of GDP per capita and the average wage. Secondly, there is a clear trend of volatility and instability of economic processes, and vulnerability to internal and external shocks. Thirdly, the weak productivity of the main factors of production – labour and capital with a high level of education of the workforce, and the presence of one of Europe's largest engineering corps and scientists – highlights a component that has not yet been sufficiently formalised; thus, the country's institutional system is the main brake on stable economic progress.

Conclusions

The theoretical and methodological foundations of productivity have been laid by the classical authors of economics, who considered these processes through the prism of the division and cooperation of labour, and the relationship between the employee and the owner of the means of production. Over time, the focus has shifted onto the productivity of the two main factors of production, labour and capital, based on the Cobb–Douglas production function, taking into account the Solow balance and factors such as innovation, education, market efficiency, infrastructure, institutions and so on. On this basis, the main indicators of productivity nowadays have become the TFP and MFP. At the same time, the creative heritage of Toynbee, Porter and others indicates an expanded interpretation of productivity as the productive capacity of individual nations and countries. In this case, in addition to purely economic and technological nation-building components, others such as anthropological, psychological, mental, socio-cultural and institutional components, etc. are also considered.

References

Acemoglu, Daron and Robinson, James A. *Why nations fail. The Origins of Power, Prosperity, and Poverty*, trans. from Engl. Kyiv: Nash format (In Ukrainian).

Agrell, Per J. and Wikner, Joakim. 1996. "A coherent methodology for productivity analysis employing integrated partial efficiency." *International Journal of Production Economics* 46-47: 401-411.

Bachtler, John et al. 2019. "Towards cohesion policy 4.0. Structural transformation and inclusive growth." *Regional studies policy impact books* 1, 1: 17-28.

Barath, Lajos and Ferto, Imre. 2016. "Productivity and Convergence in European Agriculture." *Discussion papers MT-DT26*: 3-34.

Castels, Manuel et al. 2017. *Another economy is possible. Culture and economy in a time of crisis.* Malden: Polity.

Convergence of economic models of Poland and Ukraine. 2010. Edited by Dmytro Lukianenko, Viktor Chuzhykov, Michal G. Wozniak. Kyiv: KNEU (In Ukrainian).

Convergence and Divergence in Europe: Polish and Ukrainian Cases. 2013. Scientific editors Dmytro Lukianenko, Viktor Chuzhykov, Michal G. Wozniak. Kyiv: KNEU.

Deleidi, Matteo, Meloni, Walter P. and Stirati, Antonella. 2020. "Tertiarization, productivity and aggregate demand: evidence-based policies for European countries." *Journal of Evolutionary Economics* #30: 1429-1465.

Federal Reserve Bank St. Louis. *Economic Research.* Accessed October 30 2020.
https://research.stlouisfed.org/fred2/series/CTFPPPUAA669NRUG#.

Filipenko, Anton S. 2017. "Productive ability of nations: theory and methodology." *Proceedings of the conference. Productive ability of nations: the case of Ukraine.* 29 June 2017. Kyiv.

*Global Productivity. Trends, Drivers, and Policies.*2020. Edited by Alistair Dieppe. Washington DC: World Bank.

Groth, Charlotta, Gutierrez-Domenech, Maria and Srinivasan, Sylaja. 2003. *Measuring total factor productivity for the United Kingdom. Bank of England.* Accessed October 30 2020.
http://www.bankofengland.co.uk/publications/Documents/quarterlybulletin/qb040106.pdf.

Hideaki, Aoyama, Hiroshi, Yoshikawa, Hiroshi, Iyetomi and Yoshi, Fujiwara. 2008. "Productivity Dispersion: Facts, Theory, and Implications." *The Research Institute of Economy,* Trade and *Industry.* Accessed October 30 2020. http://www.rieti.go.jp/en/.

Keynes, John M. 2007. *The general theory of employment, interest and money. The selected works*, trans. from Engl. Moscow: Eksmo (In Russian).

Kim, Jungsuk and Park, Jungsoo. 2017. "The Role of Total Factor Productivity Growth in Middle income Countries." *ADB Economics Working Paper Series*, 527: 3-29.

Kim, Young Eun and Loayza, Norman V. 2019. "Productivity Growth. Patterns and Determinants across the World." *Policy Research Working Paper. Development Economics* 8852: 1-69.

Koszerek, Douglas, Havik, Karel, McMorrow, Kieran, Röger Werner and Schönborn, Frank. 2007. "An overview of the EU KLEMS Growth and Productivity Accounts." *European Economy. Economic Papers* 290: 105.

Leontief, Vasiliy. 2006. *The selected works in 3 vol. (vol. 2). Special investigations on the ground of "input-output."* Moscow: Economica (In Russian).

Measuring productivity. 2001. Measurement of aggregate and industry-level productivity growth. Paris.

Mill, John S. 2007. *Principles of Political Economy with some of their applications to social philosophy*, trans. from Engl. Moscow: Eksmo (In Russian).

Morris, Ian. 2018. *Why the West rules – for now. The Patterns of history and what they reveal about the future*, trans from Engl. Kyiv: Klio (In Ukrainian).

Nelson, Richard. 2006. "What makes an economy productive and progressive? What are the needed institutions?" *Working Paper Series 24. ONS Productivity Handbook. A Statistical Overview and Guide.*2007. Edited by Dawn Camus. New York: Palgrave Macmillan.

OECD 2019. "Productivity Growth in the Digital Age". Paris: OECD. Accessed 30 October 2020. www.oecd.org/going-digital.

Office for National Statistics 2021, https://www.ons.gov.uk.

Porter, Michael E. 1990. *Competitive Advantage of Nations.* Boston: Harvard Business Review.

Schwab, Klaus. 2016. *The Fourth Industrial Revolution*. Geneva: World Economic Forum.

Smith, Adam. 2001. *Inquiry into the nature and causes of the wealth of nations*, trans. from Engl. Kyiv: Port-Royal (In Ukrainian).

Spence, Michael. 2013. *The Next Convergence: The Future of Economic Growth in a Multispeed World*, trans. from Engl. Moscow: Publishing Gaydar institute (In Russian).

Tarscott, Don and Tarscott, Alex. 2018. *Blockchain revolution. How the Technology behind bitcoin and other cryptocurrencies is changing the World.* New York: Portfolio/Penguin.

The Economics of Productivity. 2009. Edited by Dawn W. Jorgenson. Cheltenham: Edward Elgar Publishing Limited.

Total economy data base key findings. July 2020. Accessed October 30 2020. www.conferenceboard.ca.

Toynbee, Arnold J. 1995. *A Study of History*, trans. from Engl. Kyiv: Osnovy (In Ukrainian).

Weber, Max. 1994. *The Protestant Ethic and the Spirit of Capitalism*, trans. from German. Kyiv: Osnovy (In Ukrainian).

Witztum, Amos. 2012. "The firm, property rights and methodological individualism: some lessons from J. St. Mill." *Journal of Economic Methodology* 19, 4: 339-356.

Wolff, Edward N. 2014. *Productive Convergence. Theory and evidence*. Cambridge: Cambridge University Press.

CHAPTER TWO

THE FOURTH INDUSTRIAL REVOLUTION AS A MOTIVATOR FOR A QUALITATIVE LEAP IN A COUNTRY'S PRODUCTIVE CAPABILITY: INTERNATIONAL EXPERIENCE, AND CHALLENGES AND RISKS FOR UKRAINE

YURII K. ZAITSEV

With regard to philosophy of the development of the global economy and society in the context of the Fourth Industrial Revolution, William James believes: "The greatest revolution of our generation is the discovery that human beings, by changing the inner attitudes of their minds, can change the outer aspects of their lives" (Coombes 2011). I absolutely agree with William James's opinion. Note that the most powerful technological revolution in the history of modern society, creating the background for meeting the entirety of critical and long-term needs of economic and social life subjects across the globe, is simultaneously providing brand-new manufacturing capabilities and tools to affect the processes of managing the life of these "human beings" and their mind, desires, emotions, etc. This is an extremely relevant challenge for and threat to the existence of both the individual and the whole society in the institutional field of our civilisation's values.

The establishment and application of a new modern technological and economic paradigm – the nature and functions of which have been revealed by several contemporary researchers (see Schwab 2016; Schwab and Davis 2018; Blommaert, Van den Broek and Kolthof 2017; Skinner 2018; Huateng, Zhaoli, Delhi and Huali 2019; Zaitsev and Moskalenko 2020; Reinert 2020; Drexler 2013; Ford 2015; Brockman 2015) – is obviously insufficient to understand urgent problems and ways of further development of the productive capabilities of globalised society in the long run.

This is because, firstly, *global economy* in the context of Industry 4.0 means not only the concentration of humankind's possibilities based on joining efforts, better interaction between national economies and societies, and formation of philosophy and real basics of pluralist economics[1], but also a new philosophy of values, methods and forms of economic growth, which is a key factor for a change in the paradigm of the worldview by scientists, policymakers and public authorities. It requires dramatic changes by society, individual social groups and people worldwide that preclude civilisational resonance; in other words, systematic equilibrium between the needs of and possibilities for the further existence of humankind as particular integrally institutionalised forms of social and socialised life.

Secondly, the interrelated process in time and space of Industry 4.0 and the globalised economy's expansion complicates not only the subjective perception of deep changes taking place across the globe, but also the depth of potential opportunities, real challenges and contradictions accompanied by these changes, posing mega-threats to preservation of the core values of human civilisation. This is because of the misconception of very possible ethical and specific limits of the transformation of these values. This is true even under conditions of unlimited technological resources of nanotechnological revolutions, and economic, political, mental and ethical freedoms caused by these revolutions.

Thirdly, "[c]ontemporary theory", according to E. Reinert (2020, 55), with whom one should probably agree with, "experiences issues concerning taking into account qualitative economic changes to be the framework for quantitative changes in the future." Besides, he also believes that "society falls into confusion in the age of paradigm transformation. A similar

[1] A ***pluralist economics*** refers to: 1) a result and form of the objective evolution process of the economic system, during which various institutional and legal models of national economies occur, function, coexist and advance, even in the institutional field of a single globalised economic system; and 2) economies and economic policy models whose fundamental theoretical backgrounds consist of paradigm approaches based on different theoretical and methodological views of scientists and policymakers regarding ways of solving same-type problems and tasks of further economic growth. Different scientific schools and different subjective approaches to the analysis of methods for solving relevant issues and contradictions, and satisfying the needs and interests of economic life subjects, cause not only pluralism of thoughts, conceptual views and theoretical development models but also pluralism of approaches to the establishment of practical economic policy for ensuring such a development (Keynesian theory, neoliberalism, ordoliberalism, new institutionalism, post-neoliberalism, contemporary political economy, etc.).

situation is also relevant to modern science: we have a significant amount of research and conclusions while some of them contradict each other" (Reinert 2020, 55). At the same time, he stresses, "a combination of different paradigms can lead to the situation when we will choose something based on our national or other interests. If it is profitable for us, we will say that the Earth is round; if not, we will state that it is flat" (Reinert 2020, 55).

Thus, dramatic qualitative changes in the technological method of production, organisational and economic architectonics of the present-day world, and economic, social and civilisational development are coursed by the overload of resource and ecological capabilities of the planet. It is crucial that these changes are followed by individualisation and atomisation of intellectual work,[2] and that rapid robotisation of the full cycle of social reproduction creates prerequisites for new philosophical and paradigmatic comprehension of prospects, and potential options for the further existence of human beings and society.

Economic science has only recently stipulated, on the basis of the interdisciplinary approach, the principles and nature of the human-centred paradigm of economic and social growth, whose primary concepts include understanding the fact that, firstly, "the catalyst of historical evolution is in methods for harmonic coordination of the activity of freely acting humanitarian creatures"; secondly, "new philosophy of history, being a general civilizational non-ethnical, non-class ideology of humanity self-establishment, does not have any historical framework"; thirdly, "the value of life is in the implementation of its fundamental social constants; humanitarian absolutes. Division of Truth and Good results in instrumentalism"; and fourthly, "the axis of life is in worthy movement to material and spiritual relaxedness, full self-actualization via the social and existential progress, rising to humanitarian high values" (Ilyin 2003, 27, 40, 41).

Unfortunately, the above-mentioned philosophical principles of understanding the essence of the human-centred paradigm as a motivator for developing up-to-date economic and social systems, concepts and goals for applying its productive capacity – as described by a globally recognised philosopher, V.V. Ilyin, and other contemporary scientists – do not deny the contradictory nature of the human being that the above-cited author characterises in the following manner: "A human paradoxical feature is ambivalence: it is a subject constructing the world and an object

[2] A. Nazaretian (2018, 170) believes: "the development of technologies accompanied by the increasing potential effect of individual actions and the decreasing internal social stability (which fulfillment requires more and more cultural self-limitations) is a logical consequence of the technological and humanitarian balance model."

existing in the world" (Ilyin 2003, 35).

By the way, in this context, what we deem appropriate is the actualisation of investigating the dialectics of interrelations between human-centred and transhumanistic paradigms as core motivators, conceptual systems of views, and approaches to the definition of primary objectives and ways of applying new productive capabilities of society generated by Industry 4.0.

Essential features of the transhumanistic paradigm are directly related to specific views of a significant group of scientists, policymakers and businesspeople on the nature, possibilities and functions of people in a technologically united globalised society. In particular, proponents of this approach, according to researchers of this issue, refuse any dogmatic interpretations (primarily religious ones) of human existence. They understand the evolution of scientific knowledge as a prerequisite for technological and biological advancement of people. They also perceive an individual not as the final product of evolution, but as an intermediate stage on the way from a biological person to a cluster of informational and cybernetic fields and supreme intelligence. "In fact, transhumanism…is a desire to overcome limited human physiological characteristics, to perceive an individual as a potentially unlimited essence in terms of development" (Dubrovskyi and Klimova 2014, 96).

At the same time, other critical researchers of the nature of the transhumanistic paradigm of the economic and social growth of globalised society in the context of Industry 4.0 express their opinions more frankly, relying on expert views. They maintain that "the implementation of the eugenic idea – to create an overhuman by advancing the current person – is the main goal of the whole technological activity while the rest is just a 'cover operation'" (Bielkina, Frolova and Korsakova 2016, 185).

We believe that ambivalence to the human essence is a basis for the whole range of motivators and risks related to the development of nanotechnologies in the process of the Fourth Industrial Revolution. Its results simplify transitions of human beings and society from one reality to another – the ambivalence of the human functional essence can turn people, by using advanced technologies and values of leaders of the brand-new progress wave, from subjects into objects of modified economic and social life – in order to gain harmony, systematic equilibrium and steady growth of the productive capacity of national economies, etc. Reasoning: for the comfortable life of anything and for anybody – not an innovative technology, it is as old as the hills.

Trends in changes in the system of values and motivators of the economy and society, particularly regions, social groups and certain subjects of globalised economic life across the globe caused by the nanotechnological revolution, result in serious concerns about the quality of paradigmatic orientation. This is both in the field of scientific research of the nature and prospects of current processes, and in the field of political activities and economic policy, from the perspective of preservation and the best possible orientation of human civilisation's development.

In my opinion, the state of dualism, uncertainty and risks regarding predictions of the future place and role of a human being in social production, and in spiritual, cultural and civilisational global fields, dominates in approaches to formation of, first, the paradigmatic focus of scientific research in social sciences, second, the paradigmatic orientation of policymakers and economic policy, and finally definition of the paradigm of globalised society's economic growth. However, to my mind, it should be remembered that, in any conditions, a person remains human only in the case of learning and possessing all the achievements of the human mind in the socialised environment: the ability to work and understand the necessity to participate in social production in a certain form; the ability and necessity to constantly communicate with other people, feeling and using your and the other person's emotions, emotional potential and emotional capital; and the ability to feel joy and bring joy to other people, etc. A nanotechnological person is no longer a full individual.

Well, the transhumanistic development paradigm aimed at applying the achievements of the Fourth (and not the only) Industrial Revolution in order to turn a person into the overhuman actually directs this growth towards completion of the existence of natural human civilisation, without even trying to answer the questions: what internal productive capabilities and development reserves of human beings are still not revealed; what will happen to society, the world of people, and what will happen to hundreds of millions (billions) of people (and whether they will be able to remain human) in the context of rapid robotisation of all life spheres across the globe? Such conclusions drive the need, in the process of defining strategic goals of economic growth and the desired results of the nanotechnological revolution as a primary motivator of this development, for philosophical understanding, forecasting and encouraging potentially irreversible ethical, spiritual and social losses of human civilisation. The level of risks from making rapid fateful decisions is beyond human imagination.

Modern scientists have a consolidated idea about the institutional essence of motivation as being about the process of inclining employees towards activities; "the complex of internal factors that determine and direct the activity of a person, team, individual social group, or society to achieving the conscious goal" (Mishurova and Kitelev 2003, 7). I guess it will be helpful to supplement such an idea about the essence of motive and motivation with definitions that deepen the understanding of their nature and functions, with an emphasis on the fact that motive is "a driving reason, a ground for any action", or "in favour of any action" while motivation is "reasoning, rationale, grounds for actions" (Spirkin A. G. et al. 1986, 324).

This supplement suggests that motives and motivators for the process of inclining towards activities should, firstly, rely on the understanding of the essence of driving reasons and, secondly, recognise that such an incentive is not necessarily the outcome of the internal factor actions. On the contrary, the process of inclining towards activities is frequently formed because of the emergence and development of irreversible external factors that only later turn (or do not turn) into internal factors. This incentive can be illustrated by the development of the Fourth Industrial Revolution becoming a challenge and an impetus for activities of the majority of countries in the globalised world.

At different historical development stages of economic systems and society, the accumulation of internal and external factors can be qualitatively different depending on challenges, demands and possibilities of national economic systems, the level of interrelation and interaction of national economies in the field and within the global economic space. At the same time, under any conditions, according to Steven Landsburg, people respond to impetuses, everything else is details.

Factors determining the productive and manufacturing capabilities of countries can be conditionally divided into two categories: a) *traditional* – technical, economic, organisational, motivational (including the level of and reasons for conflicts of interests of core population groups, possibilities to reconcile these interests using the motive and impetus system, etc.), institutional, social, mental (providing the level of human and social passionarity), intellectual, spiritual, civilisational (that define the values of life activities by people, authorities and businesses); and b) *innovative* – (primarily at the macro-level) related to the development of scientific and technological revolutions, particularly the Fourth Industrial Revolution, and nanotechnological revolutions, which actually generate brand-new productive capabilities of these economies and the globalised economic system, as well as simultaneously forming new, sometimes dangerous, motives for the further development of globalised society (we have already mentioned above the emergence of dualism caused by technological revolutions in human civilisation's evolution – the human-centred/transhumanistic orientation of the development, etc.).

As a consequence, it is probably worth mentioning the opinion of D. Rodrik who stresses in his *Economics Rules: The Rights and Wrongs of the Dismal Science* that economists frequently "…do not see the difference between the efficiency and other socially significant goals," and they "tend to take the world for granted, including human selfishness, and make decisions given this limitation. They will say (and will be right) that this work is defined by their focus on empiricism and has nothing to do with values and ethics" (2016, 223-224, 229).

In the minds of numerous economic subjects and economists, according to Rodrik, if there are market values, "all of them come to the same thing: efficiency. The only thing an economist can say about the market, and just about the properly operating market, is that it ensures the efficient allocation of resources with the maximum accuracy" (2016, 226).

The warning of this well-known scientific theorist and methodologist is definitely not useless in the context of changes triggered by the Fourth Industrial Revolution in architectonics, and the goals and methods for ensuring the productive capacity of nations. On the one hand, qualitative changes caused by the Industry 4.0 revolution, including the formation of the digital economy, provide great opportunities for overcoming the system of limited economic development of globalised society, which is definitely a powerful motivator for economic activities of businesses, society and the state. According to researchers, "all countries, especially catching-up ones, have the chance of a non-linear breakthrough in the national economic growth if they focus on wide informatization of society and efficient digital transformation of business processes" (Golovenchik and Kovalev 2019, 365). According to McKinsey's estimates, China's GDP might increase by up to 22% by 2025 due to Internet technologies. The USA's expected value growth caused by digital technologies is also impressive: it might reach $1.6–2.2 trillion (10% of GDP) by 2025 (Golovenchik and Kovalev 2019, 369). McKinsey's estimates show that the potential economic effect from digitalisation of the Russian economy will increase the country's GDP by RUB4.1–8.9 trillion (at 2015 values) by 2025. The effect of digitalisation will represent between 19% and 34% of the GDP's general expected growth, while the share of the digital economy will reach 8–10% of the GDP (Golovenchik and Kovalev 2019, 370).

According to the Huawei Global Connectivity Index (GCI), the volume of the digital economy was estimated at $12.9 trillion in 2018, which was 17.1% of the global GDP (Golovenchik and Kovalev 2019, 370). However, according to scientists, such impressive results of the digital economic growth in its current form are primarily caused by the Internet aimed at consumers. The next wave of rapid growth in the digital economy will be caused by the digital transformation of manufacturing industry aimed at creating more integrated relations among all things and people.

Researchers believe that a total transformation of the field will be based on an intelligent Internet connection allowing all manufacturing sectors to benefit from unprecedented opportunities for growth. On average, if all countries annually increase their investments in the ICT infrastructure by 8%, it will give new economic potential of $23 trillion by 2025 (Golovenchik and Kovalev 2019, 370-371). According to the forecasts of Huawei and Oxford Economics, the increase in the GCI by 1 percentage point is equivalent to an increase in competitive ability by 2.1%, an increase in national innovations by 2.2% and an increase in productivity by 2.3% (Golovenchik and Kovalev 2019, 371), which shows the steady growth of the productive capacity of national economic systems and, consequently, can encourage the sustainable prosperity of nations and people.

All of these cutting-edge possibilities for businesses, the state and individuals are efficient and convincing motivators for the active involvement of national economies in processes of revolutionary change deepening in the technological methods of manufacturing and transformation of valuable traditional benchmarks of social development in order to relieve social tension, social exclusion, social deprivation, etc.

On the other hand, the Fourth Industrial Revolution, the digital economy, on the basis of which there are transformations of economic management processes, and the creation of economic goods are becoming motivators that, by increasing the productive capacity of people and nations, generate a dangerous trend in economic dehumanisation, in forming motives and impetuses for the emergence of a transhumanistic focus aimed at the creation and dominance of artificial intelligence, and overhuman, post-human being as well.

Establishment of a post-industrial, information type of economy and society leads to qualitative changes not only in all structural elements of the economic system, but also in the entire system of levers and factors ensuring its functioning and development. Such changes are manifested initially in the enrichment of economic development goals and socialisation of all institutional forms of economic life. However, Friedman, in his well-known work "The Methodology of Positive Economics" (1953), stresses: "A fundamental hypothesis of science is that appearances are deceptive and that there is a way of looking at or interpreting or organizing the evidence that will reveal superficially disconnected and diverse phenomena to be manifestations of a more fundamental and relatively simple structure" (Friedman 1994, 43).

Dani Rodrik, the above-mentioned methodologist of economic science, emphasises the danger of such deceptiveness of the paradigmatic character, particularly in the approaches of contemporary neoliberals to one of the most relevant problems of the market economy and society's functioning: their efficiency. He stresses the following: "The majority of economic models stipulate the selfish behaviour of individuals. They aim to maximize their (and, perhaps, their children's) consumption possibilities and do not care about what will happen to others" (Rodrik 2016). Furthermore, Mason emphasises that the main message of neoliberalism is the fact that it has no alternative (Mason 2016, 10).

However, there is an alternative: a humanistic paradigm of understanding the nature and regularities of economic and social growth. The framework for this humanistic paradigm of investigating the laws of economic and social functioning from the perspective of ensuring their dialectical unity in the integral and efficient meta-system, to my mind, initially consists of the objective centripetal principles of its values-based orientation: intellectualisation, morality, spirituality, responsibility, socialisation of economic and social life subjects, and a focus on the best possible correlation of market and social fairness at micro and macro levels, etc.

The question is whether these principles of value-based economic and social orientation are ensured and developed by the Fourth Industrial Revolution that intersects with nanotechnological revolutions and generates such specific forms of understanding, perception and functioning of the reality as cyberculture, cyberpunk and cyber libertarianism, identity virtualisation, culture as technoculture, people and cyborgs from a transhuman to a post-human, technological transhumanism totalitarianism, cybernetic modernity, technological social Darwinism and technoeugenics, etc. (Yemelin 2017, 187-199, 330-336).

Above-cited Klaus K. Schwab, as well as the majority of scientists and policymakers, believes that technologies should expand opportunities rather than limit them; that the future should be formed by people and for people; and that values should be benefits rather than disadvantages of technologies. Improvement of living standards should be a priority. If the Fourth Industrial Revolution leads to a rise in inequality, poverty, discrimination, instability, environmental danger, marginalisation, enslavement or devaluation of people, it will mean that we chose the wrong way (Schwab and Davis 2018, 45).

So, in my opinion, internal factors, potential achievements and consequences of the Fourth Industrial Revolution, depending on global society's understanding of the essence of strategic goals, can serve as both motivators for the development of global contradictions, and motivators for the value-based advanced growth in the welfare of all countries and each person across the globe.

We I agree with K. Schwab about the definition of the essence, content and role of dialectics of interdependence and interrelation between technologies, values and necessity for conducting the policy of prioritising social values during development, adoption and application of advanced technologies and their systematic use. K. Schwab and N. Davis (2018, 48-49) specify the following fundamental principles of defining the essence of such interdependence: 1) Any technology involves the reflection of values, goals and beliefs of its author. The more powerful the technology, the more important it is to realise what it consists of; 2) Economic motives most frequently determine what technologies are reasonable to develop, as well as how to implement and apply them. These motives can be recognised by social consequences; 3) In political negotiations between representatives of society, technologies and businesses, we should define how much attention would be paid to social values; and 4) With technologies being closely integrated into society, we are responsible for the definition of their development areas and the announcement of the social value priority.

Challenges for employment and labour motivation in the context of the Fourth Industrial Revolution. Labour as a key civilisational feature of a person, individual and society

Exploration of the essence of the driving forces of civilisational factors of economic development suggests the unity of their deep, substantial forms of all historical development stages of society's productive capacity.

In my opinion, *labour*[3], *culture*[4] and *passionarity* (Gumiliev 1993,

---

[3] At the same time, the content and character of labour and specific features of involvement of a certain civilisation's entity in the social reproduction process; labour ethics; ethics of the relationship between economic entities; tools for the spiritual impact on the motivation system and labour efficiency, on principles and the process of selection and decision-making, on the character of interaction between key economic entities and social relations, etc. are directly related to historical features of forming these deep institutional forms of human civilisation's functioning in each nation. Therefore, consideration of such features is a crucial condition for ensuring a synergetic effect of social advancement of humankind and people in the strategic prospect.

509) of people play a key role among such forms. The existence of time, and spatially continuous dialectic systematic relations and dependencies between the above-mentioned substantial forms of civilisation's functioning, in their different modifications, according to tasks and possibilities of a certain historical development stage of people, a nation and humankind, provide the conditions and grounds for setting strategic goals of this civilisation, and motives and ways to reach them. According to philosophers, "civilization that exploits, but does not cultivate, has no future" (Ilyin 2003, 18).

Motivation

For a long period, the ultimate principles of labour motivation of any economic entity in the capitalist market economy have included the following: 1) There is no compelling reason for work without richness; 2) The only thing that is of lasting benefit to a man is that which he does for himself; 3) Money that comes to people without effort on their part is seldom a benefit and often a curse (Brown 2015). These principles are scientifically explained and creatively revealed by J.A. Schumpeter in his book *Capitalism, Socialism and Democracy* (1995).

Contemporary challenges of human civilisation based on labour, culture and passionarity of members of society

In my view, the new historical age related to the Fourth Industrial Revolution with its incredible technological possibilities and focus on the mass use of robotics in the context of the capitalist market economy will not just solve issues of fulfilling human and social needs, but will also cause an increasing risk of civilisation's death. This is because of decreasing possibilities to satisfy these needs by one's own labour, which is a key institutional form distinguishing us from the animal world, making us people and forming society. The rapid integration of nanotechnologies, atomistically precise manufacturing and robotic automation result in the dynamisation of qualitative changes in labour

[4] During the meeting of government representatives from 150 countries in Florence (October 1999), the World Bank stated that culture is the most significant component of economic growth and, from that moment, it will increasingly determine and affect the bank's economic activities, although almost 200 years ago, Wilhelm Roscher (historical school of political economy) believed that the higher the culture, the higher the labour appreciation.

requirements, conditions to ensure the quality of human labour, etc. At the same time, there is an increasing number of external challenges, in particular technological, structural, geopolitical, technologically geopolitical, global-ecological and civilisational challenges. This is in addition to those related to mass social mutations (glam-capitalism, downshifters, a long-term unemployed population, internal 'unemployed – principals', 'unemployed – migrant principals' as a widespread phenomenon); and politics and economics (aggravation of social and socio-technological competition, and the emergence of a dualistic development paradigm (human-centred or transhumanistic) of the economy and society).

According to Cowen (2015), technological, structural and geopolitical changes in the context of a globalised economy lead to the division of the economically active population into two categories, deepening the inequality in the technological evolution of certain countries and regions. In these circumstances, in my opinion, reservation of human rights to labour will be the main motivator, motive and impetus for work at the micro-level in the system of horizontal relations of the globalised economy. Following the results of research conducted in 2013 at Oxford University, 47% of professions out of 702 in the USA could be automated, and 35% of professions in the UK and 49% in Japan have already disappeared (Huateng, Zhaoli, Delhi and Huali 2019, 210). Other investigations show that 90% of relevant vocational professions will be performed by smart machines by 2030 (Huateng, Zhaoli, Delhi and Huali 2019, 210).

The competition of intelligence and intellectual potential of workers, and the struggle for possibilities to ensure conditions for forming, applying and developing our own intellectual capabilities, will prevail in the system of internal motivating factors of the majority of employees and in the system of social competition on the labour market. Passion for money accumulation and for richness as a stimulating reason for work, as described by Rockefeller, will take a back seat, because people will enter into competition not only with each other but also with machines and robots, in order to remain human. Human civilisation without labour will initially degrade and then disappear.

Eventually, we I believe that eventually there will be an inextricable connection – the interdependence between labour quality and life quality – and the belief of economic entities in the possibility to ensure this connection is the key value and motivator for the advancement of the market economic system in the context of revolutionary changes in productive capacity of businesses, human beings and the state. Under any conditions, labour, the attitude to which formed the whole complex of economic and individual values, was a key value and a factor for the progressive growth of economic and social systems in the majority of the world. While this value is kept in a fairly wide area of interests, opportunities, and hopes of the majority of members of society and the authorities, capitalism – and its economic, social and political systems – will be quite resistant to both internal and external challenges, disturbances, and temporary disruptions, even of the systematic equilibrium whose recovery takes place during qualitative internal transformations.

Problems and risks of Ukraine's integration into the global economic space in the context of digital globalisation

Systematic adoption of microprocessor engineering, telecommunications and digital technologies at the end of the 20th and beginning of the 21st centuries, multiplied by the principles of neoliberal economic policy, became the framework for the rapid establishment of the three-stage globalisation model of financial flow regulation processes, cheapening the affordability of loans for global economic entities, and simultaneously meaning greater dependence and control over their activities by international financial institutions and certain developed countries. In the 1980s and 1990s, it was possible to see the ultimate system of institutions and tools for the impact of the global economy on financial flows in all significant sectors, including: national, international and private financial institutions; the world's reserve currency; global debt; and the global risk phenomenon. As a result, over the last decade of the 20th century and at the beginning of the 21st century, the annual volume of global financial transactions was estimated at the astronomical sum of about half a quadrillion dollars, which caused the situation of a credit risk on a global scale that could lead to a general systemic crisis, according to researchers.

At the same time, it should probably be admitted that the long-term focus of the transnational corporation on the technological and financial strategy, as well as the delocalisation production policy in the modern conditions, are mainly coincident with the demands and interests of national economies of post-colonial and post-communist states (including Ukraine).

On the one hand, objective globalisation processes accelerated by subjective efforts of the most economically powerful countries significantly reduce possibilities for independent selection of options and tools for establishing one's own competitive national economic systems of developing countries. However, on the other hand, transnational corporation operations somehow encourage the development of such systems: by large investments, arranging the manufacturing of contemporary products, and involving national enterprises and entrepreneurs in the circle of specific manifestations of international division of labour, etc.

There is a situation with the fulfilment of a transnational corporation's interests and national economic policy goals where the authorities have managed to ensure their more-or-less civilised combination encouraged the advancement of developing countries in terms of industrialisation, steady rates of economic growth, integration into the global economic community and the system of free trading relations. Structural changes in the national economic complex affected by the transnational corporation and the economic policy of interacting national states, and national capital, resulted in at least two positive trends: 1) the addition of numerous *new economies* contributing towards the global commodity turnover, and entering into a single informational space as competitive and, to some extent, equal entities and partners; 2) the socialisation of economic life in these countries. Meanwhile, it is worth noting some brand-new trends caused by the globalisation process at the beginning of the 21st century: during this period, a new institutional form of the functioning of the globalised economy is being dynamically established, which directly and indirectly affects the methods of controlling all areas of social life; an institutional system of digital globalisation is emerging and developing.

Indeed, according to China Info, the rates of digital economic growth in developed countries significantly outpace the GDP growth rates. In 2016, the former reached 6.8% in the USA, exceeding the GDP growth rate of 1.6% (Huateng, Zhaoli and Huali 2019, 210). In Japan, the digital economic growth rate of 5.5% outpaced the GDP growth rate by 0.9% within the same period (Huateng, Zhaoli and Huali 2019, 210). The rate of digital economic growth in the UK of 5.4% considerably exceeded the GDP growth rate of 2% within the same period (Huateng, Zhaoli and Huali 2019, 210). The rates in China are 16.6% for digital economic growth and 6.7% for GDP growth (Huateng, Zhaoli and Huali 2019, 210).

Such results of the development of the information economy can cause over-optimism regarding possibilities for and prospects of the functioning of the "informational, digital technological production method" and the establishment of the global information society. However, these possibilities can only be fully implemented if "the equality of rights in relations between states does not depend on the equality of powers, but depends on the equality of sovereign statuses" (Blischenko and Dori 2001, 16). Besides, e-commerce reduces not only expenses for promoting products – and thereby rapidly increasing volumes of them, which is definitely a positive phenomenon from an economic perspective – but also jobs, leading to additional unemployment and decreasing the effective demand. This is clearly a contradictory dialectic.

The digital globalisation process also creates prerequisites for the total automation and atomisation of economic life subjects, and thus a person remains face to face with a virtual, fetishised capital. It eventually deepens social exclusion and gaps in human–society relations. Digital globalisation increasingly disrupts the interrelation and cooperation between the state, businesses and society, and takes consumers and producers beyond social values and principles to the world of falsified and misleading institutional forms and relations. Moreover, the above-mentioned statistics do not take into account the fact that the advantages of digital globalisation are primarily felt by developed countries, transnational corporations and higher social classes in these countries.

Conclusions and forecasts of Thomas Barnett's (2004) concept, suggesting that technological development creates a zoned division of all territories worldwide, structuring in its way the global strategic space where the core zone – the USA and the EU – will always dominate while other countries, in the best-case scenario, are destined for the "user attitude to networks", also do not encourage optimistic expectations from the advancement of new institutional forms of the capitalist information economy. Such a development (if it definitely takes place in the coordinate system of Barnett's concept), to my mind, will likely encourage an increase in political and social tensions, and exclusion in the global social space. These trends can also be enhanced by a neoliberal market approach to the use of planetary resources in favour of the world's most powerful economies, which definitely deepens ecological threats for humankind.

So, as stated above, the rapid growth of globalisation processes in the context of the extensive advancement of information and the digital economy based on the capitalist market is an ambiguous phenomenon, which leads to dualism and entropy features in the global economy and society, requiring political and economic analysis and reasoning of conclusions and recommendations, and new political and economic paradigms and principles for forming the concept and model for the further existence and development of Ukraine and other states, in terms of maintaining the sovereign statuses of countries, regions and individuals.

Transformation of labour's civilisational functions in the context of nanotechnological revolutions and the digital economy

Any social form of human existence is directly related to economic life and the economic activities of people. Therefore, when it comes to the essence, content and key features of any civilisation, one should rely on the analysis of the particularities of historical conditions for forming social production, labour processes, and the system of economic, social and labour relations. A civilisational approach, especially in the context of the qualitative leap to the development of the essence and motivating factors of productive capabilities of certain national economies and countries, and the whole globalised society, primarily implies detection of the complex of certain common human values. It also implies the analysis on this basis of special features of forms of their manifestation and application in all social sectors of people or nations. This can be carried out from the perspective of determining their common human potential and possibilities for use by other people in order to ensure the most efficient growth of the economy and culture.

Systematic research of the essence of driving forces of civilisations and the economic growth factors allows discussion about the unity of their substantial forms, where the key roles initially belong to labour, culture (Throsby 2001, 25) and passionarity of people; in other words, their ability in the process of labour functioning, in all its forms and varieties, to constantly advance (simultaneously conserving forms and features that define and strengthen the constructive personification of civilisation), highlight promising strategic goals and objectives of this civilisation, and ensure their attainment by the efficient application of previous civilisational achievements in the system of social and economic relations.

Both material and spiritual cultures encourage the establishment of a particular social culture, and directly affect principles and institutional forms of manufacturing, allocation and consumption of products. A specific character of the development of spiritual culture of certain nations, countries and civilisations directly affects not only the intellectual content of labour, and its application boundaries that define possibilities for innovative advancement of people, businesses and the national economy, but also the determination of strategic goals of economic and social development, methods for their achievement, the essence of motives and impetuses of manufacturing and economic activities, and the ethics of relationships between economic entities within a separate civilisational field and during interaction of different civilisations.

These principles formed the civilisational functions of labour, where the key ones, in my opinion, include the following: 1) recognition of continuity of labour activity reproduction (regardless of the kind, form, content and character of labour) to satisfy increasing social demands. Henry Ford mentioned: "A business that makes nothing but money is a poor business. It seems that everyone looks for the shortest way to money and avoid the straightest one – through labour" (Ford 1922)[5] 2) realisation and acknowledgement of the need for interaction of different people, teams and states in the labour process; 3) an understanding of the role of labour for socialisation of human beings and society; 4) realisation and recognition of the role of responsibility for organisation processes and labour results at all levels and in all areas of economic life; 5) the establishment, in the process of developing the social division of labour, of the character and content of work, social and labour relations, and trust between economic entities, as an institutional tool that is a fundamental condition for obtaining steady positive results in any economic field, as stressed by Confucius; and 6) the formation and realisation by people and society of the role of the creative character of labour for the self-actualisation of a human being as a creator. Defining the meaning of this civilisational function of human work, Confucius said: "Choose a job you love, and you will never have to work a day in your life" (Bugromeev and Bugromeev 2010).

However, in the context of technological revolutions, rapid evolution of robotics and the digital economy, and the need for some of the above-mentioned civilisational labour functions, either disappears or transforms unrecognisably, taking on falsified, misleading forms. Nowadays, the whole range of leading corporations, such as MagicLeap, Microsoft, HoalohaRoboticus, Google, DeepMind and others, are shifting to the next technological wave, described as Society 5.0 in Japan (the fourth one was informational; the third one was industrial), which "will be based on the integration of physical space and cyber space technologies into a single complex." (Lebedeva 2019, 22-23). It means "the association of robotic systems, bio- and nanotechnologies, photonics, quantum equipment, human-machine interface with cutting-edge achievements of engineering cybernetics, artificial intelligence, big data, Internet of Things, etc" (Lebedeva 2019, 22-23). A huge group of European experts suggest the

[5] He insisted on the fact that "labor and only labor is able to create values. The economic principle is labor. Labor is a human element that benefits from fruitful seasons"; "A moral principle is the human right to labor…only work leads to the right way to health, wealth and happiness"; "As for me, there is nothing more disgusting as leisure life" (Ford 1922).

following challenges and threats caused by the dynamisation of such processes: 1) unpredicted technological changes leading to the sharp transformation of the labour market (3D printers, robotic automation, digitalisation, closed digital systems, etc.); 2) a political factor related to weakened international collaboration; and 3) recession of Western values – democracy, solidarity, humanity and current European integration principles (Lebedeva 2019, 22-23).

In these circumstances, according to A.A. Grytsenko, Ukraine's leading economic theorist, "The development of economic digitalization and capitalization processes will give a positive effect for society only in case of combining with economic socialization processes. It implies fundamental changes in the social system, evolution of activity types related to free time and formation of new human capabilities, which leads to a range of problems and challenges for society" (Lebedeva 2019, 22-23). This warning regarding the premature adoption of advanced technologies is also expressed by Guo Kaitian, Senior Vice-President at Tencent (a leading company engaged in digital technologies estimated to be worth $256.6 billion) and Head of the Supervisory Board at Tencent's Research Institute. He believes that adoption of technologies is quite an expensive process, while its deep impact on society is much more complicated than people can imagine. This impact of technologies does not only relate to the enhancement of manufacturing efficiency, because it goes far beyond its boundaries, destabilising the structure of social division and allocation of labour. Statistical figures show that daily consumption of scientific and technological progress products results in the loss of the key thing – a human being, their needs and demands. Evidence suggests that the majority of people cannot keep pace with the extreme development of technologies. At the same time, Guo Kaitian stresses that "society as a group of individuals has to advance, mature and become controlled" (Lebedeva 2019, 22-23). Furthermore, "the scientific and technological progress is one of the main forces of human society advancement. Another similar force is human propensity to self-analysis" (Lebedeva 2019, 22-23).

The main problem, to my mind, in the context of scientific revolution and the digital economy is the decline, or even the loss, of the totality of such civilisational labour function, as its affordability and continuity of reproduction for a significant number of people worldwide – which will complicate human socialisation processes, and conditions for self-actualisation and creative development (because of narrowing possibilities for the application of your own potential productive capacity) – turn many into outcasts or pariahs within the operating society (Lebedeva 2019, 22-23).

We can see the substantial transformation of such a civilisational labour function in the realisation and recognition of the need for interaction among different people, teams and states in the labour process due to the emergence of a new form of human interaction in productive economic activities: human beings and artificial intelligence, robots and the system of robots. How will this aspect affect human adaptation to new relations in the labour process, what will this relationship look like – subject-to-subject or subject-to-object – and who will play the role of the subject in these relations?

Following the logic cited by Guo Kaitian, this question can be answered only by using self-analysis. What requires comprehension are the focus and boundaries of such a civilisational labour function for the development and assurance of the space for trust between economic (and social in its new forms and conditions) life subjects. But how should we deal with trust in artificial intelligence and robots when they make managerial, controlling or organisational decisions? What will their attitude be to decisions made by people in the manufacturing process? What if this will cause a decline in the role of trust in social and labour relations at all levels of social division of labour? Who will define the degree and viability of the creative character of labour in the new technological and economic system?

Perhaps, we should just start by understanding the following: human labour is actually the wealth of nations, an obligatory and single condition for remaining human, maintaining human civilisation, and a real motivator for social growth in the context of revolutionary technological transformations.

References

Barnett, T. 2004. "New Map of the Pentagon". *Russia in Global Affairs*. No. 3.

Bielkina, G.L., Frolova M.I. and Korsakova S.N. (eds.). 2016. *Problem of human advancement (in the context of new technologies): Transhumanism and social risk problem. Reductionism as a temptation of human sciences. About idols and ideals of biotechnological human self-invention. How is a perfect human being possible?* Moscow: M LENAND.

Blischenko, I.P. and Dori, G. 2001. *Economic Sovereignty of the State.* Moscow: RUDN Publishing House.

Blommaert, T., Van den Broek, S. and Kolthof, E. 2017. *Management in Singularity: From Linear to Exponential Management.* Kindle Edition.

Brockman, J. (ed.). 2015. *What to Think About Machines That Think: Today's Leading Thinkers on the Age of Machine Intelligence*. New York: Harper Perennial.
Brown, A. 2015. "25 Life Lessons From 100-Year-Old David Rockefeller, The World's Oldest Billionaire" *Forbes*. June 12. URL: https://www.forbes.com/sites/abrambrown/2015/06/12/25-life-lessons-from-100-year-old-david-rockefeller-the-worlds-oldest-billionaire/?sh=648807fa52f3.
Bugromeev, V.P. and Bugromeev, V.V. (eds.). 2010. *Confucius Wisdom: Aphorisms and Lessons*. Moscow: OLMA Media Group.
Coombes, F. 2011. *Successful Self-motivation*. Hachette UK.
Cowen, T. 2013. *Average is Over: Powering America Beyond the Age of the Great Stagnation*. New York: Dutton.
Drexler, K.E. 2013. *Radical Abundance: How a Revolution in Nanotechnology Will Change Civilization*. Perseus: Public Affairs.
Dubrovskyi, D.I. and Klimova, S.M. (eds.). 2014. *Global future 2045: Anthropological crisis. Convergent technologies. Transhumanistic projects: Materials of the First All-Russian Conference, Belgorod, April 11-12, 2013*. Moscow: Kanon+ Regional Society of Disabled People "Rehabilitation".
Ford, H. 1922. *My Life. My Achievements*. URL: http://library.manipaldubai.com/DL/My_Life_and_Work.pdf.
Ford, M. 2015. *Rise of the Robots: Technology and the Threat of a Jobless* Future. New York: Basic Books. URL: http://digamo.free.fr/marford15.pdf.
Friedman, M. 1994. "The Methodology of Positive Economics." *THESIS*, 4: 43.
Golovenchik, G.G. and Kovalev, M.M. 2019. *Digital economy*. Minsk: Publishing Center of Belarusian State University.
Gumiliev, L.N. 1993. *Ethnic Sphere. History of people and history of nature*. Moscow: Express.
Huateng, M., Zhaoli, M., Delhi, Y. and Huali, W. 2019. *Digital transformation of China. Experience in transforming the infrastructure of the national economy*. Translated from Chinese. M.: Intellectual Literature.
Ilyin, V.V. 2003. *Philosophy of history*. Moscow: Moscow University Publishing House.
Lebedeva, I.P. 2019. *Japanese labour market in the 21st century. Economic and social problems*. Moscow: Institute of Oriental Studies at Russian Academy of Sciences.

Mason, P. 2016. Postcapitalism: A Guide to Our Future. URL: http://pinguet.free.fr/mason2015.pdf.
Mishurova, I.M. and Kitelev, P.V. 2003. *Management of personnel motivation: Workbook*. Moscow: Mar T, Rostov-on-Don.
Nazaretian, A.P. 2018. "21st century and 'out-of-date philosophy' (in regard to the anniversary report to the Rome club)." *Social Sciences and Modern Age*, 4: 160-177.
Reinert, E.S. 2020. "Industrial policy: A long-term perspective and overview of theoretical arguments. *UCL Institute for Innovation and Public Purpose: Working Paper*. 04. URL: https://www.ucl.ac.uk/bartlett/public-purpose/sites/public-purpose/files/final_industrial_policy_reinert_16_jun.pdf.
Rodrik, D. 2016. Economics Rules: The Rights and Wrongs of the Dismal Science. New York. London: W.W. Norton Company. URL: https://www.economicas.uba.ar/wp-content/uploads/2016/03/Economics-Rules-Dani-Rodrik.pdf.
Schumpeter, J.A. 1995. *Capitalism, Socialism and Democracy*. Translated from English. Kyiv: Basics.
Schwab, K. 2016. *Fourth Industrial Revolution*. Geneva: World Economic Forum.
Schwab, K. and Davis, N. (eds.). 2018. *Shaping the Future* of *the Fourth Industrial Revolution*. London: Penguin Random House.
Skinner, C. 2018. Digital Human. *The Fourth Revolution of Humanity Includes Everyone*. West Sussex: John Wiley & Sons Ltd.
Spirkin A. G. et al. (eds.). 1986. *Vocabulary of Foreign Words*. 13th edition, stereotype. Moscow: Russian language. (Rus.).
Throsby, D. 2001. *Economics and Culture.* Cambridge: Cambridge University Press. URL: http://catdir.loc.gov/catdir/samples/cam031/00063072.pdf.
Yemelin, V.A. 2017. *Identity in the information space.* Moscow: Kanon+ Publishing House Regional Society of Disabled People "Rehabilitation".
Zaitsev, Y.K. and Moskalenko, O.M. 2020. *Contemporary political economy as a theoretical foundation for social economic development*: in two books. Book 2. *Contemporary political economy as a methodological paradigm of economic development policy in globalized society*. Kyiv: KNEU.

CHAPTER THREE

THE INSTITUTION OF TRUST IN THE SYSTEM OF FACTORS OF A NATION'S PRODUCTIVE ABILITY DEVELOPMENT

ANATOLII M. KOLOT,
OKSANA O. HERASYMENKO

It would not be an exaggeration to say that at the turn of the millennium the economy and society, intensively transforming, changed before our eyes and appeared in a new format. The world economy and modern society with their inherent asymmetries of development now are, figuratively speaking, a new "fabric" woven of potential opportunities, new risks and threats, unknown or unconscious trends, and dominant ideas.

The phenomenon of instability, uncertainty and turbulence of the Ukrainian economy and society has a ***dual nature***. The phenomena and processes under consideration are formed, on one hand, under the influence of the world economy's globalisation and, on the other hand, in the context of increasing openness of national economies. Globalisation in its current format as a global trend and a factor of economic and social development produces instability, uncertainty and unpredictability on the global scale.

The traditional tools and mechanisms for ensuring positive socio-economic dynamics are losing their significance, and thus there is a need for new ones and, at the same time, a large-scale use of those that have hitherto played a secondary role. The relevance of this study is due to the increasing role, significance and functional load on social capital, the basis of which is the institution of trust.

Literature review

One of the modern gurus of sociology, A. Giddens, considers the economy and society of today as a kind of elusive world. In one of his recent monographs (Giddens 2000), he constantly emphasises that the term "runaway world" reflects the feelings of people who at the turn of the millennium are witnessing large-scale and multi-vector changes in all spheres of social life.

The problem of instability, unpredictability and new parameters of changes in modern societies is thoroughly reflected in the fundamental works of another famous sociologist of modernity, Z. Bauman. In one of them – *Liquid Modernity* – Z. Bauman (2000) emphasises that fleeting, unpredictable changes create uncertainty in most members of society, and their social platform is perceived as volatile and unreliable.

Considering the genesis of the concept of trust, it is necessary to emphasise that the issue of trust was studied by representatives of different scientific schools mainly in general philosophical terms, in the context of the functioning of society as a whole and general patterns of human behaviour. From the standpoint of an economic category, the concept of trust was first considered by A. Smith as a natural feeling of the individual. According to him, the desire to gain trust, persuade, guide and direct other people is one of the strongest human passions (Smith 1759). Another world-renowned scientist who addressed the issue of trust in the economy was the English economist A. Marshall, who considered it to be an immanent component of the formation and development of market relations, emphasising that the main principles of trade are the principles of trust. According to A. Marshall, trust is interpreted as a social habit and is associated with rationality, while trade and financial crises are explained by fluctuations in trust (Marshall 1993). However, this issue has not been systematically addressed in the scientific heritage of A. Marshall and other representatives of the "mainstream" of economic thought.

In the second half of the twentieth century, the issue of trust in the economy attracted the attention of many world-renowned scientists in various fields and it is associated with the increasing role of this phenomenon in ensuring sustainable economic development. The role of trust is studied in an article by K. Arrow (1972), who emphasised that, in essence, every commercial transaction contains an element of trust, especially if it takes a certain time. According to K. Arrow (1972), it would be plausible to say that most of the economic backwardness in the world can be explained by a lack of mutual trust.

An important milestone in the development of the theory of trust was the publication of the monograph *Trust and Power* by N. Luhmann in 1979. In this paper, trust is defined as the generalised expectation that another party will maintain its freedom and its disordered potential for various activities, acting in harmony with its personality or, rather, with the personality it represents to others, making it socially imaginary (Luhmann 1979). In brief scientific terms, it is the expectation that the actions of another party in the relationship will be predictable and will correspond to the characteristics of the "image" formed by a person who trusts and who is the primary carrier of trust. It should be noted that N. Luhmann distinguishes between the concepts of "trust" and "confidence", believing that they carry different "loads". In this regard, N. Luhmann (1979) emphasises that "trust remains vital in interpersonal relationships, but participation in functional systems such as economics and politics is no longer a matter of personal relationships. It needs confidence, not trust."

The modern classics of the theory of trust include work by A. Giddens. According to his concept (Giddens 1990), there are two types of trust. The first is the trust in people, which is based on personal obligations between individuals ("personalized" trust). The second is the trust in abstract systems, which implies impersonal obligations. Under abstract systems, A. Giddens understands institutional structures and symbolic signs such as money as a tool of exchange.

The development of the theory of trust can rightly be associated with the work of J. Coleman, in which trust emerges as a result of a rational choice of interacting economic entities. This is fully reflected in his work published in the early 1990s (Coleman 1990). Similar views are held by R. Hardin (1993). The unifying concept of these authors in understanding the nature of trust is the emphasis that this phenomenon arises from the counterparties' awareness of the benefits of cooperative behaviour and the achievement of a common goal.

An important milestone in the study of trust is the publication of the fundamental work of F. Fukuyama (1995), who consistently argues that the phenomenon of trust is the result of long-term cultural evolution. According to F. Fukuyama, the climate of trust in a country depends on the so-called spontaneous socialisation, the manifestation of which is the creation of amateur associations of citizens, occupying an intermediate position between family and the state. Being participants of such associations, citizens not only get used to trusting each other, but also acquire skills of self-organisation and competence that help them to start and develop entrepreneurial activities. F. Fukuyama argues that the deficit of trust can be reduced, but not overcome, by state intervention in economic activities.

The latest fundamental publications on the issue of trust in the late twentieth century were supplemented by a monograph by A. Seligman (2000). A. Seligman relates the actualisation of the issue of trust to the growth in the number of social roles, which leads to a vagueness of expectations related to the roles of the subjects of trust. A. Seligman, like many other researchers of the issue, distinguishes between the concepts of "trust" and "confidence". In his view, central to defining the phenomenon of "trust" (as opposed to confidence) is that it involves a person in a relationship, in which the actions, character or intentions of another party cannot be assured. In other words, trust is required in cases where there is no comprehensive information to make informed decisions.

In the late 1990s and early 2000s, scientific papers on the issue of trust were supplemented by a series of works by the famous Polish sociologist P. Sztompka (1999; 2002; 2007). Many of the definitions of trust proposed by P. Sztompka are dominated by the message that the category of "trust" is a kind of ***bet*** on the future; a mandatory element of human activity in conditions of uncertainty and risks. Trust reduces uncertainty and assumes that others will act to our advantage or at least neutrally (Sztompka 1999).

In the foreword to the bestseller by K. Schwab and N. Davis (2018), Microsoft CEO Satya Nadella notes: "The main thing in today's world is trust. We need a new regulatory climate, without which the confident application of innovative technologies is impossible. The outdated legislation is poorly adapted to address the issues at hand – this is a huge obstacle."

Methodology

The scientific and theoretical substantiation of building trust relationships in the context of productive development is carried out by the authors on the basis of interdisciplinarity. The productive ability of modern nations as a phenomenon and process occurring in the field of economic development requires philosophical, socio-cultural, socio-spiritual and non-economic understanding. At the same time, social, philosophical and political problems require organisational and economic evaluation, measurement and interpretation.

The constructive synthesis of theoretical research involves not just interdisciplinary cooperation, but also mutual enrichment at the methodological level, and the formation of a systematic, holistic vision of the economy and the problems and contradictions of its development. The problem of constructive synthesis has universal roots. "We stand," writes O. Toffler (1981), "on the verge of returning to large-scale thinking, to generalizing theory, to the combination of individual parts into a single whole…The desire to consider individual quantitative details taken out of the general context makes us learn more and more about less and less."

In our understanding, interdisciplinarity appears as a real tool for uniting sciences (disciplines), the emergence of integrated products, projects and interdisciplinary objects of study, the further mastery of which is fundamentally important for both science and education. It should be noted that the institution of interdisciplinarity is especially relevant for economic fields of knowledge and economics. This is due to the fact that the focus of our research is an economically active person, his economic activity and the relationships that accompany this activity.

The rationale for the current state of the institution of trust as a determinant of social change in Ukrainian society is based on the results of national annual monitoring surveys conducted under the auspices of the Institute of Sociology of the National Academy of Sciences of Ukraine. We analyse changes in the level of trust towards the leading public institutions – the government, Verkhovna Rada, the President, political parties, courts and the prosecutor's office – over the last decade. Changes in the relationship of "trust–distrust", which have a large-scale planetary manifestation, are confirmed by the results of public opinion polls conducted by the Gallup Institute.

Trust as a non-economic factor in the formation of a new matrix of the economy and society

It should be noted that Ukrainian society has been in a state of political, economic and social instability for almost three decades, which is reproduced and permanently intensified by global external trends and internal crisis phenomena. The internal component of instability in Ukrainian society is closely linked and is largely the result of inconsistency, uncertainty and unpredictability of domestic and foreign policies. The inconsistency of political and economic reforms, the lack of positive results, the disappointment of the vast majority of the population of Ukraine with their financial situation, and the unpredictability of prospects for a better future continue to reproduce the division of society on various grounds. However, while some believe that low living standards and growing social dangers are the consequence of insufficient liberal reforms, and the lack of new institutions in the economy and society and/or the inefficiencies of the existing ones, other people associate better prospects with the restoration of the command-and-control system, with a return to the values of the previous economic and political system.

There is every reason to believe that the economic problems at the turn of the millennium are only the tip of the iceberg. In our opinion, most of the social macro problems are non-economic in nature. An increase in scientific knowledge to ensure social dynamics through fuller use of non-economic factors has been achieved in recent years. More can be achieved if the absolute majority of politicians, the so-called elite and ordinary citizens believe in the importance of strengthening the role of moral, ethical and spiritual components in the development of the country's productive capacity.

In a situation when the two worlds of the economy and society become less controlled, turbulent and out of control, the institution of trust cannot but change and lose its potential.

A set of new phenomena and processes that have technical, technological, institutional and socio-cultural origins form a new matrix of the economy and society, in which trust becomes not only desirable but also a leading system-forming element that must be "woven" into a complex social framework, which keeps the economy and society in a viable condition.

In the opinion of the authors, the concept of "trust" – as well as everything related to the mission, meaning and true role of this institution – did not find a deep and objective understanding, or the perception of it as a leading social value by the majority of society. Instead, this phenomenon continues to be formed and reproduced in the public consciousness in a distorted form and associated with the manifestation of utopianism, moralising and dreaming of what is desirable. However, without it, society cannot survive and cope with threats and challenges. It should be noted that the issue of trust is addressed by many populists and demagogues of various stripes, for whom the phenomenon of trust is a screen, while their true intentions and goals remain "behind the scenes".

The authors are convinced that new sources and ways to solve the most acute socio-economic problems are connected to the potential use of non-economic factors, among which trust has a special role. In the new development trend, which is gaining momentum, there is an actualisation of the moral and spiritual non-economic component. In their recent research, the authors proceed from the fact that purely economic postulates are appearing less and less in the form of material from which to build the current and future economic lives of the country, households and each person.

It is necessary to form other coordinates of economic thinking in the direction of better and more comprehensive consideration of non-economic phenomena and processes – including the institution of trust, which until recently was not studied by economists – but in fact they have a decisive impact on economic and social development. It is necessary to convince society that the era of ethical economics is coming, in which trust, morality and personal responsibility for creating conditions for sustainable socio-economic development come to the fore. Using the potential of non-economic factors and in particular the institution of trust is the link that can help overcome the deepest crisis of our time.

There is an axiom that under the conditions of democratic society and market orientation of the economic system, neither political transformations, economic reforms, other socially significant transformation processes, or sustainable development of the country's productive capacity in general can take place without the dominance of trust relationships. There is always a certain margin of trust and distrust in the relationship between members of society and its institutions. The scale of the latter is a consequence of the manifestation of diverse phenomena and processes that have economic, political, legal and institutional origins.

Therefore, solving the problem of increasing the trust level involves identifying and neutralising a set of factors that give rise to negative expectations. Before developing a "road map" for building a society of trust, it is necessary to master the philosophy of this phenomenon, and understand its basics, nature, functions and development trends. At the same time, it is fundamentally important to find out what new trends are appearing at the stage of formation of a new (digital) economy and, in fact, what is the primary reason for increasing the "burden" on social capital and, consequently, on the institution of trust.

Factors that increase the role of trust

In general, the list of factors and circumstances of an internal and external nature that determine the increasing role of the institution of trust and the need to strengthen trust in the formation of a new (digital) economy is as follows:

- development of processes of the social system's democratisation, limiting the scale of state influence as a global trend today; transfer of a number of powers traditionally exercised by public authorities to the local level; intensive development of civil society; growing role of citizens in the formation and implementation of socio-economic policy;

- growing uncertainty and risks that are intensively produced by the world economy's globalisation and the conditions of the new (digital) economy;
- increasing complexity and non-linearity of the development of network societies;
- loss of economic development stability, which necessitates the formation of new pillars and the use of new factors of economic dynamics;
- exacerbation of the problem of competitiveness, which necessitates the search for new ways and means of gaining competitive advantages;
- increasing competition for resources, especially for the most valuable and productive ones – human resources – and those that have a non-economic, moral, spiritual or ethical nature;
- dissemination of liberal concepts of the social and labour spheres and mass manifestations of desocialisation of relations in the labour sphere;
- inadequate understanding of the dialectic of economic and social development by many representatives of both business and government agencies;
- exacerbation of environmental problems bordering on cataclysms on regional and national scales;
- deepening asymmetry of economic and social development, which is increasingly threatening economic and social security;
- emergence of new zones and spheres of economic activity, in which formal institutions and norms increasingly demonstrate "failures of the state" and the inability to regulate the relations inherent in the new (network) economy;
- increasing share of creative employees in the structure of the labour force, who prefer informal methods of regulating relations in different spheres of human life;
- expansion of spheres of economic activity, especially at the international level, in which formal institutions are inferior to informal ones in efficiency and, accordingly, informal relations;
- expansion and intensification of feedback between civil society institutions and institutions of state power and local self-government;
- intensive development of structures built on the network principle;
- development of global markets;
- expanding the scope of trust-based social contracts;

- the need to reform the political and economic systems, which can only be achieved with a high level of trust;
- increased importance of inclusive development and, consequently, the need for a new level of trust, which can provide a critical stock of trust relationships.

Factors that hinder the development of trust relationships

We have presented in brief the mega-reasons and mega-trends that necessitate the increased role of the institution of trust in the functioning of the new (digital) economy and network society. At the same time, it should be noted that today's conditions reproduce those old, and also generate new circumstances and processes that hinder the development of trust and appear as a kind of "thrombus" in the development of the institution of trust. The latter include the following:

- weakening of socio-cultural and moral guidelines in social activities of many business entities and members of society as a whole;
- formation of individualised societies; erosion of "cultures of solidarity";
- prevalence in public life of the concept of "homo economicus" over the concept of a "socially responsible person";
- diminished role of social capital; inadequate understanding of the contribution of social capital in ensuring sustainable development;
- inadequate scientific support for the development of the institution of trust;
- permanent "failures of the state", which in practice do not appear as an exception but rather as a rule.

Almost everything that has signs of disharmonious development creates asymmetries and disruptions in life, increasing the potential for mistrust. However, the nature of distrust must be considered at a higher level of generalisation and, above all, through the prism of failures in the system of socio-economic relations. At the beginning of the millennium, Ukrainian society became doubly unbalanced, as it was simultaneously destabilised both by factors inherent in the entire globalised world and by factors of national social turbulence.

Over the last quarter of a century, as a result of a set of political, economic and social factors, Ukrainian society has become even more varied, unbalanced and unstable. More attention should be paid to the main features of the socio-economic system of Ukraine, including:

- anomalous property stratification of society;
- increase in poverty;
- increased merging of power and property;
- the phenomenon of state privatisation by big capital;
- growing influence of big capital on the state's socio-economic policy;
- active lobbying of the interests of big capital at all levels, from local to national;
- extreme levels of ownership concentration;
- the power of bureaucracy over business;
- legal nihilism, asymmetry of rights and responsibilities of different social groups.

To this, one must add the losses borne by society in the field of moral and ethical principles and culture in its broadest sense.

In the monograph devoted to an assessment of the current state of Ukrainian society and an elaboration of the vectors of its modernisation, the well-known Ukrainian sociologist M. Shulga (2018, 57) notes: "The moral degradation of society has become total. It permeates all social strata and groups. Particularly dangerous is the fact that amoralism and cynicism have deeply affected the people in power, and have taken root in all echelons of power, including the highest. The most resonant crimes are committed by those who, according to their position, must ensure law and order, be a model of moral and legal behavior." The author further emphasises: "The imbalance of relations, the instability of institutions, the passivity and amorphousness of the social environment have led to the emergence of numerous bifurcation points, the overcoming of which is stressful for society. The lack of a large-scale strategy of social movement, which would be supported by the majority of citizens, testified to the failure of the social matrix. The Ukrainian society faced the historical challenge of finding its own path of development and its place in today's complex world" (Shulga 2018, 67).

Is there an awareness in society of the true importance of the institution of trust?

To answer this question, it is necessary to return to the theoretical foundations of the category itself. The concept of "trust" is so common that it would seem that all the "i"s should already have been dotted. However, the paradox is that the more often the term "trust" is used in the scientific and applied arsenal, the more blurred and ambiguous this area becomes. As S. Castaldo (2002) rightly points out, "the common feature of trust research is the diversity of conceptual typologies, the lack of a clear and general definition of the concept of trust." The works of this scientist contain five main generalisations, built on the basis of definitions that are most often cited by researchers on this issue, namely:

1. Trust is seen as expectations, relying on others, beliefs, expressions of will, or commitment to interaction and cooperation.
2. Trust is manifested in relation to various objects. The latter may be other individuals, groups, organisations and social institutions.
3. Trust is characterised by action or behaviour, and, consequently, emphasises the activity aspect of the trust phenomenon. It is about the action of the subject as a way of showing trust.
4. Definitions of trust include the results and consequences of its manifestation. It is believed that the actions of the partner should be positively assessed.
5. The definitions emphasise the riskiness of the trust/distrust decision-making situation.

Gurus of the theory of trust, such as N. Luhmann and P. Sztompka, emphasise the close connection of trust with the conditions of its functioning and, above all, with the reproduction of conditions of uncertainty, risks and dangers. P. Sztompka (1999), the well-known Polish researcher on the issue of trust whose works have received worldwide recognition, defines trust as "a bet on future unforeseen actions of others". At the same time, this scientist, like most researchers on the phenomenon of "trust", emphasises that trust or distrust is always associated with favourable and acceptable, or unfavourable and unacceptable, ***expectations***. At the same time, P. Sztompka (1999) adheres to such a broad formulation of the considered phenomenon: "Trust is an expectation in relation to the partner that his reactions will be beneficial to us, in other words, a bet is made in conditions of uncertainty that the partner's actions would be favorable to us." A "red line", which passes through the fundamental studies of P. Sztompka (1999; 2002; 2007), is a concept according to which the essential basis of the notion of "trust" should include the paradigmatic triad seeing trust as:

1) your expectations of honest behaviour of other people towards you;
2) your obligation not to violate the expectations of others regarding your actions;
3) limiting your interests in favour of those you trust and, consequently, solidarity.

In 1995, F. Fukuyama, a prominent contemporary sociologist and prophet of the "end of history", presented his own concept of the theory of trust as a condition for sustainable development in a world-renowned monograph. According to Fukuyama (1995), only societies with a high level of trust are capable of development and prosperity, unlike those that lack trust.

According to the definition given by Fukuyama (1995), trust is the expectation of community members that other members will behave more or less predictably, honestly and with attention to the needs of others, in accordance with some general norms. Some of these norms belong to the sphere of "fundamental values" (for example, the understanding of God or higher justice), but they also include such completely secular things as professional standards and corporate codes of conduct. "Trusting a doctor and hoping that he will not intentionally harm us, we count on his fidelity to the Hippocratic oath and the established rules of the medical profession"(Fukuyama 1995). Emphasis should be placed on the close connection between the concept of "trust" and the concept of "social capital". "Social capital," writes Fukuyama (1995), "is a certain potential of society or part of it, which arises as a result of trust between its members. It can be realized in a small basic social group and in whole nations, as well as in all groups that exist in between. Social capital differs from other forms of human capital in that it is usually created and transmitted through cultural mechanisms such as religion, traditions and customs."

Domestic scientific schools of socio-economic, philosophical and political sciences faced significant difficulties in explaining and assessing the phenomena of trust/distrust. Having encountered cognitive problems in the field of trust and related phenomena and processes – low levels of society's consolidation, and social incoherence – scientists often demonstrate everyday ideas, situational concepts, verbal stereotypes and superficial schemes of social relations.

Types of trust at all levels and their interaction

Trust – like social capital, which is formed on its basis – maintains and harmonises relations in the economy and society, taking into account individual and social interests, and considering its nature and mission, trust appears as an institutional alternative to the state.

Turning to the issue of society's hierarchical structure, it should be noted that trust permeates the whole range of horizontal and vertical relationships that are formed in society. In practice, all types of trust are interconnected and mutually influential. Therefore, public distrust of state institutions at the same time creates distrust of financial structures, as poorly functioning state institutions make it impossible for the financial sector to function reliably. It should be noted that the population's trust in business is largely due to, first, its trust in the state and the latter's socio-economic policy, and, second, the ability of the state to harmonise legislation in the field of entrepreneurial activity and ensure control over its implementation. It should be emphasised that trust between employers and employees is mediated, on the one hand, by the trust in business in general and the former's willingness to take into account the interests of employees, and, on the other hand, the trust in the state and, above all, in social and labour policies it carries out.

The interaction and interdependence of these types of trust is largely due to the fact that most economic agents simultaneously exist in many capacities. For example, the state – as a subject of trust – appears simultaneously as a legislator, guarantor of rights, employer, consumer, producer of public goods, investor, arbitrator, social partner, etc. An economically active person appears in many capacities: a member of society; an employee, self-employed or entrepreneur; consumer; potential or actual lender or borrower; member of public organisations, etc. Therefore, the existing types of trust in the economy and society cannot be considered in isolation from each other and, therefore, confidence-building measures must be interconnected and unidirectional. This means that it is necessary to build investor confidence by creating a general climate of trust, because this type of trust requires attractive investments, guarantees of property rights, the willingness and ability of economic agents to repay loans, a general business culture and high competitiveness of businesses, etc.

It is difficult to overestimate the importance of trust in business. A high level of trust creates preconditions for simplification, or even complete abandonment, of formal procedures in relations with partners and generally establishes a favourable climate for doing business. With a socially acceptable level of trust, time saving is achieved, capital turnover is accelerated and transaction costs are reduced. It would not be an exaggeration to say that business processes have a chance to succeed only if there is the minimum necessary level of trust between their participants. This applies primarily to financial and credit operations, insurance, the stock market, and investment activities.

Is it possible for society and the economy to ensure a country's productive capacity in the absence of a minimum level of trust?

Theoretically, this is possible on the basis of large-scale involvement of formal norms, rules and other regulations. But in order for a set of formal norms to be put into effect, effective institutions of state power and governance are needed. The functioning of these institutions is associated with significant costs and a high probability of exceeding the maximum allowable limits of state intervention in the economic of economic entities. If the latter situation becomes a reality, then society receives a command-administrative economy, the consequences of which are well known. Therefore, it is quite problematic to make up for the losses borne by economic agents and society as a whole in the absence of the minimum necessary level of trust, even in the presence of extensive government tools and a powerful apparatus of coercion and control.

However, it should be noted that modern economic history has not witnessed cases when, in the absence of the minimum necessary trust, economic agents and society as a whole demonstrate sustainable development of productive capacity and high competitiveness. Therefore, a society that relies on sustainable development and strives to occupy leading positions in the world competitiveness rankings must combine the potential of informal and formal norms and rules to strengthen institutional preconditions for trust relationships.

The institution of trust as a tool for regulating relations between economic agents

The discussion above gives grounds to conclude that trust in the economy is based on an extensive system of formal and informal norms and institutions/organisations. There is every reason to consider the institution of trust as a tool for regulating relations in the triad of "market – state – business", the formation and development of which in the context of the interaction of participants in the coordinates of the new economy were substantiated by the authors in previous publications (Kolot and Herasymenko 2017a).

It should be noted that under the influence of technical, technological and social effects, which are intensively developing, a fundamentally new configuration of the entire market structure is formed. The established market boundaries are blurring, while previously disparate network and even non-network industries are becoming interconnected segments of the single economic space. We are all witnessing the emergence and intensive development of fundamentally different types of markets.

Market space and its main link – the market – are no longer a monolith, where purely market mechanisms dominate. The modern market is increasingly reminiscent of high-quality aged cheese, which has many large and small holes in which there is no substance to the market. These "holes" do not have working market laws, but have completely opposite rules and motives of behaviour of people and institutions. Therefore, these holes (as market failures) are increasingly filled with non-market instruments while the role of the non-market is growing.

There are good reasons to say that the new (digital) economy is acquiring the characteristics of a large-scale global network market, the configuration of which acquires other properties and modifications. Business entities, and especially the economically active person, are becoming increasingly dependent on communication and information networks. New types of interaction are emerging that are radically changing the landscape of the world economy and society, creating new opportunities and challenges. In the new configuration of the social phenomenon of the "market – state – business", the institution of the "state" acquires significant transformations, while the forms of its interaction with other components of the triad acquire other properties.

In today's globalising world – which is changing under the influence of information, communication and other technologies of the 21st century – in establishing new values, the state cannot but change itself, to transform its functions and tools to influence economic and social development. At the same time, it should be noted that the formation of a new (digital) economy and network society has nothing to do with the abolition, or overcoming, of the state. Under the conditions of globalisation and a number of other external and internal factors, one can observe not a simplification but an increasing complexity of the state's functions. At the same time, the boundaries between domestic and foreign policy are blurring, and the need for partnership between the state and the institutions of the economy and society is emerging.

In recent decades, cooperation between the state and business has been carried out in new forms and new methods are being used with a deepening of bilateral relations. In our opinion, it is becoming increasingly difficult to operate with concepts such as "strengthening the role of the state" or "weakening the role of the state", as they decreasingly reflect the essence of the processes taking place in the market economy. After all, in practice, a different format of interaction between the state and capital is established, with a simultaneous strengthening (in some areas) and weakening (in others) of state participation in solving the complex problems of ensuring the development of the country's productive capacity. It is becoming increasingly difficult to assess the current symbiosis of bilateral relations between the state and business with long-established criteria and approaches. Therefore, it is necessary to master other approaches and a new type of thinking.

An unbiased analysis shows that public–private partnerships as an institution of a mixed economy enhance the country's ability to develop its productive capacity. But what does this mean? The partnership between the state and business makes it possible, first of all, to attract additional financial resources to the public sector and to reduce the severity of the problem of budget financing, to create new jobs. It is also fundamentally important that economically and socially significant objects remain in state ownership, otherwise state institutions will have control over them. Therefore, the resilience of the economic system can be strengthened by combining the resources and capabilities of two actors: the state, which owns the property and various ways to maintain and gain competitive advantages, and business, which has the capital and the best practices of management and innovation.

In most publications on the issue of trust, the reasons for the lack of it are presented in fragments, with a large number of eclectic statements. This is because the methodological basis is ignored: identification of the reasons for a lack of trust should be preceded by the development of an idea of ***who trust is addressed to and what it depends on***.

If we consider the macro level, the trust at this level is a symbiosis of a number of different types, each of which is an expression of trust between certain groups of economic agents. At this level, the most massive and influential groups of economic agents include: the population, business structures and business in general; state institutions and the state as a whole; employees and employers; creditors and borrowers; investors; intermediary structures; financial structures; and public associations.

The most representative group of economic agents is the population. This group's trust in other economic agents is determined by economic motives and interests, as well as a number of non-economic factors and, above all, the idea of moral and ethical values, and social rules of conduct. Indeed, public trust in an economic agent such as business depends not only on the level and conditions of employment, and adherence to the principles of decent work, creating conditions for opportunities, but also on the extent to which the behaviour of business structures is consistent with cultural values and "works" to promote social justice.

The trust of the population in the state and its institutions depends on: the perfection, stability and predictability of the "rules of the game" created by the legislative and executive authorities; the quality of services provided by the state; the protection of the rights and interests of everyone, regardless of their status, origin, religion, etc.; and compliance with socially recognised norms of social justice.

The state's trust in the population and business is determined, first of all, by the observance of current legislative acts and other norms of life adopted by society, and also by the ability of leading economic agents (the population and business) to serve as a source of income necessary for the implementation of national functions.

Trust/distrust between employees and employers is formed: under the influence of conformity of the structure of supply with the demand for jobs; working conditions that fall under the definition of "worthy"; the creation of conditions for staff development; and compliance with the current labour legislation.

The modern philosophy of decent work is proposed to be considered as a democratic requirement of society for governmental structures, for social partners of all levels to create decent jobs, and to expand access to them and create proper conditions (legal, organisational, economic, institutional, psycho-physiological, etc.) for productive employment (Kolot et al. 2020).

The lack, or low level, of trust – including trust between the population and business structures, between partners, and between the population and the state – is a source of the growth of structural social costs and economic losses. The latter can be traced in all spheres of public life, while their manifestations are very diverse, such as capital outflows, dollarisation of savings, low share prices of business organisations, diversion of funds for 100% prepayments, low rates of private savings in the banking system, etc. Since economic interests have a priority role in economic activity, the primary impulse of trust/distrust is not sympathy or antipathy towards the partner, but the expectation of profit from cooperation. Therefore, trust in the economy is always a certain positive expectation regarding the behaviour of economic agents. Trust in the economic sphere should neutralise risks, and create preconditions for confidence and predictability.

The sufficient trust potential in business makes it possible to abandon many formal procedures in dealing with business partners.

Attention should be paid to the close connection between informal norms caused by the development of civil society institutions, the level of trust and their interaction. For example, the tendency of society members to create public institutions to defend their rights and achieve socially significant goals implies a certain unity of moral and ethical values, or at least the minimum required level of trust and willingness to cooperate. At the same time, the participation in self-regulated associations promotes the development of moral consensus and skills of self-organisation, forms new values and interests, increases the level of mutual trust, and helps to increase social capital.

It should be noted that trust has an impact on socio-economic development in the "horizontal" field, in contrast to the state which operates in the "vertical" field. At the same time, trust appears as a socially significant resource, on the supply and the use of which depends the efficiency of social production. It should also be emphasised that the atmosphere of trust creates preconditions for improving the efficiency of formal institutions and the system of state administration. Therefore, it is correct to say that trust and social capital are in the "vertical" field of socio-economic development.

Trust and social capital, which is formed in the presence of the former institution, can influence economic development through a multichannel system. The task of this system is to reduce transaction costs due to:

- reduction of expenditures on economic and personal security;
- reduction of costs of finding partners.

According to the traditional canons of economic theory, the reduction of transaction costs is the prerogative of the state and its institutions. According to the statement by D. North (1991), which has already acquired the status of a classic, as a tool of coordination, institutions establish "rules of the game" in society, which reduce transaction costs. Social capital, especially its social norms of behaviour, and the values of trust can be considered as a special institution of informal origin. Hence the following statement: formal institutions and social capital as an informal institution solve related problems and are interchangeable. It can also be argued that in the presence of significant amounts of social capital, the need for direct state intervention in the economy is reduced and the economy requires less involvement of formal institutions.

It should be noted that in a similar scenario, the use of corporate social responsibility reduces the need for state participation in many areas (environmental protection, regulation of social and labour relations, etc.). The presence of trust is a condition for the manifestation of social responsibility. Indeed, only under the condition of trust, i.e. acceptable and positive expectations about the behaviour of others, a certain institution or person can respond to the needs of others. Therefore, the presence of trust produces socially responsible actions, and the lack of it makes it impossible to engender, or significantly limits, socially responsible behaviour. It should be noted that the institutions of trust and social responsibility are mutual. Socially responsible activities of different entities determine the scope of trust (see Figure 3-1).

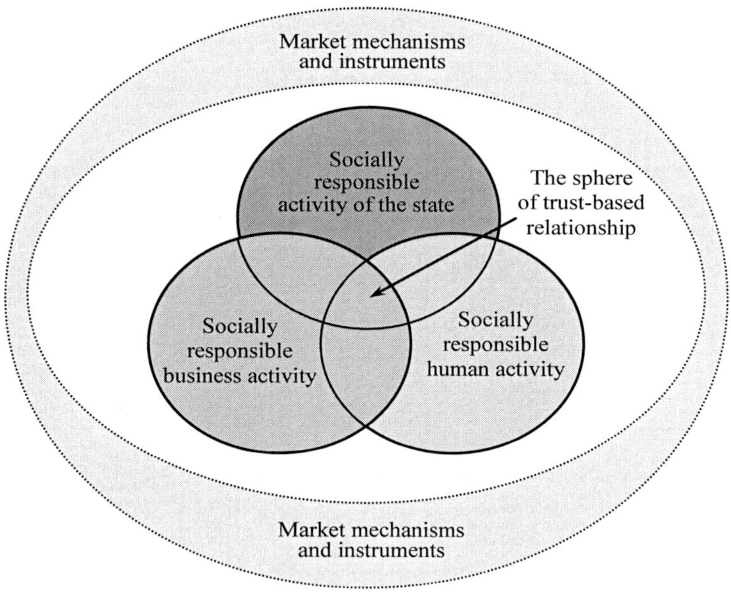

Figure 3-1. The sphere of trust relationships of institutions in society

The most effective and efficient way to build a society of trust is a consistent transition from state control over the individual and society to the control of civil society over state authorities. A society of trust does not need excessive regulation of rules by the state. At the same time, a society of trust creates preconditions and the general background, which help form a legal culture and, consequently, the observance of rules and laws becomes the norm. In contrast, a lack of trust breeds legal nihilism.

The elaboration of a system of rules introduced to regulate different spheres of economic and social life, and to use them in such a way as to prevent "failures of the state", is an art. Not all states at certain stages of their development have managed to master this art. "Failures of the state", as evidenced by both Ukrainian and international experience, are permanent in almost all countries.

Considering the fact that, despite all the "ebbs" and "flows", the levers of state influence on economic development are becoming more liberal and smaller in scale. This global trend is one of the reasons to believe that the role of trust should be strengthened both now and in the future.

It should be noted that regardless of political and ideological colours, most scholars recognise that the state should formulate rules in the field of economic and social development. At the same time, the norms of the minimum necessary and the maximum allowable intervention of the state in the economic life of society must be observed (Kolot and Herasymenko 2017b).

According to the Constitution (Article 1), Ukraine is a social state (Constitution of Ukraine 1996). The analysis of almost 40 constitutions of countries that fixed the institution of a social state makes it possible to highlight its following attributes:

- broad regulatory intervention in socio-economic processes and the formation of socially responsible political institutions;
- social orientation of economic policy and socialisation of the state budget;
- the existence and functioning of civil society institutions;
- equal opportunities for all citizens to realise their rights;
- availability of systems of state social transfers, social protection, social security and social insurance;
- an active state policy in the labour market;
- assistance to the state in developing the social partnership system;
- development of democracy and the rule of law;
- availability of social support for all categories of the population.

The modern concept of a social state proclaims new priorities of a state-organised society and the importance of:

a) integration of social and economic policy;

b) shifting from a redistributive role of the state towards a stimulative role;
c) intensification of innovative economic development on the basis of intensive growth of human capital.

In our opinion, the characteristic features of the post-industrial social state should be:

- ✓ a continuous, lifelong nature of learning, retraining and mastering the competencies required by the rapidly changing, mobile and flexible global economy;
- ✓ a continuous, lifelong improvement and maintaining of health, when people are the object of health care throughout their lifetime;
- ✓ a combination of socialisation and individualisation of social services, when, with the help and assistance of public and state institutions, people have the opportunity to choose their own educational trajectory, as well as the trajectory and mechanisms for maintaining health by choosing from the list of individually acceptable medical services. The pension system should also be diversified while preserving socially recognised guarantees;
- ✓ increasing the role of private social payments in the development of human capital, meeting social needs (above the levels defined by state social standards);
- ✓ development of public–private partnerships in the social sphere, with a leading role for the state in the formation of social policy;
- ✓ globalisation of social services and development of international competition for customers;
- ✓ the emergence of new social technologies that radically change the content and nature of social services.

The social state as an institution and as a form of social activity does not disappear; it actively transforms the methods and tools for the implementation of social functions in view of contemporary challenges.

Therefore, all of the above clearly shows that at the present stage there is an urgent need for radical changes in the practice of trust and in the intensive development of it.

M. Shulga (2018) notes that in modern mass society, with its branched social groups, dozens or even hundreds of which include the same person, it is increasingly difficult to form a high level of intra-group trust: “In the unstable Ukrainian society of the last two decades, a public atmosphere of total distrust has been formed.” This thesis is confirmed by the results of national annual monitoring surveys conducted under the auspices of the Institute of Sociology of the National Academy of Sciences of Ukraine (Ukrainian Society 2017; 2019). During the period 2010–2018, the level of trust in the leading public institutions – the Government, Verkhovna Rada, the President, political parties, courts and the prosecutor's office – decreased significantly. Instead, due to the aggravation of the political situation in eastern Ukraine, there was a fairly high level of trust in the army, charitable foundations and public associations. The success of V. Zelensky in the presidential elections in Ukraine in 2019, with a subsequent "reset" of power, significantly increased the level of confidence in the President, Verkhovna Rada, the Government and political parties (see Figure 3-2).

According to the results of monitoring in 2019, among public institutions, the population of Ukraine expressed the highest level of trust towards volunteers: 3.4 on a 5-point scale. The total level of public trust ("I completely trust" and "mostly trust") towards volunteers as representatives of civil society in 2019 amounted to 56.4% (Ukrainian Society 2019, 465), which confirms their leadership positions among civil society institutions. After the 2019 elections and amid high electoral expectations, one could observe a new trend of a marked increase in public confidence in the institutions of power: i.e. the President (46.9%), Verkhovna Rada (16.7%) and the government (17.4%) (Ukrainian Society 2019, 460-461).

The monitoring of social changes in Ukrainian society convincingly demonstrates that in the public consciousness in Ukraine "uncertainty, confusion, frustration, uncertainty, nihilism and indifference prevail. However, the processes of moral degradation, increasing aggression, cruelty and violence in society are of particular concern. Against this background, there is a weakening of the level of mutual trust and solidarity in society" (Shulga 2018, 11).

According to the results of the national monitoring in 2017, the growing tensions in Ukrainian society were caused by: the fighting in eastern Ukraine (67.8% of respondents), rising unemployment (48.1% of respondents), impoverishment of the population due to rising prices and tariff increases (46.3% of respondents), corruption and bribery (44.4% of respondents), impunity and arbitrariness of officials (40.9% of respondents), distrust of the government and frustration with its inability to change anything (34.0% of respondents), and the unavailability or low quality of medical care (26.5% of respondents) (Ukrainian Society 2017, 527).

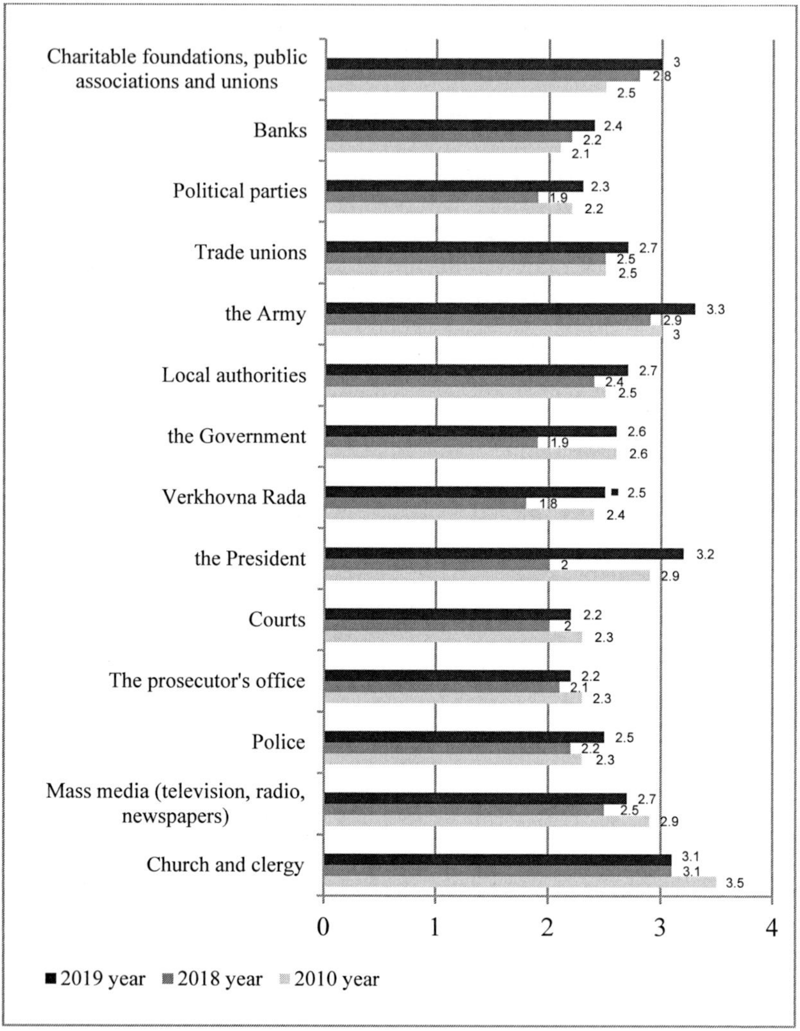

Figure 3-2. Levels of trust in Ukrainian society
(Average score* given on a scale of 1–5 points)

** The average score was calculated on a 5-point scale, where 1 is complete distrust and 5 is complete trust. Accordingly, the higher the average score (the closer it is to 5), the greater the level of trust. The average score was calculated for those respondents who answered the posed question.*

Source: (Ukrainian Society 2019, 458-464).

M. Shulga (2018, 83) notes: "In this atmosphere, society is experiencing a crisis of solidarity within traditional social groups. It is clear that in such society it is more difficult to create networked modern formations. It is even more difficult to understand the strategic interests of social groups. In addition, the biggest social groups are in a state of reformatting."

Unwanted changes in the trust–distrust relationship, which have a large-scale, planetary manifestation, are confirmed by the results of a public opinion poll conducted by the Gallup Institute. Numerous representative studies by this institution show that in the United States there is a tendency towards a reduction in support for trade unions, as well as a reduction in the trust of Congress, big companies, banks, newspapers, political parties and many other institutions that occupy leading positions in the economy and politics (Confidence in Institutions 2020). Even the US Supreme Court, an institution that has long enjoyed the support of citizens, has found itself among those losing trust. According to surveys, the level of support for this institution decreased from almost 70% in 1986 to 40% in 2012 (*New York Times* 2012).

The research conducted by numerous international organisations shows a steady trend of declining public confidence in most government institutions, political parties and NGOs in the vast majority of countries. The economic crisis of the late 2000s has only deepened the distrust of governments, and of financial institutions in particular and the banking system in general.

Social tension as a factor of failures in the system of trust relationships

The phenomenon that produces failures in the system of trust relationships is the preservation and permanent deepening of *social tensions* in Ukrainian society.

The presence of social contradictions and social tensions is an immanent reality of modern societies, which manifests itself in the violation of the coherence of interests of social groups, exacerbation of differences between social interests and, consequently, leads to complete imbalances in the social system. Differences in societal values and value orientations increase the potential for mistrust.

In his novel *The Man Without Qualities* (1995), R. Musil wrote about distrust, which can affect all groups in society: "It is a fundamental characteristic of civilization that a man most profoundly mistrusts those living outside his own milieu, so that not only does the Teuton regard the

Jew as an incomprehensible and inferior being, but the football-player likewise so regards the man who pays the piano."

"This is the main feature of culture – that a person feels a deep distrust of a person who lives outside his own circle, which, therefore, not only a German Jew, but also a pianist football player considers a creature incomprehensible and inferior" (Musil 1995).

Failures in the social matrix as one of the main reasons for negative developments in the system of "trust–distrust"

As mentioned above, the formation and development (or underdevelopment) of the institution of trust occurs under the influence of a number of reasons of a different nature and the manifestation of economic and non-economic factors. However, there is reason to believe that the main factor among the determinants of stable trust formation is a condition of stable positive dynamics. Regarding the current situation in Ukrainian society, M. Shulga (2018, 22) notes:

> "The Ukrainian society is characterized by the growing total breakdown of the social matrix. Crisis symptoms exacerbate the conflictogenic points of society. Since our society is one of the most complex among its neighbors in terms of its social and socio-cultural structures, there are objectively potential points in it that can provoke the breakdown of the holistic social matrix. A sign of the growing total failure of the matrix is the fragmentation of citizens into big value groups, which are not in a state of cooperation or at least respectful coexistence, but of confrontation, has noticeably increased in society. Each of the fragments (for example, the regional one) has different value syndrome complexes, including culture, languages, religions, ideologies, etc. Such division of society into socio-cultural fragments significantly weakens and depletes its viability, constantly maintaining a high potential level of social and political tension. But to this breakdown others are added."

High social tensions in Ukrainian society, which have lasted for many years, are generated and maintained by political tensions. The pitiful size of pensions for the vast majority of the population, uncompetitive wages in the public sector of the economy and especially in the budget sphere, the inefficiency of medicine in the state network of institutions and unaffordability of paid medical services, the crisis of science, the lack of strong and reliable state support for education, in particular higher education, and many other conditions give rise to distrust of political parties and the government. Therefore, it is a matter of mistrust in the context of a lack of consolidation.

A general, simplified, mostly abstract answer to the question of "What has happened in Ukrainian society?" should be as follows: At different levels of the hierarchical structure of society – from the level of an individual to the societal level – there was damage to the algorithm, the matrix of healthy, stable and harmonious development. The growing distrust of the state as the leading institution of society can be explained by a symbiosis of reasons, which include the emergence of a new paternalism and the objective evolution of the social type, the nature of which is not understood by many members of society.

In this regard, M. Shulga (2018, 11) notes:

> "The erosion and destruction of the principle of collectivism in social relations and its replacement by the principle of individualism and social atomization of society gave rise to the phenomenon of a new paternalism, which means that the disadvantaged person, deprived of many social guarantees, places his hopes on the state, which is built on the principles of private property and market relations. In a crisis society, when the opportunities for self-realization of the individual are reduced, when social institutions that ensure the satisfaction of primary human needs are deformed, people lose faith in themselves, try to externalize the reasons for their failures. Such features of the state of Ukrainian society naturally interact and create new defects in the functioning of social institutions."

It is a matter of great concern that society is gradually becoming resigned to the primitivisation of the Ukrainian economy, the degradation of many economic activities, the de-intellectualisation of labour, the anomalous stratification of society by income and the spreading of jobs that do not fall under the definition of decent. There is a growing feeling that society is losing the spirit of optimism, solidarity, diligence, justice, compassion and joint participation.

In general, we consider the real state of the social and labour spheres in Ukraine to be extremely difficult and threatening. Behind the rhetoric of stabilisation and declared growth of social standards, one can see a departure from the European standards, both economic and especially non-economic – opportunities for participation, morality, justice and social inclusion, when trust is becoming the biggest deficit. Unexpectedly, Ukraine is approaching the characteristics of third world countries with anomalous income polarisation, unnatural mergers of power and property, privatisation of the state by big capital and the dominance of monopoly in almost all its forms.

We are learning to tell the truth. Everyday eloquence and real life develop in parallel realities, but increasingly in opposite directions. Poverty is becoming not the exception but the norm and it is increasingly impacting the country's economically active population.

In our opinion, at this stage of development of Ukrainian society, the key task on the national scale is not the expansion of the state's social obligations, but the harmonisation of relations between major social groups through the use of trust potential.

It should be noted that the idea of harmonisation of relations and harmonious development is not new. Even the works of ancient philosophers contain the justification for the importance of harmony of interests. In the scientific treatises of modern thinkers, one finds calls for the development and promotion of the idea of harmony, although its content has its own nuances.

The Ukrainian realities are such that the idea of the social state is mostly declared but very slowly filled with real meaning. The establishment of harmonious social relations should become a strategic vector for further social transformations.

In our view, the development of trust relations, or widespread mistrust, is based on the following interactions: "trust ↔ consolidation; distrust ↔ confrontation; social irresponsibility ↔ distrust".

It should be noted that harmonisation processes must be based on new values and principles. Among the latter, the principle of complementarity of interests should be key. The point is that there should be no hierarchy of interests. These interests must be equal and consistent. Trust does not appear after the proclamation of good intentions, the emergence of slogans, or declarations that call for building trust relationships. Figuratively speaking, trust grows on the "ground" of social harmony. Therefore, the increasing harmonisation of relations between the main subjects of social relations should become dominant in the development of the economy and society. Contradictions and problems, which appear as "clots" blocking the development of trust in Ukraine, are caused by the fundamental features of the existing socio-economic system.

Growing distrust in the context of the coronavirus crisis

The national economies of most countries and the international economy as a whole are currently experiencing the so-called coronavirus crisis caused by the COVID-19 pandemic.

Given the new socio-economic reality, the scientific community is actively searching for ways to restore sustainable development. It should be noted that researchers are examining two areas for overcoming the problems posed by the pandemic that must be addressed both nationally and globally:

1) measures to be taken to return to the situation of the recent past, which include restrictions on free trade, strengthening protectionist policies, expanding the economic functions of nation states, etc. The authors of such propositions consider the recent past as the "golden age" of mankind;
2) perception of the current socio-economic reality as a new normality and the desire for sustainable development within the new epidemiological conditions.

We support the view of those scholars who believe that economic and social consequences of the COVID-19 pandemic may be similar to those caused by the Great Depression: the strengthening of protectionism, autarkic tendencies and the "second breath" of state capitalism.

The expected strengthening of international cooperation, which should be taking place during this planetary disaster, is not being observed in practice. A clear example of antisocial behaviour of players in the international space is the competition that has erupted among the manufacturers of COVID-19 vaccines and consumer countries for obtaining it.

As after the Great Depression of the 1930s, there is a **growing mistrust** between countries and economic actors.

The cessation of production of numerous goods in many areas due to quarantine restrictions testified to the vulnerability of the pre-coronavirus production chains, which was exacerbated by the application of different and inconsistent norms of national regulation, and uneven distribution of profits and losses among the participants of international cooperation.

The awareness of the vulnerability of production chains, "breakdowns" occurring not only during the early stages of the coronavirus crisis but also likely in the future, leads to the creation of back-up production while reducing economic efficiency. Similar considerations apply to further measures aimed at developing protectionism and restricting free trade.

Therefore, the pandemic and post-pandemic reality is such that social distancing, which is manifested not only at the individual level but also at the corporate and national levels, is steadily developing. There are many examples of modern pandemic practices, when at the level of business structures and individual countries there is a trend to provide themselves with everything they need. There is a high probability that this will be the impetus for mergers, acquisitions and the formation of conglomerates.

It should be noted that the politicum and expert environment in different countries is actively forming public opinion regarding the need to locate socially important infrastructure and relevant industries on the territories of nation states, which should eliminate the risks associated with the cessation of production and potential "disruption" in cooperation.

These trends are not limited by the growing distrust at the local and other levels. Global society can witness a paradigm shift in global economic progress: from the values of free trade and the post-industrial world order towards the institutionalisation of restrictions, regionalisation, decentralisation and fragmentation, the signs of which could already be seen in the pre-coronavirus period.

There is another ambiguous consequence of the coronavirus crisis. Social distancing in its broadest sense, the manifestations of which can be seen with the naked eye, means a reduction in the intensity of social contacts and, consequently, the interaction between different strata of the population. The latter may result in the reduction in social capital and the number and quality of social elevators. At the end of this process, there will be another social and labour reality, which also occurred in the 1930s. All these are signs of the new reality that must be faced.

Conclusions

Along with the formation of a new (digital) economy and network society, there is a dynamic multi-vector transformation of relations between the subjects of economic and other types of activities. The composition and hierarchy of factors for acquiring undeniable advantages are changing. At the same time, traditional tools and mechanisms for ensuring positive socio-economic dynamics are losing their significance. There is a need for new mechanisms and, at the same time, large-scale use of existing mechanisms that have hitherto played a secondary role.

Examining the nature of modern transformations of socio-economic development, the authors concluded that in a set of measures aimed at ensuring the development of a country's productive capacity, the primary role should belong to the institution of trust. The authors are convinced that trust is a fundamental phenomenon; a process of both socio-economic relations and the functioning of social institutions permeating the full range of horizontal and vertical ties that are formed in society, filling them with new qualities and values.

Within the concept of trust, which is held by the authors, the primary carrier of relationships is an individual who is active and conscious; has knowledge, ethical standards and motivational guidelines; and is the bearer of socially significant moral and cultural values.

Given the realities of today, the task of clarifying what is "behind the scenes" in a society of distrust and its components is becoming increasingly difficult. On the one hand, this complication can be explained by the absence of a reliable theory that can explain the current state of Ukrainian society in its social trust dimension. On the other hand, it should be noted that the changes in Ukrainian society at the turn of the millennium are extremely contradictory. In the current Ukrainian society, the processes that cause development, upliftment and stabilisation, and the processes that cause the deepening of instability, degradation and decline, are unfolding at the same time.

The studies conducted by the authors, including those of which the results have been published earlier, suggest that the primary function of the considered phenomenon is to ensure the building of horizontal and vertical interaction between the subjects of trust relationships. Thus, trust is directly related to: the formation of group identities, and the relationships of cooperation and solidarity; and the adoption of new, and the reproduction of existing, forms of public associations. And most importantly, the culture of trust strengthens an individual's connection with the family, state, church, nation, and other institutions of the economy and society, and also contributes to the stability and integrative nature of society. Hence the leading role of trust in the formation and reproduction of social capital.

It must be stated that modern Ukrainian society is extremely complex, divided on many grounds, diverse and multifaceted, which increases its instability and affects the dynamics of trust relationships.

The authors have repeatedly emphasised that the central message of the ideology of society's consolidation should be the institution of trust. In the new (digital) economy, trust ceases to only be a desirable institution of normal life and acquires the role of a basic platform, which creates favourable conditions for the development of the productive capacity of a country.

References

Arrow, K.J. 1972. Gifts and Exchanges. *Philosophy and Public Affairs*, vol. 1, no. 4, pp. 343-362.

Bauman, Zygmunt. 2000. *Liquid Modernity*. Cambridge, UK: Polity Press; Malden, MA: Blackwell.

Castaldo, S. 2002. Meanings of Trust: a Meta Analysis of Trust Definitions: *Paper presented at Second Euram Conference*. Stockholm.

Coleman, J. 1990. *Foundations of Social Theory*. Cambridge: Mass, Harvard University Press.

Confidence in Institutions. 2020. URL: http://www.gallup.com/poll/1597/confidence-institutions.aspx

Constitution of Ukraine. 1996. URL: https://zakon.rada.gov.ua/laws/show/254%D0%BA/96-%D0%B2%D1%80#Text.

Fukuyama, F. 1995. *Trust: The Social Virtues and the Creation of Prosperity*. New York: Free Press.

Giddens, A. 1990. *The Consequences of Modernity*. Cambridge: Polity Press.

Giddens, A. 2000. *Runaway World: How Globalization Is Reshaping Our Lives*. Routledge.

Hardin, R. 1993. The Street-Level Epistemology of Trust. *Polities and Society*, vol. 21, no. 4, pp. 505-529.

Kolot, A. and Herasymenko, O. 2017a. Market, state and business in coordinates of the new economy. *Problems and Perspectives in Management*, 15 (3), 76-97.

Kolot, A.M. and Herasymenko, O.O. 2017b. Social welfare state: genesis and prospects of development. *Social and labor relations: theory and practice*, 1, 8-36.

Kolot A., Kozmenko S., Herasymenko O. and Štreimikienė D. 2020. Development of a Decent Work Institute as a Social Quality Imperative: Lessons for Ukraine. *Economics and Sociology*, vol. 13, no. 2.P. 70-85.

Luhmann, N. 1979. *Trust and Power*. New York: Wiley.

Marshall, A. 1993. *Principles of Economics*, vol. 1, Moskva: Progress.

Musil, R. 1995. *The Man Without Qualities*. Knopf.

New York Times. 2012. “Americans’ Approval of the Supreme Count is Down in a New Poll.” 8 June.

North, D. C. 1991. Institutions, institutional change and economic performance. New York: Cambridge University Press.152 p.

Schwab, K. and Davis, N. 2018. Shaping the Fourth Industrial Revolution. *World Economic Forum*. 287 p.

Seligman, A. 2000. *The Problem of Trust*. Princeton University Press. 240 p.

Shulga, M. 2018. Social matrix disruption: monography. Kyiv: Institut of Sociology, NAS of Ukraine. 284 p.

Smith, A. 1759. The Theory of Moral Sentiments.

Sztompka, P. 1999. *Trust: a Sociological Theory*. Cambridge: Cambridge University Press.

Sztompka, P. 2002. Socjologia. Analiza społeczeństwa. Kraków, Znak. 656 s.

Sztompka, P. 2007. Zaufanie. Fundament społeczeństwa. Kraków, Znak. 420 s.

The Future Society. Conversation with Dirk Baecker. 2012. URL: http://www.russ.ru/Mirovaya-povestka/Obschestvo-buduschego-kakoe-ono.

Toffler, A. 1981. *The Third Wave*. London, Pan Books Ltd.

Ukrainian Society. 2017. Monitoring of Social Change. Results of the national annual monitoring surveys.

Ukrainian Society. 2019 Monitoring of Social Change. Results of the national annual monitoring surveys.

CHAPTER FOUR

NOOSPHERIC THINKING AS A FACTOR IN ECONOMIC DEVELOPMENT

IGOR G. KHANIN

Today, the paradigm of digitisation dominates in the field of information phenomena, to which the economy belongs. The essence of this paradigm lies in the application of physical technologies for data processing in a variety of mainly social and economic practices. Nowadays, this paradigm is close to the depletion, if not exhaustion, of its innovative potential.

Within the framework of the digitisation paradigm, technologists should explore the field of information practices in order to find among them those that can be easily digitised; whereas sociologists and economists need to make their own decisions about digitisation, having little idea of how it might end. Simulation modelling is put forward as an alternative, but it also applies to practices and does not go beyond digitisation, like artificial intelligence, which also uses modelling. The alternative can only be a tight integration of both IT components based on their convergence. In particular, information, primarily business practices, should be deepened to the same level as scientifically grounded data-processing technologies. However, neither the natural scientific thinking of information technologies nor the humanitarian thinking of information practices is suitable for this. The noospheric thinking initiated by Vernadsky is required for this purpose. Noospheric thinking is presented here by its ontological basis in the form of the Quasi-Physical Model of Cognition (QPMC) of the noosphere. The model is convergent, since it is assumed that the noosphere includes the biosphere and the biosphere includes the physiosphere.

Until now, understanding has been dominated by the model of scientific cognition of nature, inherited from the era of the natural scientific revolution and, at the same time, not fully articulated. The humanitarian model uses empirical and heuristic methods and modelling.

Moreover, natural and human sciences, and in particular the economy, are in different phases of development. In general, neither the natural science nor the humanitarian model is relevant to the current tasks of cognition. The QPMC is based on the ideas and views of Vladimir Vernadsky, Georg Wilhelm Friedrich Hegel, Karl Marx, Alexei Losev, Merab Mamardashvili, Anton Filipenko, Vadim Yefimov, Charles Peirce, Ferdinand de Saussure, Friedrich von Hayek, Ronald Coase, Alain Badiou, Bertin Martens, Allen E. Caille and others. These ideas are constantly the focus of attention, but due to the absence of an empirical base, they lack proper interpretation and practical application.

According to the QPMC, the noosphere in the epistemological sense is a materially embodied form of consciousness – the result of conscious cognitive and creative, and particularly economic, activity. The activity creates primary empirical (practical) knowledge in the form of quasi-physical effects of conscious phenomena that needs scientific systematisation. This process is never fully completed, as there is always a time and place for such activities as art.

Ontologically, the noosphere is arranged in the form of signs, where consciousness establishes and maintains a correspondence between the signified (structural units of the physiosphere and biosphere) and the signifier (symbols, texts and hypertext). The QPMC model includes the structure of the noosphere as a relevant scheme of the object of cognition with horizontal (interdisciplinary) connections between the spheres of phenomena (physiosphere, biosphere, noosphere). Vertical relations are established between the levels of abstraction (philosophy, methodology, mathematics, fundamental and applied knowledge, technology, practice).

The model of ontogenesis of knowledge (Vertical Integration and the Parabola of Knowledge, or VIPK) describes the process of vertical integration of homogeneous phenomena. As a result, the qualitative state of cognition in the sphere of phenomena is changing in accordance with the model of Paradigmatic Innovative Development (PIDev).

Until knowledge is integrated into holistic horizontal and vertical structures, their division into spheres and levels of abstraction is premature, since the ascent from the abstract to the concrete is based on abstractions obtained by immersion from the concrete into the abstract. These processes are constantly alternating. The abstract and the concrete are interdependent.

From the point of view of the QPMC and agreeing with Bertin Martens, the economy can be presented as a symbolic machine for the production of embodied knowledge. The separation of knowledge and economic management is relative and not constant. After vigorous activity invades a new sphere, practice – above all, the economic one – becomes a leader in innovation. Following the formation of a sufficient empirical base and a phase of revolutionary paradigmatic innovation (Kuhn 2012), leadership returns to the scientific knowledge.

QPMC, at least, can serve as the basis for strategic planning, forecasting and optimisation of economic management and cognition. It can also be considered as the basis for the scientific systematisation of knowledge about the infosphere, including the economy, which is given the opportunity to turn from a set of socio-economic projects into knowledge that makes it possible to understand the socio-economic reality, without which reforming the economy will not only be useless but also dangerous (Caille 2007; Yefimov 2011).

This model was tested for its intended purpose in the process of solving the problem of sign ontology. At the same time, the results of the experience of spontaneous formalisation of software applications and databases, which are actually the simulation models of economic organisations and networks, were used as an empirical base. The ontology of a sign is the core of the fundamental science of signs as a phenomenon of consciousness. On this basis, developments are underway in terms of optimising the network architectures for programmes and business organisations, creating the data infrastructures that raise the barrier of acceptable data diversity and reduce data fragmentation, as well as an augmentation of meanings in text artifacts for various purposes.

Literature review

Today, economic activity all over the planet is facing the most complex practical problems, the solution to which requires the development of economic theory. Meanwhile, as Yefimov (2011) writes in the *Journal of Economic Regulation*, "Economists are engaged not so much in a detailed study of the processes actually occurring in the economy, as they are trying to influence these processes. And we must admit that they have succeeded greatly in this." He further quotes Allen Caille (2007):

> "The modern world to a large extent is the realization of dreams, prophecies and preaching of economic science. Sometimes it's just a nightmare. And every day this becomes more and more true on a planetary scale, when nothing else is considered as a reality, except for economic and financial restrictions, except for the search for personal material enrichment. In the face of all this, any value, any belief, any action performed for their own sake, just for the sake of pleasure, any existence

> that is not devoted to the search for usefulness – all this henceforth seems illusory, inoperative, not worth the effort, useless, unreal."

Kaye's quotation is taken from his introductory article to an almanac entitled *Towards the Creation of Another Economic Science (and thus Another World)?* Yefimov seems to agree that an attitude that is too utilitarian towards the science of economics hinders its development and thereby ultimately reduces its usefulness for economic management. However, he worries that this name can be understood in such a way that changing the point of view on reality can change reality itself. Although, there is nothing strange about this. Human consciousness intersects with reality and one cannot change without changing the other. The physics of Aristotle, Galileo, Einstein and what will follow them – all these are the realities of their time, denied or expanded by new knowledge. In our opinion, without this thesis it is impossible to understand what is happening in the sphere of non-physical phenomena. The problem of a utilitarian attitude towards the science of economics can have various aspects (subjective, objective, social, psychological, political, ethical, etc.), but the most important point is the absence of an obligatory empirical base and productive abstractions (paradigms) for the formation of an ontology (essence) of economic management relevant to the empirical base.

The role of shifts from a superficial to a deeper understanding of reality can be demonstrated in the historical example of biology. The work of Timofeev-Ressovsky (2009, 196) is well suited for this:

> "How do biological systems evolve over time? Once upon a time, in the last century, there lived crocodile No.17, and, in this century, there lives crocodile No.187, already a completely different crocodile, and what's left? 'Crocodilism' is left. This is what Plato was talking about: that fools understand very well what a horse is, but they do not understand 'horseness'. So, there was a 'crocodilism', and what is it? It is not teeth or tails at all, and not even an area of distribution, but this is a kind of initial control systems. Over time, 'crocodilism' exists in the form of certain codes of hereditary information. Just as certain codes of hereditary information are something that is implemented in any form in ontogeny, so these codes of hereditary information are the only ones that flow in biological time and pass from generation to generation. And it is quite natural that the evolutionary significance is not something that has changed in crocodile No.17, for example, but something that has changed in 'crocodilism'. The problem needs to be put upside down."

If we replace "crocodiles" with a set of phenomena and "crocodilism" with the invariant of this set, determined by "a certain type of control systems", then a methodological formula, being suitable wherever there is multiplicity and development, is obtained. This means that, in economics, it is necessary to look for such bodies. Timofeev-Ressovsky (2009, 197) continues:

> "For modern theoretical biological reasoning it is necessary to start from the beginning, not from the end. Put everything from head to foot. Not from the crocodile tail, but from the fact that in time supports the existence of crocodile tails – the corresponding information codes that determine a specific set of features. And this is the basis of the modern concept, which is absolutely necessary for the correct, effective and rapid development of biology in the near future."

An invariant that, practically, does not change in space (on the set of phenomena) and over time is the "corresponding information codes". Information (messages, data) is signs. On the other hand, economic management is a kind of informational, i.e. sign, practice. Thus, there is an analogy between the methodologies for biology and economics at the level of not only schemes but also their implementation.

It can be concluded that information, i.e. signs, lies at the foundation of the biosphere and economic management, and the concepts such as ontogenesis and phylogenesis are applicable to the sphere of economic phenomena.

Timofeev-Ressovsky stated that, in Soviet biological science, much effort was spent on obtaining results, the relevance of which was negligible. In his opinion, "In order to avoid this low efficiency and short lifespan of the results of scientific work, a correct natural-historical methodological setting is needed, and one must proceed from the modern general scientific concepts. In biology, this happened later than in physics" (Ibid. 203). The result is a clear modern flourishing of biology and medicine. The science of economics is looking for similar ways of understanding economic management and cognition (innovative development) itself.

Evgeny Saburov (2010) writes:

> "A completely different drama, a completely different collision, is already coming to the fore. And this speaks of a greater maturity of the economy, of deeper roots of confrontation. They no longer touch upon the issue of conducting, regulation, etc. What is this science all about? What is economics in general? And here two other figures arise: the drama is always personified, this is its law. These figures are of colossal size. It is impossible to say about them that someone is right and someone is wrong.

> This is a completely different formulation of problems. I mean H. Becker and R. Coase."

Comparing their views, Saburov (Ibid.) comes to the following conclusion:

> "How can I relate to Coase's words that the science of choice is no longer economics? I must say that Coase himself is also no longer economics, that in fact, understanding the firm, understanding the market, understanding the language, understanding responsibility, etc. are already going beyond the economy. And if we talk about the creation of a unified humanities, then it seems to me that it will not be born only on the ideas of Becker. It will arise from ideas from both directions. But economists cannot create it if they continue to stew in their own juice. For example, for the development of Coase's direction, the participation of linguists, philologists, an understanding of the structuring of life, the structuring of language, oppositions suggests itself."

Becker represents economic behaviour and Coase represents socio-economic institutions. Institutions are structures of signs that unite the signifier and signified parts of the structures and processes of economic management. In doing so, the behaviour uses data to indicate the state of economic objects. Thus, we have found a single basis, which is significant and unites both directions – Becker's and Coase's. In other words, the information (messages as a symbolic category) is not only a resource for the functioning of the economy but also a "material" without which it cannot exist.

Mamardashvili (2008) writes that social phenomena, differing from the physical ones in some ways while also being similar in others, form the effects of non-physical phenomena, the study of which requires a quasi-physical approach. Obviously, these effects are information, understood as messages.

Claude Shannon (1963) used the term "information" as a measure of the uncertainty of a message associated with a physical characteristic known as entropy. In natural language, the word "information" is synonymous with the word "message". Thus, the term "information" has lost its uniqueness. Shannon applied it not to messages but to physical signals, i.e. to the signifier part of messages, as a result of which the situation was aggravated.

Russell Ackoff and Fred Emery (2005) used the word "information" as a term denoting one of the measures of influence by the message (sign construction) on the recipient. In my opinion, this is sufficient for any term. It is suggested to use the terminology based on the meaning of "sign" to denote information in the sense of messages and information. These are messages, information, sign formations and sign structures.

What is common and different in physical and non-physical objects of knowledge? In my opinion, Marx's concept of the transformed forms of consciousness can serve here as a unifying principle. In Marxism, such forms are generally interpreted as distorted knowledge. I propose to concentrate on the word "knowledge" in the sense that any knowledge is ultimately a materially embodied form of consciousness, despite, of course, the fact that consciousness itself is a product of cognitive and creative activity.

At the same time, non-physical (quasi-physical and one can also say hyperphysical) objects also consist of physical objects. Their distinguishing feature is that they are divided into two parts (signifier and signified), between which a relationship of correspondence is established, maintained and used by conscious efforts.

When it comes to the dynamic characteristics of knowledge, one cannot but mention the work of Thomas Kuhn (2012), which divides the development of science into three periods: pre-paradigmatic, paradigmatic and post-paradigmatic. I name the first period as empirical-heuristic. A significant role in it is played by practices, primarily economic ones, that are the first to encounter the unknown classes of phenomena. At the third stage, official science plays a decisive role. Terminological ambiguity arises. Kuhn's term "science" refers to both cognition as a whole and the period of dominance of official science in it. Terminological inconsistencies create problems for understanding and developing Kuhn's views.

Kuhn focused on the social aspects of cognition. His work (2012), especially the concept of a paradigm, generated lively discussions. Under the influence of these discussions, the book *An Arrow of Cognition* by Mamardashvili (1997) was written. The author formulated the principle of "destruction and reconstruction of understanding", which, in a more categorical form, corresponds to the change of paradigms, including the change in the model of cognition in the course of the scientific revolution (Ibid.).

Karl Popper (1957) was interested in the question of drawing a demarcation line between scientific and non-scientific knowledge. However, the primary source of scientific knowledge is not scientific but pre-scientific empirical knowledge recorded in natural language. Losev (2005) writes, "What is science? A systematic presentation of knowledge gained from experience (through the external senses), i.e. presentation and explanation of empirical phenomena." Knowledge, before moving on to its social, psychological and other aspects, should be described in terms of knowledge itself, in particular the structure and natural transitions from pre-scientific knowledge to the paradigmatic (meta-scientific) one, and further to the scientific one. It should also be noted that the empirical basis for Kuhn at that time was, first of all, the world of matter and energies, whereas today the priority has shifted to the information phenomena.

It is difficult to disagree with Peirce that the world is literally riddled with signs, if it is not a sign itself (Nöth 2001). Saussure, Hayek and Coase also paid attention to the similarity of economics and sign systems, including language (Saburov 2010). Thus, from both a practical and a theoretical point of view, optimisation of the sign structure is a paramount priority for the economy. Against this background, more than meagre reference to signs in the humanitarian sphere, in particular in the economy which is clearly riddled with signs, looks strange. For example, in the digest *The Philosophy of Economy: Anthology* (Hausman 2010), the root of "semiotic" has not been found. Given that signs undoubtedly play a decisive role in human activity, this is one of the mysteries that needs to be solved by future historians of science.

Keynes (Heilbroner 2011) described economics as a universal science:

> "…a good economist must have a rare combination of skills. In one way or another, he must simultaneously be a mathematician, historian, statesman and philosopher. He must understand the language of symbols, but use words in conversation. Considering particulars, he must keep the whole in mind and skillfully combine reflections on the abstract and the concrete. He must study the present in the light of the past, not forgetting about the future. He cannot afford to lose sight of any part of the nature of man or his products. He must be a model of purposefulness and impartiality; haughty and incorruptible, like an artist, sometimes he should be closer to the ground than another politician!"

Keynes did not note the interdependence of the economy and the science of economics with nature and the natural sciences. Moreover, according to Bertin Martens (2004), the essence (ontology) of the economy can be defined as an information (more precisely, sign) machine for the production of materialised knowledge. Through the efforts of many thinkers and people of practice, there emerges a picture, approaching the image that Vladimir Vernadsky, Pierre Teilhard de Chardin and Edouard Le Roy called the noosphere.

This is a controversial concept. Most often, the noosphere is associated with the information phenomena; that is, the infosphere. Heinrich Gruzman, a researcher of Vernadsky's work, drew attention to the fact that

Vernadsky's philosophical and meta-scientific ideas, which go beyond his positively scientific and productive interests, should be considered in the context of his works on the theory and history of science (Gruzman 2005; Vernadsky 1988). Due to the absence of an empirical base, Vernadsky could not transform his views on the noosphere into a constructive model of cognition. He spoke in terms of matter and energy, lacking sufficient experience in handling the information – or more precisely, the signs. But, at the same time, Vernadsky was able to fit the whole world into one word, "noosphere", as an object of knowledge. Lyndon LaRouche (2001) is one of those who have been able to appreciate the significance of this step.

However, what is philosophy if not a universal theory of cognition, including philosophical ontology and, moreover, epistemology? That is true, but over the time the meanings change, and therewith the relevance of objects and the phase of the genesis of cognition. Therefore, new models or theories of knowledge are required, and therewith an updated philosophy too.

Shiyali Ramamrita Ranganathan, undertaking the study of the information phenomena as a part of library activities, faced the need to answer the question of what library science is, as well as what the science is in general. This led him to look for a cognitive model that is relevant to the task at hand. Ranganathan (1957) called it the spiral of knowledge. His model actually uses the method of "ascent from the abstract to the concrete" by Hegel (Zinoviev 2002). In it, Ranganathan (1957) presented cognition as an alternation of transitions from the concrete to the abstract and from the abstract to the concrete. His idea is undoubtedly important, but it does not exhaust the range of ideas needed to build a model of cognition that is relevant to the problems facing the cognition of the infosphere.

A detailed picture of cognition, using the concept of a name (that is, in fact, a sign and information as a message), was given by Losev (1990a). It can be considered the most complete picture of the world as a noospheric object of cognition, in which matter, energy and signs (information) are present in their static and dynamic relationships. This picture is difficult to operate. To do this, it needs to be concretised in relation to the current moment and the actual tasks of cognition. The picture of knowledge created by Losev is convergent in nature. According to it, cognitive and creative activity, regardless of the nature of objects of cognition, can ultimately be defined as the embodiment of forms of consciousness in matter (here, Losev uses a more subtle category of meon).

The use of the computer in the economy and society has exposed and exacerbated the problems of the development of the infosphere, which basically determines the structure of the noosphere. In these conditions, Einstein's cognitive principle, according to which the problem cannot be solved in the context in which it arose, becomes especially relevant. Today, the infosphere uses the inherited and not always conscious models of cognition anchored in conceptually loosely coupled texts. These texts define the nomenclature of scientific specialities, standards for teaching scientific disciplines, methods of conducting scientific work and writing articles and books, etc.

The inherited models reflect the specificity of cognition in the post-paradigmatic phase of the development of natural sciences, or the pre-paradigmatic phase where the humanities or practical knowledge is. The question arises: Is it possible to bring the spheres of phenomena studied by the natural sciences and the humanities closer? Marx's ideas about modified forms of consciousness are appropriate for addressing this problem. These ideas were developed by Mamardashvili (2008), who introduced the concept of the "quasi-physical effect of non-physical (conscious) phenomena" into philosophical discourse, which is also necessary for convergence.

Today, knowledge of the infosphere has become very close to the paradigmatic phase and needs a model that will cover all phases of the development of cognition, including the pre-paradigmatic (empirical-heuristic), paradigmatic (scientific revolution) and post-paradigmatic (scientific). Such a model is necessary, in particular in order to solve the problem of the ontology of information (more precisely, the sign). This problem has a thousand-year history. Examples of the attempts to solve it in the context of modern knowledge can be seen in the efforts of the scientific school of Ronald Stemper (Gazendam and Liu 2005) and the monograph by Kumiko Tanaka-Ishii (2010).

Stemper is right when he relies on organisations as an empirical base, i.e. he immediately attempts to solve social and economic problems of the economy and society; although, in my opinion, one should start with simpler and well-formalised sign structures, which are the applied computer programs. However, even under this condition, he would need an approach to cognition that differs from the natural science and humanities.

Tanaka-Ishii uses computer programs as an empirical base, or rather programming processes. Thus, the result obtained by her, in contrast to the semiotics of programs, should be called programming linguistics, given that linguistics is actually concerned with the signifier part of signs. She knows this because she cites Nöth, who drew attention to the fact that de Saussure's model of the sign is missing the signified. However, she is right when she declares the need to move not only from the paradigms of the Peirce and de Saussure signs to practice (in our terminology, "to rise from the abstract to the concrete"), but also back, from the empirical base to the paradigms of the sign (from the concrete to the abstract). However, due to the inaccurate choice of starting points and goals for the movement, in her case, as in the case of Stemper's organisational semiotics, the synthesis did not work out. This does not mean that their efforts are futile. They mapped out the path to follow.

Knowledge of the ontology (essence) of signs is necessary, in particular for the development of the applied paradigms of computer programs, data, business organisations and economics. The applied paradigms of sign constructions will serve as a tool for optimising the information (more precisely, sign) infrastructure of the economy from the enterprise level and above by reducing its rigidity (resistance to change) and fragmentation, which are caused by the presence of a complexity barrier due to semantic diversity and data variability (Polyakov et al. 2018).

Attempts to create the models of practical work in the infosphere, including those with the elements of knowledge, have been made for a long time and constantly. Some of them are called methodologies. Examples include the Object-Oriented Analysis and Design (OOAD) (Booch 2004). The object of this methodology is software systems. Further, these are the Theory and Practice of Business Processes (TPBP), the Enterprise and Systems Architecture (ESA), the Semantic Technologies (ST) and other tools (Berners-Lee et al. 2001; Zachman 1987; Scheer 1999).

Each of these tools is usually based on some significant, and more or less adequate and principled, position. For OOAD, it is "a program as an object, not an algorithm", in TPBP "a program is a tracing of business processes", ESA is "overcoming disintegration between technologies (information) and business", and in ST "technologies must take into account the semantics of data". These tools did not become the models of knowledge that ensure the transition of the infosphere from pre-scientific knowledge to scientific knowledge. Obviously, such a model should be based on a comprehensive and well-integrated empirical, philosophical and methodological base.

In connection with cognition models, cognitology or cognitive sciences (about cognition) should be mentioned. However, the focus of attention of these disciplines is mainly the manipulation of data carrying knowledge, or the processes of spontaneous formalisation of knowledge expressed in natural languages. At the same time, spontaneous automation is based on guesses, analogies and associations.

Within the framework of modern practical economics, knowledge management is devoted to knowledge and cognition, including the functions of innovative and strategic management. According to the views expressed by Tom Wilson (2002) and Gary Gorman (2019), knowledge management differs from information management and librarianship by no more than the overestimated salary level of managers. Their views were challenged by David Pauleen (2019), who relied on the views of Larry Prusak.

Pauleen is right that knowledge and cognition management are not limited to information management, human resource management and the cost aspects of these processes. In his opinion, there is still something implicit that is difficult to express in words. We would call this management in terms of knowledge itself. However, until the implicit emerges, the success of its application will remain a matter of intuition and experience of staff. Gorman and Pauleen postponed resolving their differences by translating them from the social level to the personal level.

In fact, there are many models that have been developed specifically to learn about humanitarian phenomena or claiming universality. Among them are the tectology of Alexander Bogdanov (1989), the cybernetic approach of Norbert Wiener (1961), the praxeology of Evgeny Slutsky (2007) and Tadeusz Kotarbiński (1975), etc. These and similar developments can be considered as experiments in the search for a real model of cognition of non-physical phenomena. They completed their tasks and today are the potential objects of an instructive history of cognition, and sources of positive and negative experience.

A special place in the series of experiments on the formation of a model of cognition of non-physical phenomena is occupied by a systematic approach and systematic thinking based on it. It is used universally and is founded on the concept of a system. This concept is based on the mathematical abstraction of structure. Any ontology can be associated with it: physical or biological, including undefined. The latter, among the dissimilar elements, may include non-physical elements. This allows the constraints of the system and the systematic approach to be extremely flexible. At the same time, researchers and developers, proceeding from experience and intuition, can interpret them based on the material in the subject area in a manner that suits them. In order for such lightness and versatility to be productive, it must be complemented by the talent, experience and intuition of the subjects of the innovation process, like in the case of modelling.

Luciano Floridi's (200~~3~~4) "philosophy of information" is aimed directly at the application of philosophy to explain the phenomena of information. Its object by default, i.e. virtually without limitations, is any phenomenon to which the word "information" can be attributed. Such phenomena form the empirical basis of Floridi's information philosophy. However, according to the definition of Losev: "What is philosophy? World outlook, compiled by synthetic combination of scientific information" (Losev 1997), philosophy is not directly connected with the empirical base but through the achievements of science. This means that until the vertical of knowledge about information is formed, philosophy and theory for this area cannot be productive, if they exist~~ing~~ independently from each other and from practice.

At the same time, one can refer to Alain Badiou (2003, 16), who states: "The specific role of philosophy is to propose a unified conceptual space in which naming takes place of events that serve as the point of departure for truth procedures." At the same time, he believes that the truth is "only scientific, artistic, political or love". In fact, Badiou speaks of the type of thinking that meets the requirements of the current moment and the level of development of science, art, politics and personality. Its core should be an actual model and, ultimately, a theory of knowledge. Today, it is the noospheric thinking and the noospheric model. It is impossible to think about space without thinking about the things that fill it.

The activities of the International Federation for Systems Research (IFSR) community are aimed at the formation of the foundations of information sciences, as in the case of the cognition model. As shown, the problems of information are reduced to problems of signs. Community members, working on the Fuschl Conversations project, state: "We want to build a general theory that conceptualizes reality as a field containing meaningful human social interactions as well as technology and nature" (Brier 2001).

The goal is ambitious but is it achievable? Indeed, history and the current state of knowledge show that, due to the limited capabilities of a human, cognition of the whole is carried out in parts. Moreover, the knowledge of each part is divided into stages. Periods of continuous evolutionary development of cognition are replaced by discrete transitions between areas and stages of cognition. This means that a single object (synchronicity) and process (diachrony) of cognition need a rational decomposition that meets the current meanings of development, which are constantly refined over time. It is doubtful whether it is possible to create a "theory of everything", but it is possible and necessary to build a model of cognition, in accordance with which a large whole is in a certain way divided into parts and the processes of cognition of the parts are divided into phases. At the same time, the procedures for learning each part in each phase should be basically regulated.

Vernadsky probably thought in a similar way when, having formed the image of the noosphere, he turned to the history and theory of science to implement this image. In his papers on this topic, if properly interpreted, you can find many of the key ideas used in the proposed discussion of the QPMC. In particular, Vernadsky (1988, 87) wrote about the times that preceded the natural scientific revolution:

> "A new worldview came to replace the dying outlook, and it was carried by people who had their roots in forms that had imperceptibly grown along with the scientific organizations of that time, the foundations of which, in essence, logically contradicted the dominant views…These are people of the popular milieu, nameless carriers of the disorderly mass life. Their names are as little known to us as the names of poets who composed a folk song, composers who gave a way of peculiar, full of originality and depth of folk music."

Here, Vernadsky speaks of scientific activity as one of the phases of the cognition process. At the same time, the first in order and in importance is the phase of practical cognitive and creative activity of the great masses of proactive people, on the results of which science is based.

The following quotation speaks about the principle of the integrity of knowledge, and about the relativity of its division into objects, phases of development and levels of abstraction of cognition:

> "Only in abstraction and in imagination that does not correspond to reality, science and scientific worldview can dominate by themselves, develop apart from the participation of ideas and concepts spilled in the spiritual environment, created in a different way. It is possible to speak about the need for the disappearance of one of the aspects of the human personality, about the replacement of philosophy with science, or vice versa – it is possible only in unscientific abstraction." (Vernadsky 1988, 58)

Indeed, philosophy, methodology, and fundamental and applied theories gain meaning only when they are included in the framework of an integral structure – for example, such as the parabola and the vertical of knowledge as a part of the QPMC. And in the words of Vernadsky, when solving problems of cognition, it is necessary to proceed from practical problems and in order to solve them guided by the deepest abstractions, the QPMC sees the principle of vertical integration of knowledge.

Quasi-Physical Model of Cognition

In order to implement Einstein's aforementioned cognitive principle in relation to the infosphere, the Quasi-Physical (Noospheric) Model of Cognition (QPMC) is proposed (shown in Figure 4-1). This model embodies Vernadsky's Noospheric Thinking, transformed with due regard for the peculiarities of the current time.

As follows from the Figure, the main blocks of the model are: Consciousness, Cognitive-Creative Activity (CCA) of consciousness, the sphere of phenomena, a set of effects of CCA of consciousness, a model of knowledge ontogenesis (VIPK), a model of phylogenesis of knowledge (Paradigmatic Innovative Development), ontology of phenomena, and transformation of the sphere of phenomena. These QPMC concepts are included in the categorical apparatus of noospheric thinking.

Scientific activity of consciousness takes place within the framework of actual being, which grows out of potential being (meon, meonal environment) due to the cognitive and creative practical activity of consciousness.

CCA of consciousness evokes phenomena and forms pre-scientific knowledge of them. They are fixed in consciousness, in particular in natural language. These descriptions can be varied, integrated, differentiated, formalised through digitisation, etc. Problem-oriented vocabularies can be extracted from natural language and called ontologies. Such operations can be referred to in modelling as the relationship between the abstract and the concrete by association and fact, and not by essence and meaning. However, scientific knowledge on the model of natural sciences is different.

Pre-scientific knowledge corresponds to its embodiment in the effects caused by CCA. These can be natural or artificial objects (artifacts). First of all, they should be distinguished by their essence (ontology), which must be establish by acts of scientific knowledge (see Figure 4-1).

Cognition cycles can be repeated many times. In this case, any block can be connected to any previous block by forward and feedback loops. Thus, consciousness, arising from life, continues the practical (not yet theoretical) cognitive and constructive assimilation of potential being. The results of this activity are the formation of an empirical base of scientific knowledge in the form of a target set of physical and quasi-physical effects.

On this basis, one cannot deny the existence of empirical roots, even for mathematical knowledge, although a mathematician may have difficulty trying to establish them. There can be no science for science.

The deepest abstractions must be the quintessence of an infinite variety of empirical phenomena.

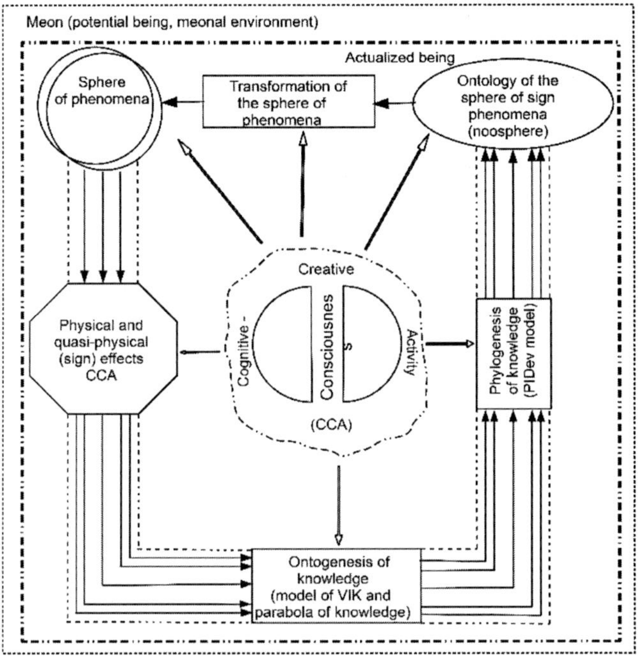

Figure 4-1. Architecture of the QPMC

Scientific cognition begins with immersion from the concrete (a set of effects; that is, the results of activity) into the abstract and continues by ascending from the abstract to the concrete. This makes it possible to optimise the existing artifacts and create fundamentally new and more efficient (optimal) ones. This is the principle of ontogenesis; that is, the Vertical Integration of Knowledge (VIK). The ontogenesis of knowledge concerns individual phenomena and their structures, forming a hierarchy up to the sphere of phenomena. The phylogenesis of the sphere of phenomena and its structures depends on the breadth of coverage and completeness of ontogenesis of knowledge about phenomena. One can say that phylogenesis is a change in the degree of paradigmatisation of these structures.

With the accumulation and ordering of practical knowledge, the investigated and transformed sphere of phenomena passes from the empirical-heuristic (pre-paradigmatic) to the paradigmatic, and then to the scientific (post-paradigmatic) phase of development. The result of these processes in the infosphere is the ontology of sign phenomena, which allows the subjects of innovative activity to think and act on the basis of understanding the essence of phenomena, i.e. essentially. Today, natural-science knowledge is closest to this. The QPMC assumes a convergence between it and humanitarian knowledge. Therefore, the construction of domain ontology is a fundamental requirement for this model.

The fundamental principles of the QPMC are the well-known laws of philosophical logic. In a generalised form, Mamardashvili formulated them as fundamental philosophical abstractions. This is the embodiment of the understood (Plato), the cogito (Descartes) and practice – the main criterion of truth (Marx) (Mamardashvili 1990+). Similar principles, on which the world is built, are contained in the law of the necessary foundation and absolute separateness, as worded by Losev (1990b). These are also the categories of firstness, secondness and thirdness of Charles Peirce, especially the relationship between them (Nöth 2001).

The classical principles in the QPMC are supplemented with ideas about the transformed forms of consciousness and quasi-physical effects of non-physical phenomena (Mamardashvili 2008). They attach to QPMC its quasi-physical character. The connection with the fundamental traditions of cognition and their development, the convergence of natural science and humanitarian knowledge, are fundamental features of the QPMC against the background of such teachings as the "methodology" of G.P. Shchedrovitsky (2005). Methodology breaks with the traditions of scientific knowledge, starting from the basics. Its foundation is thinking and activity (Shchedrovitsky 2005). However, this is by no means a firstness according to Peirce (Nöth 2001), i.e. not an ontology as "quality".

The objects of cognition for the QPMC are phenomena (manifestations of unknown entities to be determined) and structures consisting of them, up to the world level which contains all phenomena. The world structure is divided into the spheres, which consist of phenomena of one nature (one essence, one ontology). Their incarnations (effects) are physical bodies and living organisms. Since ancient times, signs have been considered as one of the fundamental entities. Charles Peirce (Nöth 2001) gave this idea a definitive form. His "firstness" (simplified "quality") can be compared with *ratio fiendi*; that is, the necessity of becoming an essence, a "physical" necessity. "Secondness" (relations) is the need for mathematics; that is, relations in space and time (*ratio essendi*), in particular the need for actualisation and activity of consciousness (*ratio agendi*). Peirce's "thirdness" means universal coherence, including consciousness. The ratio of cognoscendi of the law of foundation can be compared with thirdness. According to Peirce, thirdness is realised by signs that are studied by semiotics (Nöth 2001). Peirce gave a laconic and precise answer to the question of "What function do signs perform?" Firstness and secondness can be interpreted as the signifier, and thirdness interpreted as the signified part of signs. Then, one can say that the objective world – that is, the world as a result of scientific knowledge – is built of signs.

Vernadsky did not attach much importance to the words "sign" or "information". The idea of interconnection of world phenomena is expressed by the word "noosphere"; that is, the sphere of reason or thought. It would be naive to believe that by this he wanted to say that for some reason people will suddenly start to think better. Most likely, he meant that a thought and, accordingly, the signs that it produces have always been, are and will be elements of the world order.

Indeed, Vernadsky was a researcher of the geosphere and biosphere, and, in these areas, he gained worldwide recognition. By exploring and acting, he envisioned the world as a whole. His thinking was planetary and historical. "Public history", he argued, "is a continuation of natural history" (Vernadsky 2004). It follows from the views of Vernadsky that the biosphere contains the geosphere but is not reduced to it. This is not a coincidence, since they are composed of different entities. Likewise, the noosphere should also contain the biosphere and not be reducible to it. It should be the sphere of symbolic, i.e. informational, phenomena (if we understand information as messages).

The idea of the noosphere is encoded in Peirce's system of views and in the idea of Peirce's sign in Vernadsky's system. Their belief systems can serve as clues to one another. The biosphere is the whole world in the volume of its scientific knowledge, as it was yesterday; the noosphere is the further development of the world today. Figure 4-2 graphically presents the main features of the described model.

Figure 4-2 shows that the vertical of integration and the parabola of knowledge, which are discussed below, are superimposed on the structure of the noosphere. The full circle corresponds to the noosphere and covers the segment that corresponds to the biosphere. This, in turn, contains a segment that symbolises the physiosphere (an extension of the concept of the geosphere). The concentric rings and parabolas of knowledge show that a unified model of cognition is applied to the cognition of various spheres. It is characterised by the levels of abstraction and the asynchronous nature of the development of scientific knowledge in different areas. The physiosphere is most developed, followed by the biosphere. Scientific knowledge of the noosphere is in its early stages of development.

It should be noted that phenomena differ from effects (objects) in their uncertainty and objects differ from phenomena in a more complex structure. We can say that objects are phenomena that have found their embodiment and application.

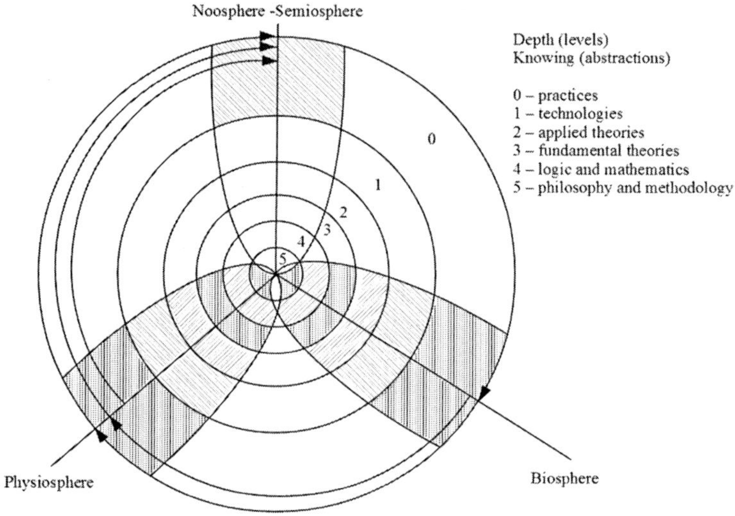

Figure 4-2. Quasi-physical model of the object of cognition
Source: Pikalov 2019.

From a comparison of the views of Peirce and Vernadsky, one can draw a conclusion about the fundamental role that signs play in the noosphere and in the world. Peirce's pansemiotism and Vernadsky's belief in the power of knowledge are also fully justified by the potential that information technologies still hide. That is why it is so important to know the ontology of signs. For this purpose, it is necessary, first of all, to separate non-physical phenomena from the physical and to establish what their fundamental difference is from each other.

The empirical base of non-physical phenomena is information. In natural language, this word is synonymous with message and intelligence. However, Claude Shannon (1963) applied it in the meaning of a measure of the influence of a message on the recipient and the word "information" became a homonym. Therefore, in order to avoid ambiguity, especially in fundamental matters, let non-physical phenomena be called signs or sign bodies, since messages (information) really consist of signs.

In order not to limit cognition to philosophising, only strongly formalised sign structures should be included in the empirical base of integral cognition. Let them be called sign constructions. Today, computer programs and the data processed by them are formalised as much as possible.

So, the physical effect is a fragment of the meonal environment (potential being). Consciousness perceives it as a whole, consisting of physical components, interconnected by physical connections. Physical effects can be natural or artificial (artifacts) objects. Natural objects are also the products, at least, of cognitive activity. However, it is difficult to separate cognitive and creative activities. An example of only creative activity is the replication of samples.

In the process and in the result of cognition, consciousness transforms being. Biological phenomena and their corresponding effects have all the properties of physical phenomena and effects. Therefore, skipping the biological effects, one can go straight to the quasi-physical effects.

Quasi-Physical Effect[1] is a fragment of actual being. Consciousness perceives it as a whole, consisting of two physical or quasi-physical components. The latter, in contrast to physical effects, are linked in consciousness by a correspondence relationship. There is no insurmountable gap between physical and quasi-physical effects (objects). For example, in the case of a computer program, by connecting the parts (loading the text of programs and data into a computer system), an object created as quasi-physical turns into an autonomous physical thing. It is a computer that operates under the control of the signals of the program text recorded on the machine medium. Of course, in order to have the right to think and speak in this way, it is necessary to postulate the existence of temporal objects, characterised by structure and states. In the sign, the process (for example, data processing), as the signified part, is connected by the static signifier part (for example, by the algorithm in the program text).

Thus, a quasi-physical object consists of physical objects, split into two parts connected with each other through consciousness by a correspondence relationship. In certain phases of its existence, a quasi-physical object can become a physical object.

The next component of the QPMC is the Paradigmatic Innovative Development (PIDev) model (see Figure 4-3), which resembles the

[1] Merab Mamardashvili proposed the term. It is used for continuity reasons, although the term "hyper-physical" would be more appropriate.

structure of Thomas Kuhn's scientific revolutions but has fundamental features.

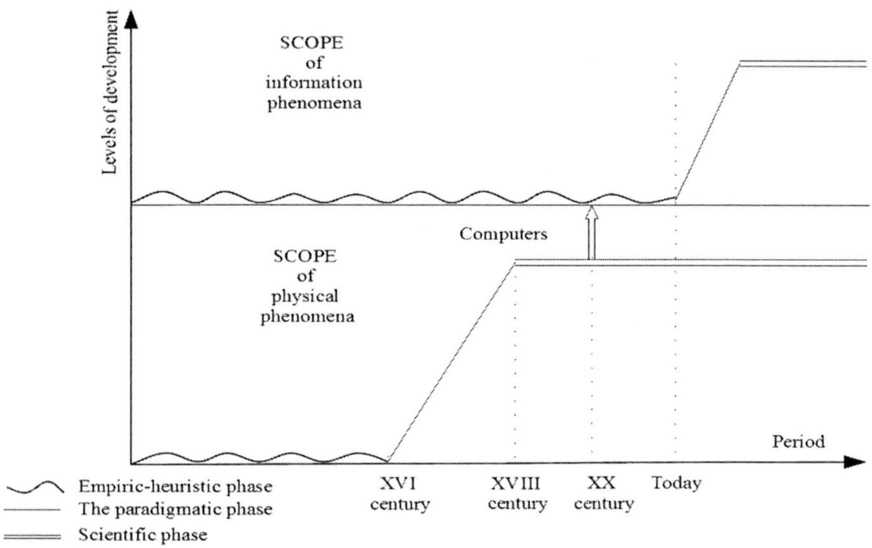

Figure 4-3. Model of Paradigmatic Innovative Development
Source: Polyakov et al. 2017.

First, PIDev is an integral model. Its objects of cognition are macrostructures. These are the spheres of phenomena or their constituent parts. The PIDev model allows one to differentiate and compare them according to the degree of cognition maturity. In addition, the PIDev model combines several phases of cognition of the sphere of phenomena. As an integral model, PIDev can be called a model of knowledge phylogenesis.

Figure 4-3 compares two PIDev models, one of which relates to the physiosphere and the other one to the infosphere. The wavy line denotes the empirical-heuristic (pre-paradigmatic), and oblique-paradigmatic, double-scientific (post-paradigmatic) phases.

The diagram shows that computers appeared in the physiosphere in the scientific phase of its development and are applied to the information practices (effects of sign phenomena) related to the empirical-heuristic phase of infosphere development. The knowledge of the infosphere lags behind the knowledge of the physiosphere. Therefore, IT is the physical technology of data processing applied to the information practices. To solve the problem of the disintegration of IT and business, it is necessary to bridge the gap in the development of knowledge of physical data-processing technologies and information practices.

Second, the fundamental features of cognition were identified by Kuhn, based on the experience of mature natural sciences that are in the scientific phase of development. The PIDev model, on the contrary, begins with the formation of the object of knowledge and the corresponding science. In this case, knowledge of such a sphere of phenomena emerges in the form of innovative development and depends more on innovative business than on official science. Business forms the empirical base that is necessary for scientific knowledge of the infosphere. At the same time, business may not be aware that it is clearing the way for knowledge. If the integration of cognition and business is implemented purposefully, it can serve as the ideal of innovative development and can be called a "knowledge economy".

Thus (third), the PIDev model is the integration of knowledge and management (business). Joint development of management and knowledge is innovative development. In the empirical-heuristic phase, its main driving force is the personnel of enterprises, from workers to top managers. Vernadsky (1988), who studied the history of cognition in Europe, drew attention to the important role of the masses engaged in economic management in preparing the natural-scientific revolution.

Fourth, the main task of the pre-paradigm phase of innovative development is a formalisation of the existing practices. These practices use the methods based on experience (analogies) or guesses (heuristics). An example is the digitisation of information practices through data-processing technologies. Although IT is called informational, it still exists without a proper philosophical and scientific justification in terms of information, or more precisely, signs. At the same time, attempts to form such justification are constantly repeated. However, the existing humanitarian models of cognition, explicit or hidden, as well as the models borrowed from the natural sciences, in the new conditions of the infosphere's development, do not allow this problem to be addressed. For the scientific revolution in the infosphere to become possible, an act of "destruction and-reconstruction of understanding" must take place (Mamardashvili 1997). As a result, a model of cognition that is relevant to the problems of the development of the infosphere can be formed.

Such a model can consist of the well-known parts and, at the same time, give an unexpected holistic picture of what is happening. Structures of cognition such as transformed forms of consciousness (Marx), quasi-physical effects of non-physical phenomena (Mamardashvili), the ascent from the abstract to the concrete (Hegel), firstness, secondness and thirdness (Peirce), information, signs, knowledge, innovation, etc. can create a holistic picture of what is really happening. Such a model can become an effective tool for intensifying the innovation. In this respect, Mendeleev's periodic table of elements can serve as a striking example of the systematisation of knowledge.

Phylogenesis, or macroscopic development of knowledge about the sphere of phenomena, takes place as a result of the accumulation of "micromutations" in the bodies of the infosphere. These are separate innovative acts. They can even use deeply abstract philosophical or scientific innovations, but, at the same time, they must end with a concrete practical, including commercial, result. The logic of the development of the empirical basis of knowledge plays a decisive role.

The process of formation of innovations, which can be called "ontogenesis of knowledge", is shown in Figure 4-4 as the model of VIPK. The upper half-plane in the figure is assigned to specific (practical, materialised) knowledge. In this case, concrete processes are considered as temporal things. The upper half-plane corresponds to the zero level of abstraction.

The lower half-plane is reserved for abstract knowledge, which does not refer to single things, but to their sets, ignoring the uniqueness of each of their elements. The plane is divided into five levels of abstraction: constructions and technologies, applied theories, fundamental theories, mathematics, and philosophy, including methodology.

The left half-plane is occupied by problems and the right half by solutions. The right branch of the parabola symbolises the ascent from the abstract to the concrete (Hegel 1970). Moreover, the very shape of the parabola (the left branch) suggests the need to supplement the Hegelian figure of cognition with a symmetrical figure, which is the immersion from the concrete into the abstract.

The nested rectangles in the figure are innovation cycles. If innovative changes affect only practical knowledge, then innovation is characterised by a zero level. This is the level of digitisation of information practices. It relies on physical data-processing technologies, the formation and development of which lies within the competence of the physiosphere and not the infosphere.

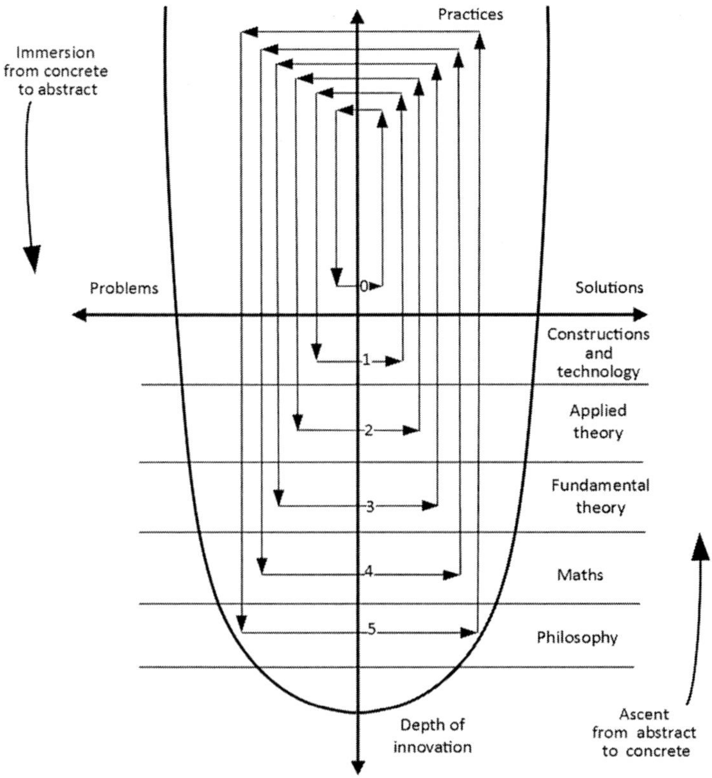

Figure 4-4. Model of the ontogenesis of knowledge (VIPK)
Source: Polyakov et al. 2017.

Figure 4-4 shows nested innovation cycles of different depths. In these cycles, analysis (immersion from the concrete into the abstract) alternates with synthesis (the ascent from the abstract to the concrete). Ranganathan's (1957) model, called the spiral of knowledge, is reduced to a similar alternation. The coincidence confirms the fundamental importance of this pattern. In addition, in the graphic model of the VIPK and in Hegel's "ascent", the concrete is higher than the abstract. This coincidence, manifesting at the figurative level, is not accidental. The empirical base of knowledge is inexhaustible and constantly expanding. At the same time, the levels of abstraction are limited. As follows from Figure 4-4, the VIPK model interprets the term "innovation" in an extended way. According to this model, an innovation is a change that can take place at any of the six levels of abstraction shown in the figure. Moreover, these changes should definitely affect the level of practice. The depth of innovation is determined by the maximum level of abstraction. Innovations that involve philosophy, methodology, mathematics and/or fundamental theory are paradigmatic. VIPK is not only and not so much a classification of knowledge, but a unit of knowledge that has a meaning and completeness. Until the vertical of knowledge is formed, it makes no sense to divide knowledge into scientific, educational and professional subjects in accordance with the levels of abstraction.

Scientific revolutions can occur in old and emerging realms. With the acceleration of development, the time intervals between them should therefore be reduced. Scientific revolutions constantly face problems that require solutions. The old sciences are struggling with these problems, creating more and more scientific subjects in the search for solutions. We have to wait until some "invisible college" finds a radical solution to the problem. In this case, the question of the formation of organisational structures that should carry out the vertical integration of knowledge will inevitably be raised. Research networks in which the corresponding vertically oriented associations can be created can serve as the prototypes of such structures.

The innovative potential of noospheric thinking

Marx's thesis about practice as the main criterion of truth takes the last (in order, but not in importance) place among the fundamental philosophical abstractions of Mamardashvili (1990). Therefore, noospheric thinking (that is, the QPMC), like any model or theory, should be evaluated in terms of its innovative potential.

The explanatory and predictive powers of models and theories are closely related. The explanatory power of the cognition model allows us to understand what is happening with cognition of the sphere of phenomena today. Predictive ability helps to anticipate what events may occur during development. This should allow avoiding false paths and goals, as well as posing and addressing the real problems.

As a communal (common) intellectual capital, the cognitive model should have theoretical and practical productivity, and serve as an environment for the formation of fundamental and applied theories, as well as the development and application of structures and technologies, which can be physical, symbolic or combined.

It is interesting to preliminarily consider examples of what the meaning of the well-known abstract propositions or practical problems looks like in the context of the QPMC (noospheric thinking). Of course, the examples given do not exhaust all the possibilities of the QPMC.

Plato's cave myth. Plato's famous cave myth can be explained in terms of the QPMC. According to the myth, people do not see real objects as they are but instead see their shadows cast on a cave wall by illuminated objects held by others stood behind them. The cave corresponds to the meonal environment of the QPMC. The light source is consciousness; people who wear objects that cast shadows are performing a practical activity; shadows on the wall are phenomena recorded in natural language; objects casting shadows are physical and quasi-physical effects of phenomena; and people watching shadows on the wall are performing cognitive activities.

According to Plato, people are divided into those who know by observing and those who act without knowing. For a slave society, this division is probably natural. The consequence of the unification of cognising and acting subjects is the connection between shadows and objects (phenomena and effects). This is primary cognition (in the QPMC, it is practical cognitive and creative activity). Its results serve as objects for secondary, scientific cognition, where the theoretical (that is, abstract) cognition plays an important role.

The cave myth is often used as an argument in defence of idealism. Mamardashvili (1990) saw it as a formulation of the problem of fundamental philosophical abstraction of the embodiment of the understood. From the point of view of the QPMC, this myth is a paradigm of cognition, which has not lost its relevance. It is associated with the zero-innovation cycle as a part of the VIK model and the parabola of knowledge.

Hegel's method of ascent from abstract to concrete. The parabola of knowledge in the VIK model symbolises the connection between knowledge, which is divided according to the degree of abstractness/concreteness. Knowledge embodied in things and processes has the maximum degree of concreteness and a zero level of abstraction.

The vertical line and the parabola of knowledge serve as an illustration of the Hegelian method of ascent from the abstract to the concrete. Hegel's movement is directed from bottom to top. This is somewhat unexpected, since abstractions are perceived as "higher" knowledge. On the other hand, in science, an abstraction is associated with fundamental knowledge, i.e. with depth. Accordingly, in the VIK model, an abstraction is also a movement towards the foundation and immersion in depth. At the same time, the symmetry of the parabola suggests that there must be a method paired with Hegel's. It really is the method of immersion from the concrete to the abstract. This method, based on empirical grounds, forms paradigms that systematise the results of empirical-heuristic cognition, bringing them to a common denominator, which are paradigms.

Thus, in the VIK model, Hegel's figurative vision and logic are explained and developed. Indeed, abstraction is an immersion in the essence of things and not a separation from them. Then, concretisation can only be an ascent.

Non-natural modelling is a simplified version of Hegel's ascent from the abstract to the concrete. Unnatural – in other words, symbolic or imitation – modelling has found a wide application in economics. The VIK model and the parabola of knowledge allow us to see the methods of non-natural, and in particular mathematical, modelling of information phenomena as a simplified version of Hegel's ascent from the abstract to the concrete. Simplification consists in the absence of intermediate steps between abstractions and practices. In the infosphere, between philosophy, methodology and mathematics, on the one hand, and practice, on the other, there are no essential (ontological) fundamental and applied theories, or sign constructions and technologies. Figuratively speaking, instead of climbing, you have to jump from the foot to the top of the mountain (see Figure 4-5).

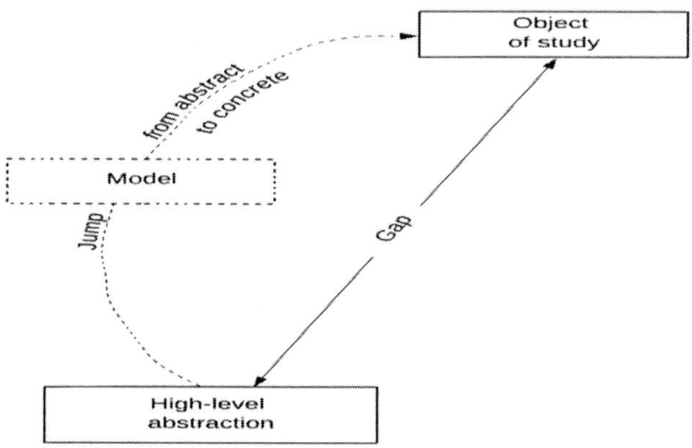

Figure 4- 5. Non-natural modelling as a leap from abstract to concrete
Source: Pikalov 2019.

Unsurprisingly, such jumps are rarely successful. Thus, a characteristic feature of non-natural modelling is the use of an abstract apparatus for a specific material based on associative links between them. Due to its low selectivity, non-natural modelling is universal but its efficiency is inversely proportional to such versatility. Proceeding from this, it is necessary to make a decision that can be much more expensive than using fundamental and applied theory, which provides a solution to a wide range of problems. The use of the QPMC tool as a transition from modelling to cognition is based on an understanding by Polyakov et al. (2019).

IT status today. A relatively recent and well-known book by Nicholas Carr (2005) sparked a discussion on whether the potential for the development of information technologies has been exhausted; they are not losing the ability to be a competitive advantage, are they? The logical-conceptual apparatus of the QPMC can be used to determine the status of IT today. First of all, it is necessary to establish to which sphere of phenomena IT belongs. It is obvious that the computer is a physical machine, i.e. it belongs to the physiosphere. The matter becomes more complicated with the program. The program text is the work of the programmer. A sheet of paper stained with paint is, of course, a physical thing. In fact, the text of the program is not physically connected with other things but, within the meaning, it is connected with the computer, data and the user of data. In the text, as you can see, there is a physical entity but that is not merely it. Probably, such objects were meant by Mamardashvili as quasi-physical effects of non-physical (conscious) phenomena. However, in reality, they should be called hypercomplex temporal physical objects. The text of the program can be compared with the design and construction documentation, according to which products are manufactured. The program should be produced at minimum cost. This production consists in transferring it to a machine medium and converting it into machine code. The project is connected with the product and the text of the program is connected with the program, which is ready to be launched, through the consciousness of the designer and the programmer by the relation of correspondence.

Whoever has seen the texts of programs and data on punched cards or punched tapes will hardly doubt the purely physical nature of these objects. Indeed, once inside the machine, data becomes a physical signal. Thus, computer data processing is a purely physical technology. There are enough physical and mathematical concepts for its implementation. The corresponding abstraction is called a (Turing) machine for a reason.

However, the processed data, leaving the machine, is transmitted to the user, who should correlate these subtle physical structures with the objects and processes that he controls, and form on their basis the influences that control information practices. Practices differ from technologies as models differ from theory. In particular, it is difficult to say without actually checking whether the practice will work in other conditions. For a complex technology to appear, an applied theory is needed, which means everything that is deeper than it on the vertical of knowledge. The absence means that, according to the PIDev model, the infosphere is in the empirical-heuristic phase of its maturity.

It follows from the above that IT can be called technology, if it is a data-processing technology. It is also possible to apply the epithet "informational" to IT but only in reference to informational practices. Thus, IT today is a physical data-processing technology applied to information (noospheric) practices.

It follows that there is no definite answer to the question: "Has IT reached the maximum limit of its capabilities?" You can answer "Yes, it has!", if you mean physical data-processing technologies. But if we are talking about real IT, then we are in the initial, pre-paradigmatic phase of development. In order for real IT to appear, the productive abstractions of programs, data and organisations are needed, which can only emerge together with the abstractions of information (signs). In other words, the vertical of knowledge should be fully developed in the infosphere.

The main contradiction of IT today. Based on the status of IT today, the main contradiction of IT, which should become a source of intensive development, is the discrepancy between well-developed physical technologies for data processing and information practices that are in the pre-paradigmatic phase of development. As a result, the potential of computer technologies for data processing is largely underutilised and the potential of information practices suitable for digitisation is almost completely exhausted. The emergence of real IT should give rise to fundamentally new information practices.

Solow's paradox. Robert Solow (1987) formulated a problem that today is known as the paradox of practical IT productivity in economics and business. He argued that computers can be seen anywhere except for productivity reports. Paul Strassman (1996) has been carrying out mathematical and statistical research for many years, attempting, unsuccessfully, to refute Solow's thesis. As a result, he came to the conclusion that IT is potentially efficient, but not used quite right.

There are other papers that argue that IT can become productive when applied in conjunction with certain organisational changes. Based on the QPMC, such functional solutions can produce only palliative results. Organisational changes will not transform information practices into technologies. The potential of physical data-processing technologies can only be fully realised if they are fully integrated with information practices. However, this requires the implementation of an ontological approach to information phenomena, which should result in a complete vertical of knowledge about the infosphere.

Interpretation of the category of "transformed form of consciousness". Consciousness plays a major role in life. However, it is almost impossible to turn it into an object of research. The active consciousness cognises by creating and it creates by cognising. The cognisable world appears to the individual consciousness as phenomena that are perceived by the philosophical consciousness as transformed forms of consciousness. This concept was introduced by Hegel (1970), and then developed by Karl Marx (1962) and Merab Mamardashvili (2008). This ideology draws attention to the fact that the content of such objects can change spontaneously or deliberately. The lag between the form and the development of content is natural but, from the point of view of the QPMC, this is not the crucial point. It is important that the results of cognition and creation of the world are created by active consciousness, which is not necessarily scientific. Scientific knowledge of being and consciousness consists in the systematisation and formalisation of such primary knowledge.

This structure of knowledge is embedded in Peirce's fundamental model, which uses the terms firstness, secondness and thirdness (Nöth 2001). Firstness distinguishes between substances (that is, quality), and secondness distinguishes between spatial and temporal structures. Thirdness consists in the fact that consciousness, according to its meanings, binds them together. The firstness and secondness can be attributed to the signifier and the thirdness attributed to the signified part of the sign. The philosophical concept of "the continuum of being-consciousness", used by Mamardashvili, found its scientific expression in Peirce's model. The fundamental philosophical abstraction of "the embodiment of the understood" corresponds approximately to "firstness and secondness", and abstraction of "cogito" similarly corresponds to thirdness (Mamardashvili 1990). We can say that the unity of being and consciousness is embodied in the sign, where thirdness means the signified. The ontology of the sign is the key to the intensification of the development of the infosphere (Polyakov et al. 2018).

Noospheric interpretation of Merab Mamardashvili's concept of "quasi-physical effects of non-physical phenomena". The scientific interpretation of Mamardashvili's philosophical concept of "quasi-physical effects of non-physical phenomena" is key to the formation of the vertical of knowledge in the infosphere. It is necessary to establish what a sign is, and, further, what a program, data and organisations are. Explaining these phenomena on a physical, biological or functional basis alone is unproductive.

Obviously, it follows from the fact that signs have a special (sui generis) nature.

Mamardashvili acted wisely. He did not give specific examples of quasi-physical effects. He did not show how they are arranged, nor how exactly they differ from physical objects. He left this task to science. By doing so, he avoided narrowing the scope of interpretation, allowing subjective, practical application. Interpretation within the framework of the QPMC is based on the empirical basis of IT. In this case, empirical programs and data are considered as quasi-physical objects or their parts.

Who creates knowledge? In a documentary film (Al Mare 2014) about the famous radiobiologist Timofeev-Ressovsky, who worked in Germany for two decades, the protagonist uttered the catchy words: "Science does not produce knowledge." Timofeev-Ressovsky was nominated for the Nobel Prize in 1950. At that time, he was a political prisoner and his location was unknown; therefore, the nomination did not take place. What did he want to say with his paradoxical words? What is the source of knowledge, if not science? The noospheric model of cognition allows us to arrive at several interpretations of his statement.

First, knowledge is produced not by science as a formal mechanism, but by scientists as creative units. Indeed, any science periodically encounters the phenomena that cannot be explained within the framework of this science (Kuhn 2012). There is a need for "destruction – and reconstruction" of understanding and the formation of another science (Mamardashvili 1997). This is usually done by individuals. Scientific schools will be founded later.

Second, knowledge is produced not by science, but by knowledge. Science is an important part of cognition, which systematises knowledge, tests it, preserves it, translates it, deduces consequences from it, implements it in practice, etc.

Third, knowledge is mined like diamonds. Such knowledge is primary and not processed. Processing is not the birth of knowledge, or it can be considered that it gives rise to secondary knowledge.

In particular, it follows from the above that it is not necessary to treat scientific revolutions and their preparation as something that will happen by itself, and organise and advance. Until now, revolutions have been relatively rare. The only major scientific revolutions took place in the 17th and 18th centuries. Scientific revolutions are studied by philosophers, but the results are rarely implemented in an applied form nor reach the broad scientific masses. Due to the accelerating pace of changes in society, scientific revolutions can occur more often and, at the same time, can become more manageable. There are sufficient objective prerequisites (empirical bases) for this. Subjective factors need to be strengthened. These include the formation of QPMC-type models and tools based on them for understanding, foreseeing, planning and regulating cognitive activity, which can accelerate the development of cognition and, with it, management.

The paradox of practical (and theoretical) productivity of semiotics. In one of the works, we formulated the paradox of the productivity of semiotics and proposed a solution using the QPMC tools (Polyakov et al. 2016).

Since ancient times, signs have been the phenomena claiming special essence and as such are mentioned in ancient Egyptian inscriptions (Taysina 2002). Our dependence on signs is increasing, and a direction of cognition, known as pansemiotism, has emerged in response to their abundance. Signs are really everywhere. Jean Baudrillard (1981) wrote the book *To the Critique of the Political Economy of the Sign*, which gained cult status. French postmodernists declared the whole world to be a text (Derrida 1997). Semiotic philosophy (Kanke 1996) appeared. For about half a century, there has been a scientific school of organisational semiotics (Stamper 2005) and papers on the semiotics of programming have been written (Tanaka-Ishii 2010). Peirce's pansemiotism, which brings it closer to Vernadsky's idea of the noosphere, stands out with a particularly deep meaning, thanks to the doctrine of "firstness–secondness–thirdness".

Semiotics explores such important empirical material that practitioners have always expected and continue to expect too much from it. Therefore, only strong disappointment can explain the opinion given in the monograph by Daniel Chandler (2007). In this paper, semiotics is called "the last refuge of academic charlatans". Of course, this is not the case.

However, on the other hand, semiotics should deal with the ontology of signs. Instead, semioticians are more interested in any processes that use signs, which are literally represented by all kinds of human activities. In this regard, one can recall the words of Seneca (2015): "Who is everywhere – is nowhere!" A scientific discipline and a scientist, due to the limited capabilities of a human, must have their own object and their own subject. According to the PIDev and VIK models, as well as the parabola of knowledge included in the QPMC, today's semiotics is still empirical and heuristic knowledge.

The state that this science of signs is in, according to the QPMC, should be considered normal for the pre-paradigmatic phase of cognition of any sphere of phenomena. At the moment, a sufficient empirical base has been formed for the transition to the paradigmatic phase of knowledge of the infosphere and the formation on this basis of the fundamental science of the ontology of signs. This science should become a derivative of well-formalised sign practices, and a productive base for the formation of applied sciences of signs and, further, sign structures and technologies. If we follow this logic of, then one of such applied sciences should be the science of economics.

Noospheric thinking as a convergence of natural science and humanitarian knowledge. Traditionally, knowledge is divided into natural science and humanities. The objects of the first group of knowledge are nature; in the second group, they are the human being and society. Traditionally, it is believed that the divergence between them in terms of objects, methods and results of cognition cannot be reduced. In the late 19th to early 20th centuries, there was a convergence of knowledge about nature, as a result of which the geosphere (more precisely, the physiosphere) and the biosphere were discovered. Vernadsky, Le Roy and Teilhard de Chardin logically continued this trend, announcing the convergence of natural science and humanitarian knowledge under the auspices of the noosphere (Vernadsky 2004). This is how the idea of the noospheric unity of the world object and the process of cognition arose.

This idea needs to be implemented; the QPMC model is its result. This model does not claim to be versatile. It is important that it comes from an empirical base that consists of well-formalised messages that include software applications and databases. Scientific knowledge (in contrast to practical knowledge or philosophy) poses only those problems for which there is a good and, at the same time, spontaneously formalised empirical basis. The results obtained form the basis for the next round of knowledge.

The QPMC does not address the issues of the biosphere. Suffice to say that the physiosphere consists of physical bodies and the biosphere consists of living organisms. They are related to each other at the level of substance. The living contains the inanimate. In this case, the biosphere cannot be reduced to the physiosphere, since life manifests itself in the living as a new quality. The noosphere includes the biosphere, with the physiosphere and the signified part in the form of texts, images, audio, video and other non-physical artifacts.

According to the QPMC with its empirical base, the noosphere, as an integral object of scientific knowledge, is also a sign structure, of which a schematic similarity is computer programs. For a program, the signifier part is its text, and the signified part is a computer and the data processing process that the computer implements or data, the signifier part is the data itself and the signified part is the area of interest of the data user.

The transformed forms of consciousness discovered by Hegel make it possible to take the next step on the path towards convergence of natural science and humanities. It consists in an understanding of the need to investigate conscious phenomena not directly but through signs (that is, non-physical artifacts) of conscious activity.

Another step is the convergence of the physical and quasi-physical effects of conscious activity. A comparison of physical bodies with the empirical basis of the QPMC has shown that quasi-physical objects differ from physical ones in that their signifier and signified parts, which ultimately have a physical nature, are connected not physically but by correspondence relations.

Convergence forms the basis for the integration of data-processing technologies and business practices.

What is information? Many famous scientists and philosophers have given answers to this question. But the research is not over. Luciano Floridi put forward 18 questions regarding the nature of information. The list opens with the question of "What is information?" Towards the end of the list, there is the question of the ontology of the sign. Floridi (2004) chose philosophy as a tool for solving the outlined problems. This happened against the background of the strengthening of interdisciplinary research – that is, the horizontal integration of knowledge. It can be considered that Floridi thereby made a step towards the vertical integration of knowledge. In a developed and explicit form, this principle is used in the QPMC.

According to the QPMC, when studying the phenomenon of information, first of all it is necessary to ask the question: "What does the empirical knowledge base of information research consist of?" The answer is obvious: it is information as messages. Claude Shannon, on the other hand, used this word as one of the measures related to messages. Russell Ackoff and Fred Emery use it in the same capacity. Along with this measure, they also introduce measures called "motivation" and "instruction" (Ackoff and Emery 2005). The development of this direction depends on addressing the problems of information as messages. It is obvious that they consist of signs and represent sign structures. But then it turns out that the problem of information is a problem of signs, which should be solved by semiotics. However, semiotics cannot solve it because it intuitively chooses between two models of cognition – a model for the natural sciences, which is in a post-paradigm phase of development, and a model for the humanities, which is in a pre-paradigmatic phase. However, to solve the problem of information (more precisely, a sign), a model obtained as a result of the convergence of the above models and covering the paradigmatic phase of the development of cognition is required. The QPMC has such properties.

What is a program? This question may seem unnecessary. Indeed, thousands of programs appear in the world every minute. It is impossible to imagine the life of a modern person and society without them. How can you, living in a forest, have no understanding of what a forest is? However, many useful and even high-quality endeavours are carried out without knowledge, or with incomplete knowledge, of their nature. Once upon a time, a master could create a wonderful thing and, at the same time, believe that he achieved it thanks to a spell bequeathed by his ancestors. Insufficient knowledge does not allow us to do things differently and make them better.

The program is a well-formalised sign effect of the non-physical phenomenon of programming. To understand the program, you need to understand the sign. To understand the sign, you need to understand the program. Therefore, it is not surprising that, following hundreds of monographs and dissertations on "What is a program?" this problem does not disappear from the registers of scientific papers (see for example the article "What is a program?"[2]). It should be noted that to understand in this case means to find a suitable abstraction – this is the key to each of the many different objects. This abstraction should make a diverse and complex set of objects uniform and simple.

From the point of view of the QPMC, data are the signified part of a well-formalised message (that is, a sign construction). Usually, data refers to the parts of sign structures that are used as objects of processing. However, "being an object of processing" or "being an instruction" is a functional, and not an essential, property. For example, the text of a program can act as either an instruction or an object of processing. Moreover, the program is a well-formalised sign construction. In order not to lose the essence behind functional terms, its signified part should also be called data.

What is data? One of the common answers to this question reads like this: "Data is the facts on the media. Information is processed data. Knowledge is interconnected information." Obviously, this chain is talking about something that goes through some kind of processing but its essence remains unknown. There are also definitions that consider data as a kind of information, and information turns out to be the interpretation of data and represents its meaning.

---

[2] https://anr.fr/Project-ANR-17-CE38-0003

However, essentially it does not change anything. All of these definitions are functional and not ontological. In order for monotonous (semantically poor) Big Data to be turned into semantically rich information, you need to be able to discern and then overcome the barrier of semantic diversity of data. In turn, for this purpose you need to answer the question of how data is arranged and built into the external environment.

This should help solve the problem of creating databases that perform the function of flexible communication between the user, his area of interest and the data-processing system. Until this happens, programmers are forced to avoid going beyond the barrier of semantic diversity and data volatility. Basically, they are engaged in digitising a monotonous and/or relatively rarely changing data structure. Otherwise, the "curse of complexity" reminds us of itself (Booch 2004). To overcome this, the data has to be fragmented, but, at the same time, the problem of its integration subsequently arises. Programmers are only able to control a limited number of elements and relationships. And constantly changing data structures can result in chaos.

Within the framework of the paradigm of the sign, obtained on the basis of the QPMC, the data is defined as a signified part of the sign construction (Polyakov et al. 2016). This, first of all, allows you to get rid of the perception of data as local phenomena inherent in consciousness. The data is a part of the signs, and it is both a consequence of the signifier and a possible reason for its change. To comprehend this, it is enough to imagine that data and data-processing tools have disappeared from the economy. Obviously, enterprises would have to be restructured too much. However, within the framework of the digitisation paradigm, this does not matter, since it is about adapting the existing data structures compatible with paper media to machine media.

Data structures mainly depend on the structure of what they represent and on the capabilities of the storage media. The capabilities of computer storage media and data-processing tools remove almost all restrictions on the data structure, which does not have to be tabular (relational). Therefore, it would be natural for economists and managers to be engaged in research and formation of data structures. This would make it possible to see in the data not only a flexible resource but also the material from which an economic organisation is built. However, the digitisation paradigm assigns this function to information technologies that perceive data only as something that is subject to adaptation but not to a radical revision.

The structure of the user's area of interest (the signified part) and the structure of the software depend on the data structures (signifier part of the sign construction). In addition, the data connects subject areas, users and data-processing systems into a single network. This is enough to recognise them as key elements, on the quality of which the functioning and development of the system of management and cognition depend.

What is an organisation? The organisation, in particular the economic one, can be defined by analogy with the program as a quasi-physical effect of the phenomenon of activity. Indeed, a software application of economic purpose is a model of the fragment of an economic organisation. All coordinated programs for all fragments of the organisation would form a complete model of the organisation. Indeed, the data structure corresponds to the architecture of the organisation and the data values correspond to its state. Data-processing algorithms correspond to the organisation management functionality implemented by data users. A similar idea about the similarity of programs and organisations was expressed by Peter Brödner (2005).

Conclusion

Today, the answer to the question of "What is an economical organisation?" is ambiguous. Bertin Martens has worked with many emerging economies around the world. In order to better understand how they would react to external influences (aid, loans or investments), he represented them through the abstraction of an information machine that produces knowledge. Such an abstraction seemed productive to him, since, in those countries where such structures were obviously better, investments in the economy yielded a greater return (Martens 2004).

Indeed, the economy is controlled by information (signs) and everything that it produces is knowledge (signs capable of generating new knowledge) embodied in things or processes (services). In this case, post-paradigm cognition (official science) can be considered as an outsourcing. The QPMC actually implements this idea in a detailed and in-depth form. It offers a convergence of cognitive and economic activities.

The QPMC is a tool for the development of information technology. It is necessary to ensure its "upgrade" to the level of iconic technologies. This requires mutual adaptation of physical data-processing technologies and economic information practices, which play a leading role. On this basis, it is possible to build an informational (more precisely, symbolic) economy, uniting the enterprises, corporations, industries and territories up to planetary scales.

Moreover, the QPMC can serve as an ontological basis for solving social issues. In particular, the fact that the economy produces knowledge embodied in the form of products and services does not mean that knowledge is always new, deep and socially positive. These parameters can and should be controlled.

The QPMC also means that primary knowledge, which is a “raw material” for science, is generated in the process of practical activity, to a large extent at the sensory level. It should be borne in mind that the inept replacement of humans with machines and robots can destroy this channel of communication between the human personality, nature and society.

The QPMC is based on ontological (essential) concepts of phenomena, and physical and non-physical effects (objects) of consciousness, including signs. Based on the QPMC (noospheric thinking), the following predictions can be made:

1) It is possible to reduce the intensity of the generation of innovative ideas in the physiosphere, which may require a search for new areas of phenomena suitable for intensive innovative development. One of these areas is the infosphere. The view that its potential has already been exhausted is not true.
2) The resources of semantically simple and rarely changing information practices suitable for digitisation by the existing data-processing technologies are close to exhaustion.
3) There is a need for, and possibility of, creating an ontological theory of signs on the empirical base of programs and data for economics and business.
4) In the near future, it will be possible to develop (“upgrade”) the existing IT to the state of truly information, i.e. iconic, technologies.
5) In the near future, it might be possible to develop methods to increase the flexibility of data structures and approximate them to the status of an infrastructural resource.
6) As the quasi-physical approach develops, modelling, as a tool for the innovative development of the infosphere, will give way to the inventions based on ontological theories.

When scientific revolutions take place, the economic organisations, claiming the title of a “corporation of knowledge”, cannot stand aside. It is the organisations that accumulate empirical knowledge, which has to be systematised. For this purpose, corporations should have relevant cognitive models capable of solving topical theoretical and practical problems of infosphere development.

Examples of the potential theoretical productivity of the QPMC are:

A. Formation of the paradigm of sign ontology and the theory of sign constructions on the empirical basis of computer programs, databases and business organisations.
B. Formation of the paradigm and theory of computer programs based on the paradigm of the ontology of the sign.
C. Formation of a paradigm and data theory based on the paradigm of sign ontology.
D. Formation of the paradigm (architecture) and theory of economic organisation based on the paradigm of the ontology of the sign.
E. Formation of the theory of the knowledge economy on the basis of the QPMC as a semiotic machine that produces knowledge in symbolic and materialised form.

Examples of potential practical productivity of the QPMC are:

a) developing flexible, unified data infrastructures that reduce the fragmentation of a single data field, from the enterprise level to the global economy;
b) development of information and software tools for semantic augmentation (formalisation and augmentation of senses) of text works, which, in turn, should provide semantic processing of texts on the Internet;
c) optimisation and unification of the architecture of computer programs;
d) optimisation and unification of the architecture of business organisations.

This article outlines the model of cognition as a tool for intensifying the innovative development of the sphere of information (symbolic) phenomena, its economy, cognition and the technologies used in it. The uniqueness of this model lies in the synthesis of various ideas, the connection of which is not always obvious. Until now, not all of these ideas have been properly understood and applied, especially in relation to solving practical problems. A choice from different interpretations of these ideas had to be made. Some transformed forms of consciousness – such as the sign and the quasi-physical effect of non-physical phenomena – have received a special interpretation. The model provides the convergence of knowledge of physical and humanitarian phenomena, abstract and concrete, and embodied and non-embodied knowledge. At the same time, it shares practical and scientific knowledge. Practical knowledge relies on experience (analogies), guesses (heuristics) and modelling (associations).

It partly ends with materialised forms of knowledge, which act as objects of paradigmatic and scientific knowledge. The QPMC model does not claim to be complete. The author is aware that, in the process of implementation, it may require changes, and looks forward to arousing interest in this topic and stimulating discussions.

References

Ackoff, R.L. and F. Emery. 2005. *On Purposeful Systems. An Interdisciplinary Analysis of Individual and Social Behavior as a System of Purposeful Events.* New Brunswick: Aldine Transaction.

Al Mare. 2014. "Timofeev-Resovsky. N. 1. Near the bison." YouTube video, 1:17. February 13, 2014. https://www.youtube.com/watch?v=elwGCME0zMA

Badiou, A. 2003. *Manifesto of Philosophy.* Saint Petersburg: Machina.

Baudrillard, J. 1981. *For a Critique of the Political Economy of the Sign.* St. Louis: Telos Press.

Berners-Lee, T., J. Hendler and O. Lassila. 2001. "The Semantic Web." *Scientific American* 5, 34.

Bogdanov, A. 1989. *Tectology: Universal Organizational Science.* Moscow: Economics (Rus.).

Booch, G. 2004. *Object-Oriented Analysis and Design with Applications.* Redwood City, CA, USA: Addison Wesley Longman Publishing Co., Inc.

Brier, S. 2001. "The Necessity of Trans-Scientific Frameworks for Doing Interdisciplinary Research." Accessed 16 August 2020. https://www.researchgate.net/publication/237477137_Fuschl_Conversations_Foundations_of_Information_Science_Towards_a_New_Foundation_of_Information_Cognitive_and_Communication-Science.

Brödner, P. 2005. "Software is Orgware – A Semiotic Perspective on Computer Artifacts." Proceedings of the International Conference on User-driven IT Design and Quality Assurance 5: 1-8. Accessed 16 August 2020. https://www.it.uu.se/edu/course/homepage/contextuse/ht08/Brodner1.pdf.

Caillé, A. 2007. "Presentation." *Revue du MAUSS* 30.

Carr, N. 2005. *Does IT Matter? Information Technology and the Corrosion of Competitive Advantage.* Moscow: Secret Firmy.

Chandler, D. 2007. *Semiotics: The Basics.* New York: Routledge.

Derrida, J. 1997. *Of Grammatology.* Baltimore: The Johns Hopkins University Press.

Floridi, L. 2004. "Open Problems in the Philosophy of Information." *Metaphilosophy* 35: 554-582.

Gazendam, H. and K. Liu. 2005. *The Evolution of Organisational Semiotics: A Brief Review of the Contribution of Ronald Stamper.* Dordrecht: Kluwer Academic Publishers.

Gorman, G. 2019. "The Uniqueness of Knowledge Management – or the Emperor's New Clothes?" Accessed 21 August 2020. https://www.emeraldgrouppublishing.com/librarians/info/viewpoints/unique.htm.

Gruzman, H. 2005. "Dogged Genius of Russia." Accessed 21 August 2020. http://lit.lib.ru/g/gruzman_g/genii.shtml.

Hausman, D. 2007. *The Philosophy of Economics. An Anthology.* Cambridge: Cambridge University Press.

Hegel, G.W.F. 1970. *The Science of Logic.* Moscow: Mysl' (Rus.).

Heilbroner, R. 2011. *The Worldly Philosophers: the Lives, Times, and Ideas of the Great Economic Thinkers.* Moscow: Corpus.

Kanke, V. 1996. *Philosophy. Historical and Systematic Course.* Textbook for High Schools. Moscow: Logos (Rus.).

Kotarbiński, T. 1975. *A Treatise on Good Work.* Moscow: Economics Publ (Rus.).

Kuhn, T. 2012. *The Structure of Scientific Revolutions.* Chicago: University of Chicago Press.

LaRouche, L. 2001. "Current Strategic Studies: The Vernadsky Strategy" Accessed 28 August 2020. https://larouchepub.com/lar/2001/2818laronvernadsky.html.

Losev, A. 1990a. "Philosophy of Name." In *From early works (collection),* edited by Aza Taho-Godi, 11-193. Moscow: Pravda.

Losev, A. 1990b. "Music as a Subject of Logic." In *From early works (collection),* edited by Aza Taho-Godi, 194-369. Moscow: Pravda. Mamardashvili, M. 1990. "Consciousness as a Philosophical Problem." *Voprosi filosofii* 10: 3-18 (Rus.).

Losev, A. 1997. "Higher synthesis.". In "*I was 19 years old ...". Diaries. Letters. Prose* edited by Aza Taho-Godi, 17-28. Moscow: Russian Dictionaries (Rus.).

Mamardashvili, M. 1997 *The Arrow of Cognition: Sketch of Naturally-Historical Gnoseology.* Moscow: School "The languages of Russian culture" (Rus.).

Mamardashvili, M. 2008. *The Experience of Physical Metaphysics.* Moscow: Progress-Traditsiya (Rus.).

Martens, B. 2004. *The Cognitive Mechanics of Economic Development and Institutional Change.* New York: Routledge.

Marx, K. 1962. *Income and its Sources. Vulgar Political Economy.* Appendix [to the Work "The Theory of Surplus Value"]. Moscow: State Political Literature Publishing (Rus.).

Nöth, W. 2001. "Charles Sanders Peirce." *Criticism and Semiotics* 3-4: 5-32. Novosibirsk (Rus.).

Pauleen, D. 2019. "Knowledge Management: a Wolf in Sheep's Clothing." Accessed 10 August 2020. https://www.emeraldgrouppublishing.com/librarians/info/viewpoints/wolf.htm.

Pikalov, Y. 2019. "Noospheric Way of Organizing Knowledge in the Knowledge Bases of Innovate Importance." Proceedings of the 11th International Joint Conference on Knowledge Discovery, Knowledge Engineering and Knowledge Management, Vienna, Austria, September 17-19: 250-257. Accessed 10 August 2020. http://www.insticc.org/node/TechnicalProgram/ic3k/presentationDetails/83473.

Polyakov, M., I. Khanin and N. Bormatenko. 2016. "Quasi-physical Approach to Solving the Semiotics Practical Productivity Paradox." 4th Annual International Conference on Philosophy: Yesterday, Today & Tomorrow, Singapore, 28-29 November.

Polyakov, M., I. Khanin, N. Bormatenko and S. Kosenchuk. 2018. "Ontology of Sign: a Key to Information and Technological Advancement of the Knowledge Society." *The International Journal of Technology, Knowledge, and Society* 14: 27-45.

Polyakov, M., I. Khanin and N. Bormatenko. 2019. "From Modeling to Technologization of Conscious Phenomena Based on Understanding." 9th International Conference on Information and Social Science: 468-477.

Popper, K. 1957. *Science: Conjectures and Refutations, Philosophy of Science: A Personal Report.* C.A. Mace, Ed., British Philosophy in Mid-Century.

Ranganathan, S. 1957. "Library Science and Scientific Method." *Annals of Library Science* 4, 3: 19-37.

Saburov, E. 2010. "Economy as Drama of Ideas." *Social Sciences and Contemporary World* 3: 83-89 (Rus.).

Scheer, A. 1999. *ARIS: Business Process Frameworks.* Moscow: Vest-Meta Technologia (Rus.).

Seneca, L. 2015. *Moral letters to Lucillus. Tragedies (collection).* Moscow: Azbuka (Rus.)

Shannon, C. 1963. *Works on Information Theory and Cybernetics.* Moscow: Foreign Languages Publishing House(Rus).

Shchedrovitsky, G.P. 2005. *Sign and Activity.* Moscow: Vostochnaja literature (Rus.).

Slutsky, Y. 2007. "An Etude to the Problem of Building Formally Praxeological Foundations of the Economy." *Economic Thought. Reader*: 498-509 (Ukr.).

Solow, R. 1987. "We'd Better Watch Out." *New York Times Book Review.*

Stamper, R. 2005. "Exploring the Semantics of Communication Acts." Accessed 25 August 2020. http://www.vits.org/konferenser/lap2005/Paper%2014-LAP.pdf.

Strassman, P. 1996. "The Value Of Computers, Information and Knowledge." Accessed 10 August 2020. http://www.strassmann.com/pubs/cik/cik-value.shtml.

Tanaka-Ishii, K. 2010. *Semiotics of Programming.* New York: Cambridge University Press.

Taysina, E. 2002. *Philosophical Questions of Semiotics.* Kazan: Kazan State Energy University (Rus.).

Timofeev-Ressovsky, N. 2009. *Genetics, Evolution, the Value of Methodology in Natural Science.* Ekaterinburg: Tokmas-Press (Rus.).

Vernadsky, V. 1988. *Works on the History of Science.* Moscow: Science (Rus.).

Vernadsky, V. 2004. *The Biosphere and the Noosphere.* Moscow: Ajris-press (Rus.).

Wiener, N. 1961. *Cybernetics: Or Control and Communication in the Animal and the Machine.* Paris: Hermann & Cie, Camb. Mass. (MIT Press).

Wilson, T. 2002. "The Nonsense of 'Knowledge Management'." *Information Research* 8, 1. Accessed 25 August 2020. http://informationr.net/ir/8-1/paper144.html.

Yefimov, V. 2011. "Discursive Analysis in Economy: Revision of Methodology and History of Economic Science." *Journal of Economic Regulation* 2, 3 (Rus.).

Zachman, J. 1987. "A Framework for Information Systems Architecture." IBM Systems Journal 26, 3: 276-292.

Zinoviev, A. 2002. Ascent from the abstract to the concrete. Moscow: Russian Academy of Sciences. Institute of Philosophy (Rus.)

CHAPTER FIVE

STRATEGIC GOALS OF THE ECONOMIC POLICY AND PRODUCTIVE ABILITY OF THE NATIONAL ECONOMY IN A GLOBALISED SOCIETY

OLEKSANDRA M. MOSKALENKO

Introduction

The productive capacities of the modern state, country and its economy are determined by a significant set of factors and conditions. These include the historical context and the path the country has taken, the specifics of its formation and development, the political system, relations with other countries, its place in the international arena given its political role and the level of influence on international politics of its coexistence and interdependence, and in particular its economic success and efficiency.

The strategic goals of economic policy are closely linked to the country's productive capacity and productivity. Productivity is a key factor in economic growth and changing living standards. Each country defines its strategic economic policy goals based on political and social consensus. Economic policy is implemented by politicians. Politics in economics is implemented on the basis of relevant economic theories and theoretical concepts that correlate with the concepts of the political system. The tools of the economic policy used must be scientifically sound and ensure the achievement of higher economic efficiency, and thus higher productivity and welfare of the population.

The growth of labour productivity implies a higher level of output per unit of employed labour (hours worked or employed persons). This can be achieved if more capital is used in production or by increasing overall efficiency, in particular in technologies through which labour and capital are used together. The latter means higher multifactor productivity (MFP) growth. Productivity is also a key driver of international competitiveness.

Thus, the objectives of this article are as follows: first, to consider the strategic objectives of economic policy, which ensure the strengthening of the productive capacity of the national economy; and second, to clarify the content of and prerequisites for ensuring the productive capacity of the national economy. The goals of the article are quite general but this is required by the complexity of the object of study: the productive capacity of the national economy. Establishing quantitative relationships between labour productivity or capital is not the task of this article. The author aims to show the qualitative aspects of the productive capacity of the country in a globalised society.

Previous research review

The history of the economic development of any country is an objective evolutionary process; a progress that humanity is moving. From the scientific point of view, the economic development of a country is a process of practical testing of theoretical concepts of economics, which are aimed at finding effective models of development, and factors, incentives and motives that determine it. Depending on the historical economic conditions in which countries were developing, those theoretical concepts of state management that were adequate to current economic situations became dominant. Most often, scientific trends in an economy came to the fore in times of crisis, when the recommendations provided by them allowed the reduction of negative phenomena in the economy, such as high inflation, unemployment, underemployment and low living standards. Or, conversely, the economic scientific schools came to the fore in periods of economic growth in countries that consolidated this state in the medium and long term, and the crisis was successfully levelled by economic policy measures.

Thus, in developed countries the key role was given to economic policy, which should be able to solve socio-economic problems of society and create conditions for positive changes in living standards. It has always been a strategic goal of economic policy pursued by the government to improve living standards, once the state has historically developed into a mature social entity. A mature state was able to ensure the development of public institutions and, above all, the institution of private property, which was the beginning of the opportunity to implement the ideas of liberalism in the economy. In this study, the author does not describe the details of the evolution of the state and social institutions, but emphasises the importance of developing the processes of civilisation and social nature necessary for the further progress of the economy. Thus, the mature institutions of the state with the concomitant development of other public institutions contributed to progress in its broadest sense. At the same time, there was a diversification of organisational forms of public institutions and the complexity of their functions. The state gained a monopoly on violence. It has become productively capable of developing the economy – regulating and controlling, protecting and competing – and improving the conditions for productivity growth in the economy.

For the purposes of this study, I turn to the theory of institutions, which determines the institutional foundations of economic policy. Institutions act as a link between different types of policies. It turns out that economic policy, independent of the results of previous policies, does not exist.

In the book *Institutions, Institutional Change, and Economic Performance* (1990), D. North makes a close link between the notions of secure property rights and credible commitment. Property rights are said to be secure when the state is able to make a credible commitment that it will respect them.

The productive capacity of the national economy is based on institutional preconditions and civilisational factors – namely, on the quality of institutions and their maturity. It plays an important role in the character of these institutions: inclusive, which promotes development, or extractive, which does not promote it (Acemoglu and Robinson 2013).

The very famous theoretical economists D. Acemoglu and J. A. Robinson (2013), who study the state and institutions, write:

> "We will refer to political institutions that are sufficiently centralised and pluralistic as inclusive political institutions. When either of these conditions fails, we will refer to the institutions as extractive political institutions. There is strong synergy between economic and political institutions. Extractive political institutions concentrate power in the hands of a narrow elite and place few constraints on the exercise of this power. Economic institutions are then often structured by this elite to extract resources from the rest of society. Extractive economic institutions thus naturally accompany extractive political institutions. In fact, they must inherently depend on extractive political institutions for their survival. Inclusive political institutions, vesting power broadly, would tend to uproot economic institutions that expropriate the resources of the many, erect entry barriers and suppress the functioning of markets so that only a few benefit. […] extractive institutions, by creating unconstrained power and great income inequality, increase the potential stakes of the political game. Because of the fact that whoever controls the state becomes the beneficiary of this excessive power and the wealth that it generates, extractive institutions create incentives for infighting in order to control power and its benefits."

A new theory of economic policy, proposed by Acocella, Di Bartolomeo and Hughes Hallett (2011), revises the approach of Tinbergen (1956; 1980) and Theil (1956), applying concepts and tools introduced by them in the development of conflict theories that can justify the conditions that contribute to the emergence of policy neutrality, the game equilibrium existence and policy uniqueness or multiplicity. The importance of the new theory of economic policy is reduced by the authors to several points. First, two fundamental proposals (on policy neutrality and equilibrium) are important for model building because they determine the conditions under which the effectiveness of policy instruments, as well as the coherence of optimal strategies of all players (and therefore the existence of equilibrium), are guaranteed. Second, the theory has important applications for the development of appropriate institutions. Third, rational expectations are not necessarily an obstacle to policy effectiveness. When politicians and the private sector share the same information about how the economic system works, this has important implications for the design of institutions and how they work. It is also important that economic policy theory, going back to the tools developed by Tinbergen and Theil and applying them to the context of political games, has become a theory of conflict, which is why it determines the properties of the game both in terms of whose tools are effective and a view of the conditions of existence, uniqueness and multiplicity of decisions of political games.

Imran Arif (2021) presents economic sophistication as a potential determinant of labour share and uses a fixed-effect model that allowed the observation of 98 countries from 1970–2015, finding that economic sophistication has a positive and statistically significant effect on labour share. The researcher proved that:

> "a one standard deviation increase in economic sophistication increases labour share by about 3 percent, which corresponds to about 1.6 percentage points increase relative to the mean."

Further, he shows that economic sophistication and human capital have a substantial interaction effect.

The author of this study proceeds from the idea that the problem of a country's productive capacity in a globalised society is expanding and absorbs economic and non-economic factors. Productive ability as an economic factor is closely related to productivity, which can be measured as labour productivity and capital productivity. At the same time, the productive capacity of the country can be viewed from the standpoint of non-economic factors, such as institutional, civilisational, social and motivational factors.

The productive capacity of the economy is closely linked to economic development and correlates with economic growth. Economic growth is a percentage increase in GDP compared with previous periods. Economic development is a more complex process and its measurement is carried out by a wide range of qualitative indicators. The theory of growth, which was developed in the 1960s and continues to develop in new and interesting areas, has become a solid foundation for applied economics in the sense that it is used to conduct quantitative research on taxation, policy and social insurance (Lucas 2008; 2013).

Our world and the productivity of the economy have definitely changed the IT sphere. Henry Lucas (1999) wrote about the three components of IT – computers, databases and communication networks – and proposed approaches and methods to assess the value of investing in information technology, emphasising that it is possible to measure the possible return on investment. Indeed, venture capital investments in IT projects have been made at a tremendous pace. However, the dot-com crisis, the revaluation of the return on venture capital, which was reflected in the revalued shares of such companies, and, consequently, the separation of the financial sector from the real sector in the 2000s and 2010s provoked not only economic crises but also created a new world – a world of inequality of economic opportunities.

In the past, theorists in the field of international relations have constantly discussed the goals of public administration. The discussions focused mainly on domestic and foreign policies aimed at maximising strength and security, and achieving economic challenges, including with regard to trade, industrial development, and maintaining macroeconomic stability and growth. According to Schmidt and Cohen (2013):

> "the goals of states will not change in the future, but their ideas about how to achieve goals are likely to be revised. There will be two versions of domestic and foreign policy: one – for the physical 'real' world, the other is for the existing online world, the virtual world."

These are contradictory versions of politics: in real life, the government can demonstrate a policy of peace, while in cyberspace it can wage war to demonstrate harsh measures against the dishonest behaviour of its subjects.

How is productivity measured?

Productivity can be measured at both the company and national levels (Gordon et al. 2015). Given the microeconomic basis of macroeconomic growth, it is clear that productivity improvements at the company level are directly translated into national economic growth, but productivity growth in the economy may exceed the growth of individual companies. This is due to the fact that competition promotes companies that are more productive and therefore the share of these companies increases, while the share of less productive companies decreases. In the process, the average level of productivity increases. This process of competitive dynamics is important for bringing the economy closer to the limits of production capacity.

Inefficient economic policies and market behaviour that undermine competition can cause the economy to fall below its potential. There is also the potential for spillover effects between companies to increase productivity. This explanation dates back to the time of Adam Smith's *The Wealth of Nations* (2002, originally published in 1775). That is, what companies do to benefit themselves also benefits other companies. Proponents of industry-specific policies (such as government support for innovation centres and clusters) often cite the importance of spillovers as sources of productivity growth.

This is achieved by increasing the share of high-tech and medium-high-tech industries, which, in turn, will provide the necessary quality of economic growth. The process of diffusion of technologies (Hirooka 2006) is described by the logistic function of the form:

$$\frac{1+c}{1+c\exp(-dt)}, \qquad (1)$$

where c is a constant determined by the initial condition; and d is the diffusion coefficient of the technology.

The process of leaching outdated technology, accordingly, can be described as a "reverse" logistics function:

$$2-\frac{1+c}{1+c\exp(-dt)}=\frac{1+c[2\exp(-dt)-1]}{1+c\exp(-dt)}. \qquad (2)$$

According to A. Akaev and V. Sadovnichy (2014), the movement of output in the field of manufacturing (YM) can be written in the form of the formula:

$$Y_M = Y_{HT} + Y_{MHT} + Y_{MLT} + Y_{LT}. \qquad (3)$$

Of course, governments seek to increase the share of high-tech and medium-high-tech industries by reducing the share of medium-low-tech industries and leaching low-tech industries. This is the strategic goal of the economic policy of advanced development. However, it is necessary to assess to what extent the spillover effects will exceed government spending to stimulate policies to support innovative industries.

The measurement of productivity is the ratio of the measure of total production of goods and services to the measure of invested resources used in production. Productivity growth is assessed by (P.C. News 2015):

$$R_{PG} = \Delta Output - \Delta Input. \tag{4}$$

where R_{PG} is the rest of productivity growth.

There are a number of ways to measure productivity. In OECD countries, the most common measures of productivity are (P.C. News 2015):

- MFP, which measures the growth of value-added production (real gross output minus intermediate inputs) per unit of labour and capital;
- labour productivity, which measures the growth of value-added production per unit of labour used.

General economic estimates of MFP reflect the growth of labour productivity of the vast majority of the economy in total GDP. There are also a number of measurement issues associated with estimating input and output and.

Why economic policy affects productivity: dependence on strategic development goals

Globalisation significantly affects the transformation of the structure of the levers of economic development of a globalised society and its strategic needs. At the same time, it determines the character of political, economic, financial, ideological and cultural relations between states, transforming them towards complication, intertwining and strengthening of interdependence.

Today, social strategic needs are being transformed due to the changing nature of the relationships between man and nature, man and the economy, and man and politics (Moskalenko 2014). Human needs are now associated with the growing cognitive abilities of a human being. They also concern the intellectualisation of the nature of mankind's activities, and the requirements for the quality of living environment, environmental sustainability, safety, etc. That is why economic policy for advanced development in the context of post-globalisation is a key requirement for a market economy. Globalised society puts forward an updated set of strategic needs to address the risks of a global nature, such as COVID-19, in addition to the requirements for global productivity to address global social and humanitarian challenges. Thus, the value coordinates of human existence are transformed.

In this study, the strategic goals of economic policy in terms of productivity are considered in terms of achieving benefits in productivity based on the principle of advancement. The word "ahead" formulates the initial conditions for a successful economic policy focused on increasing the productivity of the national economy – namely, "to have time for something earlier and faster than another."

Therefore, it allows an understanding of the strategy of economic policy as a strategy of advanced development in order to achieve a stable long-term competitive position of the country and its companies in the global economy, achieving economic leadership, providing "strength" of the economy based on innovative technological advantages and a breakthrough public administration. This encourages a comprehensive scientific approach to strategy and setting strategic goals as a social phenomenon. A long-term national economic strategy, which aims to achieve a wide range of goals for the productive development of the economy and the satisfaction of social needs, is an integral element of socio-political relations that develop under certain domestic laws. Thus, the strategy (it can be defined as a strategy of advanced development) is a set of actions of the government to achieve and use effective economic, technological and managerial results, and also to meet strategic needs, in the long run.

The idea of a hierarchy of motives that corresponds to a hierarchy of needs is universal and can be applied to any society. Motive is a tool for meeting needs. In accordance with the motives that influence the satisfaction of social strategic needs, there are the strategic goals of economic development and advanced economic development in particular.

The relationship of "needs–motives–goals" through the prism of collective motivation as an evaluative social disposition has the form of "social needs–social motives–social strategic goals". The evaluation disposition of modern society of "social needs–social motives", in my opinion, has the following indicative structure (Moskalenko 2014):

1) needs driven by the motivation of human nature;
2) the effect of the needs of society (civic position) on state policy;
3) needs driven by the interests of special interest groups;
4) needs driven by radical changes in the human worldview;
5) needs driven by environmental motivation.

To explain the social strategic needs driven by the motivation of human nature, environmental motivation, civic position, etc., it is necessary to turn to the essence of motives. Motives are a mental and conscious idea of a person about the need for a certain action or goal to be achieved. According to scientists, motive arises under the influence of need. Human life is determined primarily by needs. To understand what goals a person sets, or what motives he has, it is necessary to understand what needs he has and when the individual need arises. Hence, the goal is a person's activity in relation to the realisation of needs and motives (Chetvertakov 2013, 29). The social environment and institutions transform the behaviour of individuals and, consequently, the system of needs of the individual. In fact, between the influence of the external environment and the beginning of the action of the individual, there is always not only his motivation but also his need. Needs trigger the activity of individuals. Activities can also create needs (Chetvertakov 2013, 30-31). Herbert Spencer noted that a society exists for the good of its members, not that its members exist for the good of society (1997, 10). Therefore, the environment and social institutions are developed and largely subordinated to the needs of the average person over time. A person's needs determine his activity and work, and then determine the purpose and forms of social structures and culture, which are created on this basis. The system of social strategic needs allows consideration of high motives, including spirituality. In the process of motivation, the first element is the need. The reality of society produces the setting of goals, including long-term (strategic) goals. Therefore, the strategic goals of society are the goals of achieving its strategic needs. Humans and society both have goals that involve their needs. Public strategic needs are realised through the goals and active actions of the state, which are implemented in social practice through collective motivation (Chetvertakov 2013, 53; Zhalilo 2003; 2009).

Social motives as tools to meet social needs are formed in the development of civil society and are relatively stable value dispositions of the public worldview on: the needs of state achievements; institutional quality and efficiency of power; economic order desired by the majority;

freedom of entrepreneurship; strength reserves of the state economy on the world stage; technological superiority; and human development.

Public strategic needs require conceptualisation. In my opinion, they can be reduced to the following groups:

1) society's needs for human development:

- high standard of living;
- high quality of the health care system;
- high life expectancy;
- good quality level of education and lifelong learning;
- equal access to the benefits of scientific and technological progress for the population;
- availability of free time for creative growth of personality, realisation of cognitive and aesthetic needs, and reproduction of human health potential;
- equal access for individuals to choose educational institutions;
- realisation and observance of human rights, freedoms and performance of duties;
- gender equality;
- satisfaction of the right to live in a sustainable environment;

2) the needs of the state:

- democratisation of all spheres of public life;
- high level of legitimisation and consolidation of democracy;
- social economic order, desired and supported by the majority;
- inclusiveness;
- trust in the government and the availability of feedback;
- high level of development of institutions of partnership between the state and business, the state and society, and the state and political elites;
- high professional level of public administration management;
- fairness in the distribution of income, taking into account the level of competencies and the intensity of the use of their skills by individuals;

3) the needs of the economy:

- rational level of consumption of material resources;
- dematerialisation of both consumption and production;
- balanced development of economic sectors;
- economic efficiency of the real sector and the permanent need for innovative development of industry;

- acquisition by the economy of technological competitive advantages, and their consolidation and use in international competition;
- equal access to foreign commodity and resource markets;
- freedom of enterprise;
- freedom of the domestic market from total seizure of foreign capital;
- diversification of production;
- innovative competition;
- balanced liberalisation of international trade;
- integration of the national economy into the world economy;
- equal membership of the country in international financial and economic organisations, and governmental and non-governmental institutions;
- economic development on the basis of the latest technological method of production, relevant to the technologies of the Fourth Industrial Revolution.

Public strategic needs generate motives and incentives to meet them, and thus form strategic goals. However, strategic goals should not be just a long-term action plan. Their broad understanding in the system of universal and civilisational values of human development becomes expedient. Uncertainty, as a key characteristic of globalisation and post-globalisation in its impact on national economies, requires consideration of the ideological component in the formation of strategic goals. The ideology accepted by a society can direct actions of the economic power and political forces in the course of realisation of public needs. The strategy of modern economic development becomes the logic of the state's behaviour, which actively reacts to the actions of competitors. Social strategic goals tend to be adaptively modified in the face of a changing institutional environment and the logic of economic development in general.

The strategy of economic development of the national economy must take into account the patterns of development of modern economic systems. Public strategic needs within the strategy of their satisfaction determine the motives for the best use of market economy opportunities for advanced innovative development in improving the quality of life, improving public health (which is very important in the global COVID-19 pandemic), improving human functionality, greening production, dematerialising consumption, etc.

Thus, the strategic needs of economic development and advanced innovation development are not identical. They have a certain dialectical connection. Public strategic needs arising in the coordinate system of advanced economic development are based on the transformation of the motivation system, which is now driven by the needs of human living comfort, high living standards, humanisation of economic activity, and cognitive and aesthetic needs. At the same time, advancing development meets the societal need to achieve sustainable growth but on the basis of rethinking human development needs, as well as reducing the vulnerability of the economic system in a turbulent environment. The specificity of the formation of strategic needs of society in the Fourth Industrial Revolution determines the advanced economic development of countries and beacon companies. It is essential that the advanced development causes radical changes in the worldview of politicians, managers and citizens on the possibility of transforming ways to meet these needs that increase the productive capacity of national economies. The tools of development in the Fourth Industrial Revolution are advancing responses to the challenges and threats of the global economy and advancing the business activity of companies, including transnational ones, as well as improving the forms of labour organisation, quantitative and qualitative results of the real sector to ensure expanded reproduction, and public administration methods. The advanced development caused by the Industry 4.0 revolution and social evolutionary processes penetrates equally into the scientific, educational, cultural and social spheres, and public administration, creating the preconditions for their improvement and the growth of productive potential.

Along with this, there is the formation of an informational and dialectical worldview, which is a prerequisite for purposeful management of socio-economic processes in the formation and deployment of a new technological method of production. An informational-dialectical worldview, in turn, is defined by scientists as a system of worldviews that necessitates overcoming entropic processes in nature and the social environment through advanced information creativity.

I propose the following classification of strategic goals of economic policy to increase the productivity of the national economy and hence advanced development:

- goals (needs) of economic development, aimed at the realisation of endogenous motives for the functioning of society at the national level;
- goals (needs) of economic development, aimed at the realisation of exogenous motives for the existence of the state at the international level;

- goals (needs) of economic development of the state at the global level, which are realised at the interstate and international levels, within the endogenous and exogenous motives of its existence.

Of course, the proposed classification is quite conditional and this is understandable, because there is an interpenetration and imposition of these goals at different levels and time intervals of their setting and implementation. Also, there will be an expansion or contraction of them in different specific national conditions of countries.

Thus, the strategic goals of economic development, aimed at ensuring endogenous motives for the functioning of society at the national level, include:

- achievement of high living standards of the population, which is manifested in the presence of an effective system of income redistribution, and sufficiently equal access for the population to the necessary consumer goods, and educational and medical services, and their high quality;
- further intellectualisation of labour and the formation of the "knowledge economy";
- balanced optimal economic development, which allows advantage to be taken of Pareto improvement, which is where an improvement of the situation of some entities is achieved without deteriorating the situation of other entities;
- growth of employment and diversification of its forms;
- overcoming poverty and curbing inequality;
- increasing the share of the population covered by higher education;
- providing expanded reproduction based on new technologies;
- dematerialisation of consumption;
- bridging and reducing the digital divide.

Among these strategic goals of economic development, it is important to achieve a structure of the economy that will provide the greatest economic and social efficiency, and achieve higher productivity. The decisive role in this is played by political institutions and the level of coordination of their goals with the interests of society, which has the ability to exercise comprehensive control over the activities of political institutions through a constitutionalised system of public choice (Buchanan 1986). In the methodological field of the theory of social choice, "the level of improvement of the work of political institutions should be measured in units of providing people with all the necessary goods" (Zaitsev and Savchuk 2011, 278).

The strategic goals of economic development, aimed at realising the exogenous motives of the state's existence at the international level, include:

- guaranteeing the economic security of the national economy;
- ensuring the preservation of economic sovereignty, by which I mean the ability of the state to implement independent domestic and foreign economic policy based on national economic priorities and interests without the influence and pressure of institutional agents at various levels – states and international monetary and financial organisations;
- growth of the country's international competitiveness in the markets of high-tech products, outpacing the acquisition of international technological advantages and high productivity of the national economy;
- ensuring the stability of the national currency (for emerging markets and developing countries), and its internal and external convertibility of current and capital transactions;
- openness of the economy and markets on the basis of the principle of freedom of enterprise at the international level, in compliance with the principles of international economic law.

The strategic goals of economic development of the state at the global level, which are realised at the interstate and international levels, within the endogenous and exogenous motives of its existence, include:

- receiving benefits by the country from membership in international financial and economic organisations on the basis of partnership, justice, expediency, relevance and equality;
- involvement of the country in solving global socio-economic, environmental and humanitarian problems, and implementation of relevant international programmes, i.e. productive inclusion in global partnerships;
- acquisition by the country of a respectable status in the global economy as an influential actor, reliable partner and key player in international relations of various orientations and complexity;
- guaranteeing the international security of the country through the mechanism of integration and collective solutions of problems;

- integration into a single information digital space in priority areas of the Fourth Industrial Revolution, as well as into international scientific and technological exchange, and scientific and technical cooperation.

The strategic goals of economic entities, based on the principles of environmental motivation, anticipating the acquisition of new technological competitive advantages and the idea of dematerialisation of production, can be reduced to the following:

- reproduction-oriented production goals (providing for the creation of reproduction cycles of generation and/or disposal of products, and expanded reproduction);
- functionally oriented scientific and technical goals (focussing not on the product but on innovative functions);
- formation of a dematerialised economic paradigm (providing a focus on improving information, innovation, and the digital component of production and social systems).

Dematerialisation involves not only reducing the material consumption of groups of goods traditionally consumed, but also reducing the share of their consumption. Dematerialisation, in my opinion, is the strategic need of society to reduce the material component (material and energy resources) in the cost structure of enterprises (organisations) and each person, in particular in the transformation of the public worldview and the essence of economic policy to strengthen the information (digital) and intellectual component of production and consumption. This can be achieved only by permanently increasing the productive capacity of the national economy.

Thus, the implementation of strategic goals of economic policy, aimed at increasing productivity in the national economy, requires a new theory of economic policy, which is the economic policy of living standards. Strategic economic policy should be conducted in the national interests of the state and be aimed at: increasing the efficiency and productivity of industrial production; acquisition of new knowledge and technologies on the basis of the technological method of production of Industry 4.0; advanced development of human capital through soft investments in it; and reduction of social inequality and uneven economic development within the country, if such a situation occurs. For economic policy to be effective and conducive to productivity growth in the national economy, it must focus on the formation of a productive structure of incentives, rather than on balancing abstract macroeconomic parameters. Under these conditions, economic policy corresponds to the nature of social relations and business practices.

It is important to turn to neo-institutionalism from the standpoint of its methodology for studying economic policy as a component of state policy, as well as opportunities to assess its effectiveness. Improvements in policy can be measured in one way or another by the degree to which the strategic needs of individuals are met. If there are goals in politics that are shared by the majority, then their joint coordination is realised by the implementation of choice by individuals, i.e. by their selective motivational behaviour.

Thus, the normative theory of economic policy, which develops specific practical recommendations, is in a set of restrictive circumstances, which are manifested in the absence of any specific criteria for evaluating policy. Direct evaluation can be based on how "the political process contributes to the transformation of clear individual interests into concrete political outcomes" (Buchanan 1986). That is, improvements in the productivity of the economy should be sought in the actual implementation of economic policy and institutional shift, which will allow economic policy to clearly reflect the set of results that are desirable for its participants. Within a country, the participants are its citizens who pursue their privately defined individual interests through various institutional environments.

Thus, the degree of public agreement with a particular model of economic policy is a measure of satisfaction with its tools, which is manifested in the nature of its impact and results in a particular institutional environment (economy in general, tax system, health care, education level and quality, degree of independence in the judicial system, levels of environmental protection, wage levels, and other socially oriented and business-oriented indicators).

The theory of economic policy should provide recommendations for changes in economic processes and rules that can find support in society, as any proposal should be made on the basis of time and a responsible understanding of political reality (Sukharev 2007). That is, the government's ability to identify strategic goals of economic development and choose one or another tool of economic policy should remain within reach, and individual privately defined interests pursued through political choice should be recognised as the limits of what is possible.

In order to assess the economic policy of any country from the standpoint of effectiveness, it is necessary to review measures, tools and approaches to its planning. Growth policy and, in fact, economic growth do not arise by chance but on an organisational basis. Organising economic growth and increasing productivity in the economy requires economic resources and their involvement in priority areas, which are determined by the state using methods of foresight and forecasting. However, it should be borne in mind that creating in a short period of time a solid foundation for economic growth in a country that has problems with the institutional structure of its economy and productivity, which is manifested in the systemic economic crisis, is unlikely to succeed. Strengthening economic growth requires resources, time and mechanisms to stimulate such growth, based on a rethinking of the existing system of rules and incentives. Thus, productivity in the economy can be defined as the basic goal of economic policy, which is necessary but insufficient. A parallel structuring of all institutional subsystems should be a parallel goal along with economic growth based on increased productivity. "Institutional subsystems" should be understood as subsystems of politics, the economy and society – namely, state power as a regulatory subsystem, legislative and judicial subsystems, institutions of innovation initiatives, motivational subsystems, a subsystem of education and science, a subsystem of human capital, a subsystem of culture, a subsystem of health care, etc.

The inclusion of the health care subsystem in the above institutional subsystems meets the strategic need for a growing economy, which requires a healthy population that is able to realise its own human potential using all physical, intellectual and psycho-emotional resources at the highest level. The intensity of labour, which is determined by the degree of growth of its productivity, where the upper limits are the physical and cognitive capabilities of man, is not unlimited. However, it is the health of the nation that largely determines the resource potential of the full use of the country's human capital to achieve productivity goals.

The implementation of economic policy to increase the productivity of the national economy requires a strong state, whose presence in the economy becomes apparent if the quality of public management is high and people feel it. Public management must find a balance between recognising the interests of the people (population) as a priority over the interests of big business and financial markets, which is difficult to do in the conditions of neoliberal ideology but it is possible. Relevant on the agenda of a globalised society is the philosophy of post-globalisation on the basis of a global partnership and well-being for all, which are "policy measures in the interests of the people" (Georgieva 2020, 10).

Economic policy to increase productivity requires a government that has a vocation to solve a significant set of problems in social development (Geets 2020). Therefore, it is urgent to formulate the goals and objectives of economic policy aimed at increasing productivity through the enrichment of the goals of a globalised society based on a human-centric paradigm of development.

There is a formulation of scientifically applied and critical views on the universalisation of classical neoliberal recipes of economic policy (Streeck 2019). Thus, scholars, practitioners and "creators" of economic policy must assume that successful theories and models of developed countries cannot always be applied equivalently in emerging markets and developing economies. Such countries have their own socio-economic specifics, infrastructure, mentality and culture, which is often not taken into account by international financial institutions (IMF, World Bank, etc.) when developing economic reform packages for these countries. Thus, under these conditions, economic policy recipes that have been successful in developed countries do not work or lead to the exact opposite results.

At the same time, the importance and role of the state in the implementation of socio-economic goals of economic policy is changing and strengthening. That is, the state comes to the forefront of socio-economic relations between different groups of actors, both domestically and internationally. Of course, depending on the type of economic system, the role of the state in the implementation of its social functions is either greater or less. In economic systems with a sufficiently mature institutional structure, the function of supporting and enforcing social guarantees is assumed to a greater extent by the private sector, which is reflected in the existence and effective functioning of such an institution as corporate social responsibility and a number of well-established social insurance and private guarantees (non-state pension insurance, health insurance, etc.). In less developed economic systems from the point of view of institutional functionality and efficiency of public management, the role of the state in maintaining the social system becomes decisive, as market regulation mechanisms do not work, and corporate social responsibility does not work due to the lack of psycho-emotional readiness of corporate structures to transfer a certain share of social guarantees. Under these conditions, the particularly trusting nature of the relationship between the state and business is not established. The system operates in the institutional field of bureaucracy.

Productive ability of the national economy: modern characteristics

The productive capacity of the economy is a reflection of the health of politics and economics, and therefore of MFP and labour productivity.

Productivity is declining globally. There is controversy in academia over this slowdown in productivity. There is no generally accepted explanation for this slowdown. Experts point out that one of the most plausible explanations is that, by now, the potential of the computer revolution has largely been exhausted. That is why there have been no technological breakthroughs in the world that could be compared to the impact of information and communication technologies in terms of the impact on productivity, in particular on people's lifestyles in general (Razumokov Center 2020; Sandbu 2020). Digitalisation (Huateng 2019), the creation of artificial intelligence, the use of unmanned vehicles, etc. are considered to be the new drivers of growth after the era of the computer revolution.

Organisations that have managed to overcome the pilot phase of Industry 4.0's innovation and scale solutions have received an unprecedented increase in efficiency with minimal staff reductions. A report, presented at the World Economic Forum in 2019, emphasises that many companies are now trying to implement the technologies of the Fourth Industrial Revolution in production, but few manage to do so on a scale that achieves significant financial and economic effect. In general, the share of material production in the world is declining and thus the tertiary sector of the economy is beginning to occupy a leading position (World Economic Forum 2019).

There is a relationship between the productivity of economies and poverty levels (Fosu 2017). Thus, according to the World Bank, "Poverty decreased in EMDEs [emerging markets and developing economies] with the fastest growth rates of labour productivity in 1981–2015, and increased in EMDEs with the lowest rates" (World Bank Group 2020, 4). Globally, there is a large-scale slowdown in productivity growth (Dieppe 2020). The uneven economic development in a globalised society can be explained by the difference in productivity between developed and low-income economies. At present, "productivity levels in EMDEs remain less than 20 percent of the advanced-economy average, and just 2 percent in low-income countries" (World Bank Group 2020, 4). Experts identify the following factors that slow down productivity, namely: smaller benefits from redistribution by industry, slower improvement in many factors of productivity growth and increased frequency of adverse shocks (Ibid.).

The implications for the productivity of national economies from the Fourth Industrial Revolution are as follows (DeCanio 2016; Huateng 2019; Schmidt and Cohen 2013):

- large-scale and widespread implementation of the Fourth Industrial Revolution technologies based on the joint efforts of commercial companies and the state;
- accelerating the growth of welfare, from which the whole society will benefit;
- radical changes in value chains, industries and business models, with a key role for industrial enterprises;
- formation of close cooperation of stakeholders in order to minimise the consequences of 4IR for the labour market and employment, where there is a real danger of displacement of human labour.

"Lighthouses" are demonstrators of digital manufacturing and globalization 4.0, and exhibit all of the essential characteristics of the Fourth Industrial Revolution (World Economic Forum 2019). Industry 4.0 "lighthouses" show all the key features of the Fourth Industrial Revolution. They are an example of the concept of "Globalisation 4.0" and include companies that successfully use the achievements of the Fourth Industrial Revolution. These are companies such as Bayer, Division Pharmaceuticals in Garbagnate, Italy; BMW in Regensburg, Germany; Bosch Automotive in Wuxi, China; Danfoss in Tianjin, China; Foxconn Industrial Internet in Shenzhen, China; Haier in Qingdao, China; Phoenix Contact in Bad Pyrmont and Blomberg, Germany; and Johnson & Johnson DePuySynthes in Cork, Ireland. These companies have proven that you can get the economic effect of all factors of value creation in industry – namely, in productivity, resource efficiency, flexibility, efficiency, speed of market introduction and individualisation according to customer needs (World Economic Forum 2019).

In general, productivity in the European Union from 1995 to 2020 increased (2015 = 100), as can be seen from Figure 5-1. In 2008–2009, there was a significant decline in productivity, which can be explained by the global financial and economic crisis. In general, from 2010 to 2020, productivity increased, compared with the base year 2015; in 2010, productivity was lower by 5%. In 2015–2020, productivity in the EU increased by another 5%.

Actual	Previous	Highest	Lowest	Dates	Unit	Frequency	
103.50	103.80	104.20	75.50	1995 - 2020	points	Quarterly	2015=100, SA

Figure 5-1. European Union productivity, 1995–2020
Source: Eurostat 2020, Trading Economics.
https://tradingeconomics.com/european-union/productivity.

In terms of productivity of the national economy, the countries of the EMDE group are interesting for analysis, which is presented in Table 5-1 (2011 = 100). Table 5-1 shows that the annual growth rate of production per employee in Ukraine increased in some years, reaching its peak in 2004 at 12.3%, which was twice less than the same figure globally, where it amounted to 25.0%. The lowest value of labour productivity for Ukraine was in 2009, the decline was - 12.2%, which is more than six times compared to the decline of this indicator in the same year at the global level -2.0%.

Table 5-1. Labour productivity in Ukraine and in the world

	Ukraine (as an example of an emerging market)		World	
	Production per employee (for PPP in prices 2011), $	Annual growth rate of production per employee (in permanent GDP prices in 2011 for PPP), %	Production per employee (for PPP in prices 2011), $	Annual growth rate of production per employee (in permanent GDP prices in 2011 for PPP), %
2001	4,827.2	10.7	19,274.2	0.7
2002	5,065.1	4.9	19,465.1	1.0
2003	5,513.6	8.9	19,740.2	1.4
2004	6,192.8	12.3	20,232.2	25.0
2005	6,317.3	2.0	20,672.7	2.2
2006	6,799.7	7.6	21,241.4	2.8
2007	7,320.6	7.7	21,795.4	2.6
2008	7,528.3	2.8	21,943.4	0.7
2009	6,610.9	−12.2	21,500.6	−2.0
2010	6,831.2	3.3	22,211.2	3.2
2011	7,197.1	5.4	22,682.3	2.1
2012	7,261.7	0.9	23,006.6	1.4
2013	7,178.7	−1.1	23,381.4	1.6
2014	7,443.6	3.7	23,762.1	1.6
2015	6,712.1	−9.8	24,152.7	1.6
2016	6,959.9	3.7	24,492.4	1.4
2017	7,202.3	3.5	24,947.2	1.9
2018	7,449.1	3.4	25,354.2	1.6
2019	7,766.9	4.3	25,699.6	1.4
2020	-	4.3	-	1.7

Source: ILOSTAT, 2020. Statistics on labour productivity, https://ilostat.ilo.org/topics/labour-productivity.

Thus, productivity is the result of the general health of the economy, in particular digital production, and hence it is the result of economic policy, which implements strategic development goals aimed at achieving exogenous and endogenous motives for the existence of the state that correlate with global trends.

Conclusions

The development of a globalised society in the era of Industry 4.0, Globalisation 4.0, digital transformation and innovation of all spheres of public life leads to new formats in business and public administration. This enriches the strategic goals of economic policy. It takes the form of an economic policy of advanced development. The economic policy of the government at the present stage of development of society determines the strategic goals for economic development and growth, and hence the productivity of the national economy. Thus, the goals of economic policy should: take into account the new needs of society and the individual within it; be aimed at meeting growing needs; and focus on productivity growth.

In conditions of intensification of crisis phenomena in the global economy, which are characterised by special complexity, there is a public demand for economic policy of advanced development. Such a policy is a way of understanding the current socio-economic reality, which is the main point of view that shapes approaches to adapting countries to global instability. The key principles of such a policy are to catch up faster than others, to respond today to tomorrow's challenges, and to develop at an accelerated pace on the orders of the harmonious development of the economy and mankind, and the economy and nature. The Fourth Industrial Revolution formulates the motives for advanced development. Thus, modern economic policy has a whole arsenal of goals and tools to ensure that the economy develops ahead of schedule, creating the conditions for meeting the new needs of society, especially the quality of life and equal economic opportunities. The strategic goals of the economic policy of the modern state are formulated to ensure both exogenous and endogenous motives for its existence, the structuring of which is provided in this article. It is important that the formulation of these strategic goals of economic policy of the modern economy should be in the direction of strengthening the role of intangible, spiritual and humanistic components and "policy measures in the interests of the people" (Georgieva 2005).

The choice of a package of government measures takes place in a specific model of economic policy developed by the government for a particular state of the economic system and/or the economic situation in the country at the analysed stage of development of the global economy. Productivity at the global level is declining (ILOSTAT 2020). Thus, at the present stage it is urgent to create forms of economic policy that contain mechanisms for the effective implementation of long-term strategic goals and meet the current needs of society in advance to overcome the causes of declining productivity. Not every economic policy is able to ensure efficient reproduction, distribution, exchange, consumption and savings. Only economic policy that takes into account, firstly, the patterns of development of modern socio-economic and political reality, and secondly, the principles of different types of economic systems, in practice determines the driving forces of motivation to work and productive economic activity. Thus, an effective economic policy is one that implements the principles of development ahead of time, ensuring the achievement of the strategic goals of the state and the new needs of society in a breakthrough way.

References

Acemoglu, D. and Robinson, J A. 2013. *Why Nations Fail: The Origins of Power, Prosperity, and Poverty,* Pbk. ed, New York: Crown Business.

Acocella, N., Bartolomeo, G. D., and Hughes Hallett, A. 2011. "The theory of economic policy: from a theory of control to a theory of conflict (resolutions)," Working Paper n. 91, December 2011.

Akaev A.A. and Sadovnichy V.A. 2014. "On a new methodology for long-term cyclical forecasting of the dynamics of the world system and Russia development." In: *Forecast and Modeling of Crises and World Dynamics.* ed. A.A. Akaev, A.V. Korotaev and G.G. Malinetskiy, 2nd Ed. M.: Knizhny dom "Librikom". (Rus.)

Arif, I. 2021. "Productive knowledge, economic sophistication, and labor share," *World Development* 139, 05303, https://doi.org/10.1016/j.worlddev.2020.105303.

Buchanan, J. "The Constitution of Economic Policy, Nobel Lecture December 8, 1986." In: *World Economic Thought. Through the prism of centuries.* In 5 volumes, editorial board G.G. Fetisov, A.G. Khudokormov. In two books. Worldwide recognition: lectures of the Nobel laureates, ed. G.G. Fetisov. Book. 1, Moscow: Mysl, 2004, 767. (Rus.)

Chetvertakov, S.A. 2013. *Reconstruction of Maslow's theory.* St. Petersburg: Aleteya. (Rus.)

DeCanio, S.J. 2016. "Robots and humans – complements or substitutes?" *Journal of Macroeconomics* 49, 280-291.

Dieppe, A. (ed.). 2020. "Global Productivity: Trends, Drivers, and Policies," The World Bank, https://www.worldbank.org/en/research/publication/global-productivity.

EUROSTAT. 2020. Trading Economics, https://tradingeconomics.com/european-union/productivity.

Fosu, Augustin Kwasi. 2017. "Growth, inequality, and poverty reduction in developing countries: Recent global evidence." *Research in Economics*, no. 71, 306-336.

"OECD. 2020. "GDP per hour worked (indicator)," DOI: 10.1787/1439e590-en (Accessed on 31 August 2020).

Geets, V.M. 2020. *The phenomenon of instability – a wake-up call of economic development.* National Academy of Sciences of Ukraine, Institute of Economics and Forecasting of the National Academy of Sciences of Ukraine. Kyiv: Academperiodica, 456.

Georgieva, K. 2020. "Straightforward: There's no going back to the past. Investing in policies that benefit people will help create a better economy for the post-crisis world," *Finance & Development. The brave new world. The Future of Jobs and Opportunities* 25, International Monetary Fund. December 2020, 22. (Rus.)

Gordon, J., Zhao, S. and Gretton, P. 2015. "On Productivity: Concepts and Measurement," Productivity Commission Staff Research Note, Released February 2015.

Hirooka, M.2006. *Innovation Dynamism and Economic Growth. A Nonlinear Perspective.* Cheltenham: Edward Elgar.

ILOSTAT. 2020. "Statistics on labour productivity," https://ilostat.ilo.org/topics/labour-productivity.

Lucas, H. C. 1999. "Information technology and the productivity paradox: assessing the value of investing in IT," Oxford, New York: Oxford University Press.

Lucas, R. E., Jr. 2008. "Ideas and Growth Working Paper 14133," http://www.nber.org/papers/w14133, NBER, June 2008.

Lucas, R. E., Jr. 2013. *Lectures on Economic Growth*. (Rus.)

Huateng, M., Zhaoli, M., Delhi, Y., Hualei, W. 2019. *China's digital transformation. Experience in transforming the infrastructure of the national economy.* Moscow: Intellectual Literature, 250. (Rus.)

Moskalenko, O. 2014. *Theory and model of advanced economic development in the system of social strategic needs.* Kyiv: KNEU Publishing House, 550. (Ukr.)

North, D.C. 1990. *Institutions, institutional change, and economic performance*. Cambridge: Cambridge University Press.

Ministry of Economic Development of Ukraine. 2018. "Labor productivity and capital productivity for the second quarter of 2018." (Ukr.)

P.C. News. 2015. "What is productivity and how is it measured? A new Productivity Commission Staff Research Note unpacks the concept of productivity and how it is measured," May 2015, https://www.pc.gov.au/news-media/pc-news/previous-editions/pc-news-may-2015/productivity-and-how-measured/productivity-and-how-measured-pc-news-201505.pdf.

Razumokov Center. 2020. "Digital Economy: Trends, Risks, and Social Determinants," Project Manager Olga Pishchulina, Kyiv: Zapovit Publishing House, https://razumkov.org.ua/uploads/article/2020_digitalization.pdf.

Smith, A. 2002. *The Wealth of Nations*, Oxford, England: Bibliomania.com Ltd.

Spencer, H. 1997. *Synthetic Philosophy.* Translation from English. Kyiv: Nika-Center, 512. (Rus.)

Sukharev, O.S. 2007. *Institutional theory and economic policy: Towards a new theory of the transmission mechanism in macroeconomics. Book. II: Economic policy. Problems of theoretical description and practical implementation.* Moscow: ZAO Publishing House Economics, 804. (Rus.)

Theil, H. 1956. "On the theory of economic policy," *American Economic Review* 46, 360-366.

Tinbergen, J. 1956. *Economic policies: principles and design.* Amsterdam: North-Holland.

Tinbergen, J. 1980. *Revision of International Law*, Moscow: Progress, 416. (Rus.)

Sandbu, M. 2020. "A brave new world after the pandemic. Decisions made by policymakers during the current turmoil can shape the economy for decades to come." *Finance and Development. A wonderful new world. The Future of Jobs and Opportunities*, International Monetary Fund, December 2020, 5-9. (Rus.)

Schmidt, E. and Cohen, J. 2013. *The new digital world. How technology is changing people's lives, business models, and the concept of states.* Translation from English by Sergei Filin, Moscow: Mann, Ivanov and Ferber, 368. (Rus.)

Streeck, W. 2019. *Buying time: The delayed crisis of democratic capitalism. A series of lectures within the framework of the Frankfurt Readings in memory of Adorno.* Translation from German by I. Zhenina. Under scientific ed. M. Dobryakova. Moscow: Publishing house of the Higher School of Economics, 280. (Rus.)

World Bank Group. 2020. "HIGHLIGHTS. Global Productivity: Trends, drivers, and policies," 2020. http://pubdocs.worldbank.org/en/522491594657655028/Global-Productivity-book-highlights.pdf.

World Economic Forum. 2019. "Fourth Industrial Revolution Beacons of Technology and Innovation in Manufacturing," Informative Paper, January 2019, in collaboration with McKinsey & Company, http://www3.weforum.org/docs/WEF_4IR_Beacons_of_Technology_and_Innovation_in_Manufacturing_report_2019.pdf.

Zaitsev, Yu.K. and Moskalenko, O.M. 2020. *Modern political economy as a theoretical basis of economic development of society.* Book II. *Modern political economy as a methodological paradigm of economic development policy in a globalized society.* Kyiv: KNEU. (Ukr.)

Zaitsev, Yu.K. and Savchuk, V.S. 2011. *Modern Political Economy (Problems and Institutional Subject Field and Research Methodology).* Kyiv: KNEU, 337. (Ukr.)

Zhalilo, Y. 2003. *The economic strategy of the state: theory, methodology, practice*. Kyiv: NISR, 368. (Ukr.)

Zhalilo, Y. 2009. *Theory and practice of formulating the effective economic strategy of the state*. Kyiv: NISR, 334. (Ukr.)

CHAPTER SIX

CONTEMPORARY INSTITUTIONALISM AND INSTRUMENTS OF COMPARATIVE ANALYSIS OF THE PRODUCTIVITY OF NATIONAL ECONOMIES

VOLODYMYR V. LYPOV

The intensification of international competition in the era of the information revolution stimulated the growth of interest in studying the sources of success or failure of national economies. Provision of natural resources, capital, the level of economic development and the institutional environment are the focus of researchers. Each of these factors contributes to success. However, the presence or even a combination of several of them does not guarantee it. The modern histories of Russia and Singapore can serve as illustrative examples. It is not enough to have the right resources for economic success; it is necessary to ensure their effective use. The level of productivity of the national economy is becoming a key factor of success. But it, in turn, largely depends on the institutional environment. Implementation of information technologies largely ensured the formation of a number of successful alternative institutional socio-economic models. The desire to understand the origins of success stimulated the development of a number of areas of comparative institutional research. Among them are Regulation Theory (RT), concepts of Social Systems of Innovation and Production, Varieties of Capitalism (VoC), National Business Systems, Institutional Matrices (IM), and Institutional Complementarity (IC). The difference in approaches is due to the peculiarities of the goals set by researchers, their theoretical preferences, and the methodological apparatus and tools used.

The purposes of this section are two-fold:

- analysis of the features of the tools for studying the productivity of national economies, proposed within the main areas of comparative research of institutional models of socio-economic systems (SES);
- identification of the limitations of comparative research, and its advantages and disadvantages in the context of forming a holistic view of universal institutional mechanisms to ensure high productivity of national economies.

Methodology

The methodological basis of the study includes qualitative, structural, dialectical, historical and genetic analysis. In the process of working on the topic, logical-historical and systemic research methods were used.

Previous research review

Radical transformations of the 1990s stimulated the growth of interest in comparative studies of economic systems (ES). The accents of comparative studies change significantly over time. A milestone in the context of the reorientation of comparative institutional research was the work of M. Albert, *Capitalism Vs. Capitalism* (1993). The competition of alternative (Rhine and American) models of capitalism as the engine of ES productivity growth is recognised.

The origins of the alternative to the normative concept of comparative analysis (CA) of ES are found in the works of T. Koopmans and J. Montias (1971), and W. Duffy and E. Neuberger (1972). Economists are looking for answers to the threats of reduced productivity and loss of competitiveness of ES. Researchers compare certain phenomena of economic life in different ES. However, researchers ignore the institutional nature of ES. The publication of D. North's work (1990; 1991) gave impetus to the revival of interest in the institutional direction of economic research. The scientist demonstrates the heuristic potential of tracking dependence on the trajectory of the previous development of institutions (Path dependence). Moreover, the key evolutionary function of institutions is to ensure the growth of productivity of the economic system:

> "The central issue of economic history and of economic development is to account for the evolution of political and economic institutions that create an economic environment that induces increasing productivity." (North 1991, 98)

Later, this area of economic research was developed in the work of C. Castaldi and G. Dosi (2008). It should be noted that comparative institutional analysis (CIA) is not limited to identifying the historical preconditions for differentiating the institutional structure of the ES. V. Schmidt (2007) identifies within it such areas as historical, sociological, discursive and rational choice. The difference between them is due to the specifics of the object, logic and problems on which the researcher focuses. The focus is on explaining institutional stability and institutional change by certain factors (fixed preferences; existing institutions; path dependence; cultural norms; ideational ideas, ideas and discursive interaction).

Among the founders of the actual (historical) CIA of ES, M. Aoki (2001) and A. Greif (1993; 1994; 2006) should be noted. The generalisation of the further development of comparative institutional research is reflected in *The Oxford Handbook of Comparative Institutional Analysis* (Morgan et al. 2010).

In the context of the research topic, concepts of comparative research focusing on the comparison of institutional systems at the national level are of special interest. However, they differ in methodological approaches to the problem. But the common factor is an emphasis on the study of the specifics of institutional mechanisms for coordinating economic activity as a tool to ensure the productivity of ES (Boyer 2005). First of all, taking into account the impact on the development of comparative studies of economic systems, we should highlight the Theory of Regulation (Hollingsworth 1997; Crouch and Streeck 1997), the concept of Social Systems of Innovation and Production (Amable 2000), the Diversity of Capitalism (Soskice 1999; Hall and Soskice 2001), and the National Business Systems (Whitley 1999). A special place is occupied by the concepts of IM by O. Bessonova (2015) and S. Kirdina (2014).

A second direction of comparative research has a pronounced inductive nature. Formalisation of data and active use of quantitative methods of analysis serve as tools for generalisation and comparison. The work of B. Egert (2016) can serve as an indicator. The researcher focuses on multifactor productivity (MFP) analysis of indicators that can serve as analytical tools for developing government policy to ensure productivity growth. P. Castelnovo, C.F. Del Bo and M. Florio (2018) focus on an international comparative study of the impact of the quality of institutions on the productivity of state-owned and private property. R. Ganau and A. Rodriguez-Pose (2019) study the impact of local institutional systems on the transformation of productivity of Western manufacturing enterprises. W. Doellgast and D. Marsden (2018) turn to a CA of the impact of institutions as a resource and limit of the company's policy aimed at increasing staff productivity. C. Collin and K. Tarron (2018) conducted a comprehensive comparative study of the impact of economic structure on productivity and evolution of ES in Barbados, Guyana and Mauritius. A team of researchers led by T. Lohwasser (Lohwasser et al. 2019) turns to the study of the impact on the productivity of a firm's diversification of production strategies. M. Charilaos and S. Mona (2019) turn to the study of the impact of the possibility of hiring qualified personnel on the productivity of enterprises in developing countries. F. Ferdousi (2013) turns to the study of the relationship between development at the macroeconomic level, the development of the financial sector and the productivity of microfinance institutions. R. Mersland and R.O. Strom (2007) turn to the study of the impact of institutional mechanisms of management on the productivity of microfinance institutions. Comparative studies at the macroeconomic level are widespread. Thus, L.T. Nhan and N.V. Tung (2017) investigate the relationship between the quality of institutions and productivity in provinces and cities of Vietnam.

Definitions of generic, special and single as a basis for comparative research

Despite its significant cognitive potential, CA has limited use in economic research. Economists face several problems. The comparison of real objects, which is declared, is always an actual comparison of models that exist in the mind of the researcher. The choice of the bases of their formation acquires key value. For the classical political economy, Marxism, the historical school, the old institutionalism and RT, it is society as a whole. But the neoclassical school, neo-institutionalism and VoC are based on a separate economic entity. This choice determines the priority of opposite (deductive or inductive) methods of analysis. The need to combine them becomes an obstacle that will prevent the active implementation of CA.

Moreover, recourse to modelling involves focusing on the key components, in terms of the purpose of the study, of the comparable ES. The principle of "other things being equal" comes into force. In the case of ES, some factors remain out of the researcher's attention, and are considered equal and unchanged. However, they can differ significantly, form different contexts and affect the dynamics of systems in general in different ways. The structure of such factors can also vary significantly.

In addition, when it comes to CIA, there is the problem of quantifying objects of comparison. To what extent do we evaluate certain established algorithms of social interaction? After all, a meticulous CA of institutional systems leads to the recognition of the need to compare the social orientations of value systems on which they are based.

The negative attitude to dialectical methods of analysis also plays a role. However, CA itself essentially involves the opposition of objects of comparison. This involves defining the essential[1] and the phenomenal[2] in the ES and provides the search for contradictions as alternative elements of comparable systems. The determination of contradictions[3] is a tool to confirm the existence of a general (generic[4]) and the starting point for the study of special (special[5] in the institutional structure of the compared systems. After all, the contradictions can arise only as a result of the interaction of elements of a holistic system. It is based on a special institutional structure. The juxtaposition of contradictions becomes a tool for studying the evolution of institutional development. In turn, the ratio of general and special in the ES becomes the basis for the formation of the individual (single[6]), as what distinguishes a particular ESs from others.

Accordingly, the evaluation criterion is the overlap or distinction of the objects of comparison in this particular respect. After all, **phenomena that have a common nature**, or only their parts that have common principles, are subject to comparison. There is an abstraction from specific properties. They seem constant and unchanging. The "for other equals" assumption takes effect. E. Ilyenkov (2020, c. 229) characterises the problem that arises in comparative studies:

> "… When you want to establish a certain relationship between two objects, you always compare not those 'specific' qualities that make one object 'sound A', and another 'table', 'steak' or 'square', and only those properties which express something 'third', different from their existence as the listed things. *Things that are compared are considered as various modifications of this 'third', common to all properties, as if in it.*" (italics by VL)

---

[1] **Essential** – the inner content of a phenomenon, which is expressed in all forms of its existence.

[2] **Phenomenal** – a visible image of an object, its expression in the form of existence, manifestation of the essence.

[3] **Contradiction** – an interaction of opposite, mutually exclusive parts, sides and tendencies of objects and phenomena that are in internal unity, which predetermines the dynamics of its development.

[4] **Generic** – features inherent in all objects of a certain class.

[5] **Special** – a feature similar to some other objects of a certain class and different from others.

[6] **Single** – a feature of an object that differ from other objects of a certain class.

Examples are the approaches used by M. Schnitzer (1994) and S. Rosefielde (2002). The former attaches key importance to the systemic characteristics of the object of study: the countries that best represent the different variations of the ES. However, his attempt to identify criteria for comparison special (see chapters 16–18) faces the problem of determining parameters that are both present and sufficiently representative of the key characteristics of the developed countries of the East and West (USA, Germany, Japan), post-Soviet and underdeveloped countries (China, Mexico, Nigeria). S. Rosefielde (2002) significantly deepens the analysis of the criteria for identifying the special in the compared ES (Chapters 1–6), reduces the number of objects of comparison, for which the system characteristics (Chapters 7–12), offers a generalised analysis (Chapters 13, 14) and prospects for their development (Chapter 16). The scientist provides methods and samples of analysis, by which you can compare other countries belonging to the relevant groups. And although both works are based on the comparison of institutional systems, in the proposed approach it would be more correct to call it CA of institutions (CAI) rather than CIA.

Comparative studies of special institutional areas of the ES are widespread. However, most of them can only be attributed to the actual CIA. In addition, adherence to the principle of distinguishing the special/distinctive in comparable ES can serve as a key guideline for determining their belonging to the CA. Examples are the collective research *The Modern VAT* (Ebrill et al. 2001), *How are professors paid?* (Altbach et al, 2012), *The Global Future of Higher Education...* (Albrach et al. 2013) and *Pensions Panorama...* (Whitehouse 2007).

In the first example mentioned above, the basis of comparison (special/general) can be various institutional components of the functioning of modern VAT collection systems, the study of which is the work of IMF experts. However, the CA remains one of the additional tools that contribute to the main goal of the work: a systematic study of modern world practice of VAT collection. The aim is to determine the general characteristics as a tool of analysis of the VAT systems of the world (Ebrill et al. 2001). In the case of E. Whitehouse's study (2007), on the contrary, the first section presents the criteria for comparing the pension systems of 53 countries (the basis for determining the special characteristics as a tool of analysis of ES), and the second presents a regional country analysis. However, the "regionality" of the analysis is limited to the aggregation of the countries represented by region. Thus, the "comparison" in the proposed approach focuses on the presentation of systematic data on a single individual, that applies to a particular country.

In the case of the study of payment systems (Altbach et al, 2012), the chapters on the characteristics of payment systems in specific (single) countries are supplemented by those that substantiate the method of data collection and provide the possibility for their international comparison, identify the problems that arise, and present the results of comparative research and development trends of the world system of remuneration of higher education teachers (general, special and **single** characteristics of a system of remuneration in higher education). A prerequisite for the successful implementation of comparative research is a combination of both inductive and deductive methods.

The first fundamental work in the field of CIA ES itself was that of M. Aoki (2001). The author considers the branched structure of ES comparison criteria (general characteristics in ES) and the actual institutional tools of analysis (game theory). The first level consists of proto-institutions, which are very close in content to the basic institutions in the concept of IM. At the second level, there is a diversification of proto-institutions within the institutional areas of corporate governance, financing and innovation. It is at this level that the definitions of special and different in ES takes place. The scientist repeatedly emphasises the complementary conditionality of their institutional architecture. The practical value of the work is given in the chapters where theoretical developments are used to characterise the institutional structure of the Japanese system of major banks and the innovative model of Silicon Valley (single characteristics, specific to these models, as a tool of analysis).

The work of A. Greif (2006) in a CA of the trade networks of medieval Italy and the Maghreb also refers to the methodological developments of game theory. For a specific situation, the researcher constructs a specific model.

In the context of an emphasis on defining the special characteristics as a tool of analysis for comparable objects, which is the basis of comparative research, the method of qualitative comparative (institutional) analysis proposed by C. Ragin (1987) and revised by B. Kogut (2010) is of interest. It is based on the elements of the dialectical approach, enriched with the tools of formalisation and standardisation of economic research characteristics of the neoclassical direction. Ultimately, the results obtained can be used to confirm the validity of the original hypothesis, or to confirm a new understanding of the data that formed the basis of the analysis. An additional tool of analysis is the interpretation of the relationship between ethnic (emic) and ethical (etic) factors of behaviour.

Complementarity of elements as a basis of productivity of an institutional system

Attempts to define the preconditions for the functioning of ES as integral complexes lead to the appeal of the concepts of VoC, RT and IM to examine the phenomenon of complementarity of institutions (Amable 2016; Crouch et al. 2005).

The emphasis on the complementary conditionality of institutional systems allows a new approach to the definitions of general, individual and special in their structure. The selection of structural and functional components of institutional complementarity (IC), considered at the mega, macro, meso, micro and nano levels, allows us to focus on the basic principles of social interaction (collectivism, corporatism, individualism) (Lypov 2011; 2012). They are recognised as the initial basis of structural complementarity (SC) of institutional forms. SC defines the special in the structure of institutional systems and causes differences in the models of functional interaction (functional complementarity, FC) – complementarity of institutional functions. The whole institutional system is being built accordingly. Ultimately, these differences are embodied in the models of market, social democratic, mesocorporate and public capitalism.

In the case of SC, deductive methods of analysis are preferred. The specificity of social orientations of value systems determines the whole system of institutional forms. FC focuses on inductive analysis. Key importance acquire complementarity of institutional functions that ensure the successful functioning of institutional units of financing, corporate governance, industrial relations, training and retraining, production models, innovation systems, and the welfare state.

The methodological bases of comparative complementary research of institutions are: qualitative (analysis of the impact of economic values on the nature of structural complementarity); quantitative (analysis of indicators characterising the complementarity of individual institutions and institutional areas of SES); measurement (complementarity measure); structural (SC at different levels of SES); functional (FC elements of SES); systemic (SES in general and their individual components as integral phenomena); dialectical (dialectics of complementary relations at the level of basic SES institutions); historical-genetic (evolution of complementary principles of production methods); graphic (figures that characterise the structural and functional relationships between institutions); econometric (measurement of institutional complementarity at the SES level); ethnometric (using the results of ethnometric studies of value orientations of national cultures); and methods of constructing graphs (morphology of institutional interaction).

The advantage of comparative complementary analysis is the ability to predict the qualitative characteristics of institutions inherent in certain SES models based on knowledge of the key principle of their operation. In the case of institutional heterogenisation (within a single system, the coexistence of institutions different in their social orientations), comparative complementary analysis allows the identification of compensatory institutions that fill the institutional tension and gaps that arise when institutions borrowing - a case when an attempt is made to introduce institutions that have shown their effectiveness in other countries, countries belonging to the opposite IM.

Productivity and system integrity: ideal-typical in the institutional environment as a tool of comparative institutional analysis

The productivity of ES largely depends on the coordinated functioning of the whole complex of institutions and their complementarity. Accordingly, the way to ensure their productivity is through the formation of theoretical ideas about the internal basis of integrated ES, the institutional mechanisms of their functioning, and the relationship between the activities of individual economic entities and the productivity of the economic system as a whole. The origins of this approach can be found in G. Rickert's (1998) idea of the differentiation of methodological tools of research in the natural and cultural sciences. The natural sciences focus on the general features of the phenomenon (formation of concepts on the basis of its general features) but the sciences of culture focus on its specifics. Economic science is referred to as the intermediate zone and it recognises both options in demand, a combination of contradictory principles, that provide the formation of concepts on the basis of general features and on the basis of specific features that determine its specificity and uniqueness. (Rickert 1998, 103–111). In turn, M. Weber (1990) specifies the tools of such a combination through the formulation of the concept of ideal-typical as a tool of analysis.[7] It appears as an intermediate between the general and the individual as a tool of analysis; an interpretive scheme in which empirical facts are compared (Weber 1990, c. 397). In

---

[7] **Ideal-typical** – a methodological research tool, developed by M. Weber, which implies the formation of ideas about the ideal type of social phenomena by simplifying and idealising the complexity and diversity of social phenomena.

the case of the CIA ES, redistributive and market IM in Kirdina's IM concept, market and coordinated models of capitalism in VoC, types of social systems of production, methods of regulation and production, and modes of accumulation in RT can serve as examples of the ideal-typical as tools of analysis.

The origins of the idea of the existence of different IM organisation of economic activity can be found in the works of W. Euken (1940), K. Polanyi (1944), K. Wittfogel (1957) and S. Rosefielde (2002). In the concept of S. Kirdina (2014), the source of the formation of different IM is recognised features of the material-technological environment. The predominance of communal or non-communal characteristics determines the formation of opposite IM – redistributive X-economies and market Y-economies. They include complexes of alternative ideological[8], political[9] and economic[10] basic institutions. Understanding the system of forming principles of IM becomes the basis for building analytical tools to study the mechanism of action of the entire institutional complex and being able to ensure the productive functioning of the economy.

The work of M. Albert (1993) can be considered the first widely accepted attempt to present a CA of alternative institutional models of capitalism in order to justify the higher productivity of one of them. The starting point is to identify the contradictions between the alternative systems of capitalism. After the collapse of the socialist camp, these systems are recognised as a new engine of ES development. The criterion for the success of the latter is the level of social productivity. The scientist explores the significant differences in the institutional structure of the Rhine model, which emphasises collective achievement and public consensus, and a market model based on individual achievement and short-term profits. Criteria for CA of the institutional environment include attitudes to poverty, immigration, wage hierarchy, the role of enterprises in training, and the distribution of powers between shareholders, managers

---

[8] Collectivism/individualism; egalitarianism/stratification; order/freedom; well-being-oriented/pecuniary-oriented; integralism–holism–continuality/specialisation–reductionism–discecity.

[9] Vertical hierarchical authority with the centre on the top / self-governance and subsidiarity; appointment/election; general assembly with the rule of unanimity / multi-party system with the rule of a democratic majority; appeals to higher levels of hierarchical authority / legal suits.

[10] Redistribution (accumulation–coordination–distribution) / exchange (buying and selling); supreme conditional ownership / private ownership; cooperation/competition; employed (unlimited term) labour / contract (short and medium term) labour; cost limitation (X-efficiency) / profit maximisation (Y-efficiency).

and employees. There are differences in views on the impact of social protection on economic development and the tax system – on the growth of debt or savings. The differences between the systems of insurance (individualised / joint and several), social coordination (regulation–officials / deregulation–lawyers) and financing (bank/exchange), which dominate in these models of the institutional system, are studied. O. Gersemann's (2004) research leads to an alternative conclusion. The title of this work seems somewhat paradoxical; the author compares the models of "cowboy" (in the USA) and "cozy" (in Europe) capitalisms. However, it is claimed that the first model is not only more effective but also provides a higher level of social protection.

There is a growing attention to the CA of ES by representatives of Regulation Theory (RT). According to R. Boyer (1990), it is based on the emphasis on the dialectic of social relations, enriched by Keynesian ideas and works of historians of economics. Researchers focus on specific institutional forms of basic social relations, which are associated with the historical phases of society. Accordingly, there is interest in the institutional structures formed by them. These are based on market relations and capital/labour relations. A crisis is seen as a moment of reaching a certain limit and exacerbation of contradictions within the former method of regulation, leading to a decline in the productivity of the economic system. The task of economic theory in these conditions is to identify the causes of changing phases of the economic cycle and the proposal of adequate methods of regulating the economy. Regulation is seen as a combination of mechanisms that contribute to the reproduction of the whole, taking into account existing economic structures and social forms. The key terms RT is designed to provide a relationship between the theoretical and the empirical levels of research. These include social production systems, methods of regulation and production, accumulation regimes, structural (institutional) forms (money, labour relations, competition, ways to join the international regime, forms of state), and coordination mechanisms (markets, state, local communities, networks, associations). The basis of CA is not the national economies as a whole, but the sphere of production. RT focuses on the differences between the mass, Fordist type of production organisation, alternatives to flexible specialisation and the production of "diversified high-quality products". There are economies regulated mainly by markets and hierarchies (market capitalism) and those that use more diverse coordination mechanisms (institutional capitalism). The four main variants of capitalism include market-oriented (Anglo-Saxon countries), Rhine (Germany, Japan), state (France, Italy) and social democratic (Sweden, Austria).

The actual complementary relations between institutions and other forms of institutional interaction (supermodularity, coherence, consistency and compatibility), institutional complementarity and institutional hierarchy are distinguished. From the emphasis on the dominant value of the dual complementary relationship of production relations / financial sphere, there is a transition to the model of a three-component complementary institutional structure of effective growth regimes. It is recognised that in different countries the structure of the dominant areas, and the composition of institutional forms and functions that ensure dynamic development, can vary significantly.

The focus of VoC is the firm. The concept connects the properties of institutions with their functional contribution to inter-firm interaction. Variants of capitalism are considered as different modes of production, the key role in which is given to micro-agents – firms, owners, workers. The institutional explanation of the differentiation of capitalist models is based on the specifics of their behaviour. Firms are considered in the context of five institutional blocks: production relations, financial systems, corporate governance, training systems and inter-firm interaction. There are two basic types of production regimes: a liberal market economy and a coordinated market economy, both representing opposite ideal types. The Mediterranean version of the market economy is issued as an intermediate option.

Following M. Aoki, P. Hall and D. Soskis describe IC as the situation when the presence (efficiency) of one institution leads to the increased efficiency of another. On the contrary, if the absence or inefficiency of one institution leads to an increase in the efficiency of another, then such institutions are recognised as substitutional (Hall and Soskice 2001, 17). Scientists emphasise the complementarity of institutions between areas of the economy. The presence of a specific type of coordination in one stimulates the development of similar practices in others. So, long-term employment is complementary to long-term orientation in the financial sector. The practice of active inter-firm interaction extends to the blocks of financing and corporate governance, and education and training of personnel, and covers the system of industrial relations. P. Hall and D. Soskice (2001) argue that institutions are not established haphazardly but grouped into relatively related types of clusters. The closer they are to ideal modes of production, the more productive the economic system. The proposed models of capitalism demonstrate strong complementarity between basic institutional blocks, where the effectiveness of each institution depends on interaction with others (Hall and Soskice 2001, 28, 32).

The complementarity of economic and socio-political components of ES are recognized in the concept of social systems of innovation and production B. Amable prerequisite for the productivity of ES as a whole (Amable 2003). According to R. Boyer, it synthesises aspects of strategic interaction and equilibrium analysis, central to P. Hall and D. Soskice, with a sensitivity to social inclusion and institutional alternatives characteristic of RT (2000). The scientist considers five institutional areas: competition in production markets, the relationship between labour/wages (labour market institutions), finance and corporate governance, social protection / welfare state, and education/training systems. The classification of capitalist economies is based on their similarity (the use of cluster analysis) in these institutional areas. Four models of capitalism are proposed: market, social democratic, public (Mediterranean) and mesocorporate (Asian). The primary purpose of institutions is not to resolve problems of coordination between equal agents with similar interests, but to resolve conflicts among unequal actors with conflicting interests. B. Amable argues that institutional alternatives/configurations (and hierarchies of institutions) reflect the advantages of the dominant social bloc (2000).

Complementarity is seen as the aggregate institutional coherence of a group of institutions that arises as a result of their multilateral interaction in a single environment. It also provides increased productivity of ES. Since the institutions are in constant interaction, it is impossible to determine the effect of one of them separately from the others. The situation will change in different institutional environments. Changing one element of the system can have consequences that go far beyond the traditionally perceived IC patterns.

R. Whitley (1999) focuses on the comparison of institutional mechanisms to ensure productivity. The scientist proposed a systematic approach based on the differentiation of national business systems. They are considered as distinctive patterns of economic organisation, which vary in strength, the method of coordination of economic activities, and internal organisation of interaction between owners, managers, experts and employees (Whitley 1999, 33). At the heart of these differences in the organisation of coordination of business activity are the peculiarities of property relations or specific types of organisation that do not provide for its unification. Eight sections of institutional support for the performance of business systems are considered: methods of ownership control (direct, alliances, market); level of integration of production chains through ownership (low, medium, high); level of integration of industrial sectors through ownership; the degree of coordination of production chains through the formation of associations of producers; the level of cooperation between competitors; the prevalence of production associations in certain sectors of an economy; the level of delegation of authority and trust among employees. Based on the differentiation of strength (weak/strong) and the source (property rights / other factors) of coordination between firm interactions, six of their ideal types are identified. These are fragmented (competitive small businesses), coordinated industrial areas (cluster systems, like "Third Italy"), divided (large corporations, USA), partnerships (corporatism, Germany), state-organised and highly coordinated. The influence of property relations on the nature of coordination is of key importance in the distribution of the main types of business systems. An additional independent variable is the proposed vertical (production chains) or horizontal (economic sectors) type of coordination.

Unlike P. Hall and D. Soskice, R. Whitley carefully distinguishes between the institutional environment and organisational patterns. These institutional factors are associated with business systems through hypotheses about whether institutions stimulate or discourage the manifestation of the specifics of the latter. Thus, implicitly, the scientist moves onto the problem of complementarity.

The typology proposed by R. Whitley differs from the measurement of capitalist diversity in terms of its "deviations" from liberal Anglo-American "normal capitalism". Although the main criteria are similar to those proposed by P. Hall and D. Soskice, the introduction of different dimensions of ownership control and sectoral/cross-sectoral coordination reveals more detailed differences.

Inductive principles of comparative institutional analysis of economic systems

The methodological basis of the inductive approach to the CA of ES was initiated by the works of T. Koopmans and J. Montias (1971), and W. Duffy and E. Neuberger (1972). It can be reduced to three key statements. First, the most important economic categories have a system-specific nature and their content changes in the transition from one system to another. The terms "cost", "organisation", "planning" and "control" are not systemically neutral; in different systems, they may have different meanings. Second, the emphasis is on the "blurring" of the very concept of ES. Excessive abstraction, presentation as a specific empirical phenomenon, or identification with national economies should be avoided. It is necessary to take into account the presence of non-systemic factors (climate, geographical location, voluntarism of politicians). Third, it is recognised that the choice of the criterion of efficiency and productivity of the ES is usually determined by the value orientations of those who have the right to make decisions in the systems themselves, and of the researchers. As a starting point for research, the development of a universal language for describing ES was envisaged. Differentiation of ES as institutional structures took into account the influence of the peculiarities of the natural, material and technological, and social environments. It provided for the development of specific methods for assessing the systemic characteristics of specific economies and the recognition of their value conditionality. Focusing on socio-cultural value factors shaping the specifics of ES allows us to talk about the relationship of the proposed approach with institutional analysis.

Recognition of the greater variety of institutional ES models than those proposed by supporters of VoC and RT stimulates interest in the concept of the New Comparative Economy (Djankov et al. 2003). Its emergence was preceded by comparative quantitative studies of institutional support in the areas of finance (La Porta et al. 1998), corporate property (La Porta et al. 1999a) and public administration (La Porta et al. 1999b). The new comparative economy focuses on the study of institutional differences and their implications in areas such as enterprise management, wealth redistribution, property rights, financial relations, conflict resolution and the selection of political leaders. Thousands of references are obtained in comparative studies of minority shareholder protection systems (Djankov et al. 2008b), debt collection (Djankov et al. 2008a), private credit development (Djankov et al. 2007) and the regulation of industrial relations (Botero et al. 2004). The approaches used for quantitative CIA are becoming widespread and improved.

The eloquent study by R. Pariboni and P. Tridico (2019) can serve as an example of such an approach to defining CIA tools. The aim of the work is a theoretical and empirical analysis of the impact on the dynamics of labour productivity of European countries of key socio-economic factors. They are divided into four directions. The first characterises the rate of growth of non-residential, real, gross, fixed capital formation, excluding research and development. The second is the level of research spending. The third includes indicators that can characterise the level of encouragement for firms to implement labour-intensive technologies by deregulating the labour market and increasing the share of temporary employment. The fourth direction characterises the structural changes in the economy. Among the used indicators are: the share of workers involved in the production sector, the share of skilled workers and the share of labour in the service sector, whose wages are growing regardless of the dynamics of their productivity (manufacturing share, skilled services share, Baumol's disease of "services share") (Pariboni and Tridico 2019). The generalised analysis of separate empirical indicators of ES of the EU countries serves as a basis for formation of theoretical conclusions and practical offers concerning the improvement of institutional maintenance of growth of labour productivity in the countries of the union.

B. Egert (2016) focuses on MFP analysis of indicators that can serve as analytical tools for developing government policy to ensure productivity growth. They are divided into micro (enterprise), meso (industries), macro (national economies) and international levels. At the macro level, the starting point for assessing productivity is the absolute productivity frontier. At the meso level, as well as at the level of an individual enterprise, the initial indicator of productivity is the absolute limit of productivity. In turn, at the macro level, specific factors that can ensure productivity growth in the long run are taken into account. The key importance is given to indicators that characterise the influence of the state on innovation activity and openness of the national economy in the field of trade operations.

P. Castelnovo, C.F. Del Bo and M. Florio (2018) turn to an international comparative study of the impact of the quality of institutions on the productivity of state-owned and private property. Indicators that characterise the quality of the institutional environment are divided into internal and external groups. From the set of 50 indicators, divided into four groups (regulatory authority, regulatory mandate, regulatory regime, competition framework), the data of the first and fourth were used. In turn, a two-step procedure is used to determine total factor productivity (TFP). In the first stage, TFP is evaluated as the resulting use of all factors of the production process. The second step of the analysis involves the use of appropriate indicators to determine the impact on TFP of state ownership and the quality of state regulation.

R. Ganau and A. Rodriguez-Pose (2019) investigate the impact on the transformation of productivity of Western industrial enterprises of local institutional systems. To analyse the quality of the institutional environment, data from the European Quality of Government Index, calculated by the Institute of Quality of Government of the University of Gothenburg, are used. At the same time, to take into account the institutional specifics imposed by the region's membership in a certain national institutional system, data of the World Bank's Worldwide Governance Indicators (WGI) project on government efficiency, anti-corruption measures, the legal framework (rule of law) and government accountability were taken into account. Labour productivity is calculated taking into account the number of employees, and capital resources per employee (capital-to-employment ratio).

V. Doellgast and D. Marsden (2018) turn to a CA of the impact of institutions as a tool that can be both a resource and a constraint on the company's policy aimed at ensuring the growth of staff productivity. The study was conducted in the form of case studies on the basis of data from the telecommunications industries in Germany, France, Great Britain and Denmark. In addition to studying the relevant documentation and statistics, 109 interviews were conducted with managers (supervisors) and representatives of employees (workers' local representatives). The participants and representatives of stakeholders had the opportunity to get acquainted with the results and to take part in the discussion. The comments were used in the preparation of the final report. Institutional practices of labour market organisation and collective bargaining were compared. Emphasis was placed on the institutions for ensuring the participation of employees in the management of the enterprise (bodies, roles, single/dual channel of influence). Four models of productivity stimulation policy have been identified in the practice of resource constraints and resource provision.

C. Collin and K. Tarron (2018) conducted a comprehensive comparative study of the impact of economic structure on the productivity and evolution of ES development in Barbados, Guyana and Mauritius. The analysis of the presented case studies involved taking into account the peculiarities of the influence of geographical location and the dependence of the historical path of development on the development of economic productivity. The focus is on the patterns of evolution of the institutional system. The influence of the peculiarities of the natural economic environment is recognised as a prerequisite for the formation of the most productive institutions in this situation, and the institutional structure of the organisation of the process of social production and the distribution of results.

A group of researchers led by T. Lohwasser (Lohwasser et al. 2019) studied the impact on the productivity of a firm's diversification of production strategies. The focus is on the impact on unrelated/related diversification performance. Scientists used a multilevel meta-analytic approach. It involves taking into account the theoretical developments of concepts that use the analysis of transaction costs, agency costs and the study of the impact of resource security on the dynamics of productivity. The institutional environment is seen as a factor influencing the efficiency of market transactions. Among its key aspects are the formation of information asymmetry, increasing research costs and support for contracts. A set of hypotheses regarding the impact of diversification on productivity and its mechanisms is considered. The analysis of the block of hypotheses about the directions of influence of differentiation on productivity testifies to the possibility of both positive and negative influences. The mechanisms for determining its direction are explored through the analysis of hypotheses about the effectiveness of innovations that are interconnected or unrelated to the main activities of the enterprise.

M. Charilaos and S. Mona (2019) studied the impact of possibility of hiring qualified personnel on the productivity of enterprises in developing countries. In the research, the instrumental variables model with a GMM[11] estimator is used. The peculiarities of the institutional environment of individual countries are taken into account. They reflect the influence of institutional factors such as the level of economic and technological development, and the quality of the institutional management, financial system and education. The specifics of the geographical environment and field of activity are taken into account. The specifics of the impact of labour quality on the productivity of a firm at the micro, meso and macroeconomic levels can be traced.

L.T. Nhan and N.V. Tung (2017) investigated the relationship between the quality of institutions and productivity in provinces and cities of Vietnam. For this purpose, the possibilities of regression analysis based on the Cobb–Douglas production function are used. The net revenue of all enterprises in a given province or city is used as a measure of productivity. The quality of institutions is assessed through the Provincial Competitiveness Index of the province or city. In the regression model, this index is used as an independent variable. Regression models also take into account the total labour force that is employed and the average capital of all firms.

Conclusions

The fundamental transformation of the global economic system has led to significant changes in the theoretical and methodological foundations of the study of the environment of human economic activity. Interest in institutional theory is being restored. Analysis of the components of institutional systems is deepening. The influence of the features of the institutional structure for ensuring the growth of productivity is at the centre of attention of researchers. Deductive and inductive approaches to CA of the impact on productivity of different models of ES and their

[11] **Generalised method of moments** (GMM) is a generic method for estimating parameters in statistical models.

components are being developed. Depending on the purpose and the available information base, researchers have the opportunity to choose a wide range of methods and tools of analysis.

References

Albert, M. *Capitalism Vs. Capitalism*. New York: Four Wall Eight Windows, 1993.

Altbach, P., Androushchak, G., Kuzminov, Y., Yudkevich, M. and Reiserg, L. (eds.). *The Global Future of Higher of Education and the Academic Profession. The BRIC and the United States*. London: Palgrave Macmillan, 2013.

Altbach, P., Reisberg, L., Yudkevich, M., Androushak, G. and Pacheco, I. (eds.). *Paying the Professoriate. A Global Comparison of Compensation and Contracts*. New York: Routledge, 2012.

Amable, B. "Institutional Complementarity and Diversity of Social Systems of Innovation and Production." *Review of International Political Economy* 7, no. 4, April 2000: 645–687.

Amable, B. *The Diversity of Modern Capitalism*. Oxford: Oxford Press, 2003.

Amable, B. "Institutional complementarities in the dynamic comparative analysis of capitalism." *Journal of Institutional Economics* 12, no. 1 2016: 79–103.

Aoki, M. *Toward a Comparative Institutional Analysis*. Cambridge: MIT Press, 2001.

Bessonova, O. *Market and distribution in the Russian matrix*. M.: ROSSPEN, 2015.

Botero, C., Djankov, S., La Porta, R., Lopez-de-Silanes, F. and Shleifer, A. "The regulation of labor." *The Quarterly Journal of Economics* 119, no. 4, November 2004: 1339–1382.

Boyer, R. *The Regulation School: A Critical Introduction*. New York: Columbia University Press, 1990.

Boyer, R. "How and why capitalisms differ." *Economy and Society* 34, no. 4, November 2005: 526–527.

Castaldi, C. and Dosi, G. "The grip of history and opportunities for novelty: some results and open questions, related to the dependence on the previous trajectory of development in economic processes", *Terra economicus*. Moscow: Science Spectrum, 2008, pp. 105 - 143. [In Russian]

Castelnovo, P., Del Bo, C.F. and Florio, M. "Quality of institutions and productivity of State-Invested Enterprises: International evidence from major telecom companies." *European Journal of Political Economy* 10, no. 410, October 2018. doi: https://doi.org/10.1016/j.ejpoleco.2018.10.005.

Charilaos, M. and Mona, S. "Access to skilled labor, institutions and firm performance in developing countries." *International Journal of Manpower* 40, no. 2, February 2019: 328–355.

Collin, C. and Tarron, K. "Geography, Economic Structures and Institutions: A Synthesis. Working Papers in Technology Governance and Economic Dynamics," no. 80, 2018. Oslo/Tallin; Other Canon Foundation/Tallinn University of Technology, 47 p.

Crouch, C. and Streeck, W. *Political Economy of Modern Capitalism: Mapping Convergence and Diversity*. London: Sage, 1997.

Crouch, C., Streeck, W., Boyer, R., Amable, B., Hall, P. and Jackson, G. "Dialogue on Institutional Complementarity and Political Economy." *Socio-Economic Review* 3, no. 2 April 2005: 359–382.

Djankov, S., Glaeser, E., La Porta, R., Lopez-de-Silanes, F. and Shleifer, A. "The new comparative economics." *Journal of Comparative Economics* 31, no. 4, 2003: 595–619.

Djankov, S., McLiesh, C. and Shleifer, A. "Private credit in 129 countries." *Journal of Financial Economics* 84, no. 2, February 2007: 299–329.

Djankov, S., Hart, O., McLiesh, C. and Shleifer, A. "Debt enforcement around the world." *Journal of Political Economy* 116, no. 6, 2008a: 1105–1149.

Djankov, S., La Porta, R., Lopez-de-Silanes, F. and Shleifer, A. "The law and economics of self-dealing," *Journal of Financial Economics* 88, no. 3, March, 2008b: 430–465.

Doellgast, V. and Marsden, D. "Institutions as constraints and resources: Explaining crossnational divergence in performance management. Human Resource." *Management Journal* 29, no. 2, August 2018: 199–216.

Duffy, W. and Neuberger, E. "Toward a Decision-theoretic Approach to the Study of economic Systems." *Jahrbuch der Wirtschaft Osteuropas* 3, no. 1, 1972: 67–86.

Ebrill, L., Keen, M., Bodin, J. and Summers, V. (eds.). *The Modern VAT*. New York: IMF, 2001.

Egert, B. "Regulation, Institutions, and Productivity: New Macroeconomic Evidence from OECD Countries." *American Economic Review: Papers & Proceedings* 106, no. 5, May 2016: 109–113.

Eucken, W. *Principles of the national economy*. Jena: Gustav Fisher, 1940.

Ferdousi, F. "Determinants of Performance of Microfinance Institutions: Cross Country Analysis International." *Journal of Financial Economics* 1, no. 4, 2013: 143–151.

Ganau, R. and Rodríguez-Pose, A. "Do high-quality local institutions shape labour productivity in western European manufacturing firms?" *Discussion Paper* DP13703, Centre for Economic Policy Research, London, 2019.

Gersemann, O. *Cowboy Capitalism: European Myths, American Reality*. Washington, DC: Cato Institute, 2004.

Greif, A. "Contract Enforceability and Economic Institutions in Early Trade: The Maghribi Traders' Coalition." *American Economic Review* 83, no. 3, March 1993: 525–548.

Grief, A. "Cultural Beliefs and the Organization of Society: A Historical and Theoretical Reflection on Collectivist and Individualist Societies." *Journal of Political Economy* 102, no. 5, May 1994: 912–950.

Greif, A. *Institutions and the Path to the Modern Economy. Lessons from Medieval Trade*. Cambridge: Cambridge University Press, 2006.

Hall, P. and Soskice, D. "An Introduction to Varieties of Capitalism. Varieties of Capitalism." In: *The Institutional Foundations of Comparative Advantage*, edited by P. Halland and D. Soskice, 1–70. Oxford: Oxford University Press, 2001.

Hollingsworth, J. *Contemporary Capitalism: The Embeddedness of Institutions. Cambridge Studies in Comparative Politics*. Cambridge: Cambridge University Press, 1997.

Ilyenkov, E. "Dialectical logic: essays on history and theory." In: E. Ilyenkov, *Sobr. ess. Vol. 4.* M.: Politizdat, 2020.

Kirdina, S. *Institutional matrices and the development of Russia: an introduction to the X-Y theory*. SPb.: Nestor-History, 2014.

Kogut, B. "Qualitative Comparative Analysis of Social Science Data." In: *The Oxford Handbook of Comparative Institutional Analysis*, edited by G. Morgan, J. Campbell, C. Crouch, O. Pedersen and R. Whitley, 139–179. Oxford: Oxford University Press, 2010.

Koopmans, T. and Montias, J. "On the Description and Comparison of Economic Systems." In: *Comparison of Economic Systems*, edited by A. Eckstein, 29–41. London: Becerley, 1971.

La Porta, R., Lopez-de-Silanes, F., Shleifer, A. and Vishny, R. "Law and finance." *Journal of Political Economy* 106, no. 6, June 1998: 1113–1155.

La Porta, R., Lopez-de-Silanes, F. and Shleifer, A. "Corporate ownership around the world." *The Journal of Finance* 54, no. 2, February, 1999a: 471–517.

La Porta, R., Lopez-de-Silanes, F., Shleifer, A. and Vishny, R. "The quality of government." *The Journal of Law, Economics, and Organization* 15, no. 1, March, 1999b: 222–279.

Lohwasser, T., Wagner, D., Van Essen, M., Lander, M. and William, M. "Do Institutions Matter for the Relationship between Diversification and Performance? A Meta-Analysis," *Academy of Management Proceedings* 2019, no 1, August 2019. https://journals.aom.org/doi/10.5465/AMBPP. 2019.82 27.07.2020.

Lypov, V. *Institutional complementarity of socio-economic systems*. Kh.: Izd-vo V.N. Karazin KhNU, 2011.

Lypov V. "Institutional complementarity as a factor in the formation of socio-economic systems." *Journal of Institutional Studies* 4, no. 1, 2012: 25–42.

Mersland, R. and Strom, R.O. "Performance and corporate governance in microfinance institutions." *MPRA Paper No. 3887,* July, Munich University Library, Munich, 2007, 37. https://mpra.ub.uni-muenchen.de/3887/ 26.07.2020.

Morgan, G., Campbell, J., Crouch, C., Pedersen, O. and Whitley, R. (eds.). *The Oxford Handbook of Comparative Institutional Analysis*. Oxford: Oxford University Press, 2010.

Nhan, L.T. and Tung, N.V. "Any links between economic performance and institutional quality? Evidence from Vietnam provinces and cities." *Asian Journal For Poverty Studies* 3, no. 2, December 2017: 118–124.

North, D. *Institutions, institutional change and economic performance*. Cambridge: University press, 1990.

North, D. "Institutions." *Journal of Economic Perspectives* 5, no. 1, January 1991: 97–112.

Pariboni, R. and Tridico, P. "Structural change, institutions and the dynamics of labor productivity in Europe." *Journal of Evolutionary Economics*, 30, no. 10, October 2019: 1275–1300. https://doi.org/10.1007/s00191-019-00641-y.

Polanyi, K. *The Great Transformation.* New York: Farrar & Rinehart, 1944.

Ragin, C. *The Comparative Method: Moving Beyond Qualitative and Quantitative Strategies*. Berkeley: University of California Press, 1987.

Rickert, G. *Natural Sciences and Cultural Sciences*. M.: Respublika, 1998.

Rosefielde, S. *Comparative Economic Systems: Culture, Wealth, and Power in 21st Century.* Malden, Massachusetts & Oxford: Wiley-Bleckwell, 2002.

Schmidt, V. "Comparative institutional analysis." In: *Handbook of Comparative Politics,* edited by Todd Landman and Neil Robinson, 125–143. London: Sage, 2000.

Schnitzer, M. *Comparative Economic System.* Nashville: South-Western Pub. Co, 1994.

Soskice, D. "Divergent Production Regimes: Coordinated and Uncoordinated Market Economies in the 1980s and 1990s." In: *Continuity and Change in Contemporary Capitalism*, edited by H. Kitschelt et al., 101–134.Cambridge, UK: Cambridge University Press, 1999.

Weber, M. "Objectivity of socio-scientific and socio-political consciousness." In: *Weber M. Selected works*, 345–414. M.: Progress, 1990.

Whitehouse, E. *Pensions Panorama: Retirement-Income Systems in 53 Countries.* Washington: World Bank, 2007.

Whitley, R. *Divergent Capitalisms: The Social Structuring and Change of Business Systems*. Oxford: Oxford University Press, 1999.

Wittfogel K. *Oriental Despotism: A Comparative Study of Total Power.* Yale University Press, 1957.

CHAPTER SEVEN

EFFECTS OF FOREIGN DIRECT INVESTMENT ON LABOUR PRODUCTIVITY

OLGA V. NOSOVA

The role of foreign direct investment in a country's economy

The study of foreign direct investment (FDI) effects on the productivity of local firms addresses a research effort to assess the likely impacts of enhanced FDI activity within emerging economies. This paper aims to understand the effects of FDI on the labour productivity of local firms and to identify factors that will support the development of a more effective policy to encourage attractive FDI practices in Ukraine. Tinflow increase of foreign capital in recent years demonstrates that workers in industries with greater foreign participation experience faster wage growth. The actual relationship between horizontal and vertical FDI spillover effects remains unclear, although the available research has identified some positive correlations.

Recent studies have highlighted the considerable research efforts in developing an understanding on the subject of the investment motivation of FDI spillover effects, its impact on economic growth, competitive advantages inside the developed economies, and draw attention to short-term adjustment problems rather than to the long-term possibilities. Empirical studies of FDI spillover effects on domestic firms reflect various factors, conditions, and characteristics of the firm, at industry and national levels. The reported results do not reproduce the ambiguous effects of economic sectors on labour productivity, or undervalued labour costs per worker, and do not take into account the role of the shadow economy in the countries of Central, Eastern, and Southeast t Europe. Inadequate skills and education of workers have been considered to be a major or severe obstacle for multinational firms' operations in many developing countries.

The government policy of FDI inflow liberaliation induces incentives for foreign companies to enter the local markets of other countries. Government support for education and training, and the realisation of benefits arising from FDI have prompted governments to encourage FDI inflow. This paper discusses the challenges faced by governments in creating policies to attract FDI practices in emerging economies.

The inflow of FDI stimulates the development of new technologies, management, marketing, and the use of advanced methods of labour organisation. The FDI inflows affect and promote labour productivity changes. The higher wage rates lead to rising aggregate demand. The higher investment, along with total productivity improvements, could reinforce the current account position. The increasing technological transparency of the information society emerging in European countries, as well as growing intra-European bilateral FDI links, have contributed to a greater incidence of technology spillovers and external scale economies.

Globalisation has affected the creation and enlargement of the world's supply of a relatively unskilled labour force. The economic consequences of globalisation depict international competition in increasing labo-intensive products and trade. As a result of it, international trade for new products rises. It stimulates the redistribution of the labour force from high-skilled sectors to unskilled sectors. There is a growing number of unskilled workers in East European countries. High unemployment rates in market economies are combined with a large share of concealed unemployment in East European countries and this calls for government interventions in labour markets. It is important to mention the role of the government as the political institution that should correct market forces to provide adjustments in the institutional framework. The penetration of transnational corporations (TNCs) into the domestic market accelerates product development, creates new working places, brings in the new management of the organisation, and improves the welfare of workers. The problem of the relationship between labour quality and labour cost has been subject to many scientific works.

One can mention that low wages in developing countries attract FDI. Nevertheless, there are surveys that reveal most FDI occurs between countries with similar wages (UNCTAD 2001, 123). The majority of low-wage countries have the lowest levels of FDI. The COVID-19 crisis negatively affected the movement of international capital. In the first half of 2020, global FDI flows fell by 50% compared with the last half of 2019, to $364 billion, as a consequence of the pandemic and the resulting supply disruptions, demand contractions, and pessimistic outlook of economic actors (OECD 2020, 2020).

The physical closure of places and construction sites resulted in a reduction in international production, and disruption of supply and distribution chains. Delays of greenfield projects and the reduction in mergers and acquisitions (M&A) have prevented FDI inflows from rising, and this highlights the negative consequences of the pandemic's effects on international investment policies.

Foreign direct investment and human capital: economic analysis of the relationship

Scientists consider capital movement in the form of FDI as the major source of capital attraction. **Cross-border capital movements** may increase opportunities for investment attraction and creates challenges for agencies. Empirical surveys of the international organisations UNCTAD, World Bank, IMF and WIFO have pointed out that the basic volume of the cross-sectional movement of capital flows is carried out in the form of FDIs. Positive effects of this on the economy of the recipient country include an increase in the volume of real capital investments, an acceleration in the pace of economic development, an improvement of the country's balance of payments, receipt of advanced foreign technology, organisational and managerial experience, and the results embodied in new technology, patents, licenses and know-how. Foreign capital inflow increases the level of employment and qualifications of the local labour force, raising the productivity of the labour, and improves the standard of living and purchasing power of the population. Changes in skill structures and job characteristics demonstrate a cautious upturn in economic activities in East European countries upturn over the last decade this region has maintained its cost competitiveness, despite surging wages and occasional labour shortages, by benefiting from considerable productivity improvements (UNCTAD 2018). Negative consequences of foreign capital inflow include: suppressing local producers and limiting competition, repatriation of capital and transfers of profits in various forms (dividends, interest, royalties) which worsens the balance of payments, increasing dependence of the national economy on foreign states which threatens the economic and political security of the recipient country, and ignoring local conditions and peculiarities by foreign investors.

Questions about the size of FDI's role in the process of capital formation and total investment escalation have received ambiguous consideration in the economic literature. FDI inflows are not always accompanied by the creation and return of fixed capital. The purchase of a company by a foreign investor leads to a change in property relations.

The UNCTAD forecast for global FDI flows demonstrates a decrease by up to 40%, from a value of $1.54 trillion, and projects a further decline by 5–10% in 2021 comparing to 2020 (UNCTAD "2020a", 2020, 8). The unstable situation with the COVID-19 pandemic in the world, ineffective measures to curb the development of the virus, disruptions in the supply chain, the introduction of tough conditions in financial markets, and changes in human needs and behaviour at the markets have forced investors to delay the implementation of international projects. The reduction in production caused by the emergency in the health care system has led to greater losses of human lives. The unpredictability has affected the global economy in the acceleration of instability of international investors' economic behaviour. Uncertainty also reduces demand in the private sector, increases households' savings and reduces their expenditures (Paskeleva 2020, 76). Economic policy plays an active role in stimulating aggregate demand. The adoption of support measures for the economic development of the most vulnerable sectors in the pandemic, such as services (tourism), restaurants, entertainment and construction, provides the basis for protecting workers in affected sectors.

On average, the top 5000 multinational enterprises (MNEs), which account for a significant share of global FDI, have seen downward revisions of 2020 earnings estimates of 9% due to COVID-19. The hardest hit are the automotive industry (−44%), airlines (−42%), and energy and basic materials industries (−13%). Profits of MNEs based in emerging economies are more at risk than those of MNEs in developed countries; profit guidance for the latter has been revised downwards by 16% (UNCTAD "2020b". 2020. Impact of the Coronavirus outbreak on global FDI. P.1).

Dingel and Neiman (2020) provide estimates of the share of non-standard workers who are particularly vulnerable to the loss of income or jobs as a result of the impact of COVID-19. For the purposes of analysis, Dingel and Neiman consider non-standard forms of work and include part-time workers, the self-employed and workers hired on fixed-term contracts. Their study relates labour market disruptions, and discusses what policies can do and what policy actions governments have taken, to support vulnerable workers and promote an inclusive labour market recovery. Cavalleru Cuasa (2020) provide estimations of total employment in European countries. In the sectors most directly affected, non-standard workers represent around 40% of total employment on average across European countries, ranging from about 20% in Latvia and Lithuania, to more than 50% in Italy, the Netherlands, Spain, and Greece (Cavalleru and Cuasa 2020).

After a decline of 37% in 2019 (to $24 billion), outward FDI from economies in transition is expected to continue to decline in 2020 and 2021, as economic recessions in home economies and low oil prices affect the capacities of MNEs from the region to invest abroad. FDI flows to the transition economies of Southeast Europe, the Commonwealth of Independent States (CIS), and Georgia, hit hard by the economic downturn caused by COVID-19, are projected to decline by around 38% in 2020. These flows will not recover before 2022, according to UNCTAD 2020 b (2000).

Total investments into a fixed capital can be made in the case of financing projects with the attraction of bank credits. An analysis of the variety of points of view allows a conclusion to be drawn on the prevalence of capital formation. In particular, Dohrn and Heilemann (1996), and Graham (2000) consider FDI as one of the financial sources of fixed capital formation abroad, namely debt financing, capital market financing, and subsidies. Krkoska (2001) argues that capital formation is positively associated with FDI, along with domestic debt and capital market financing, but negatively correlated with stock market liquidity.

As the most widespread form of FDI inflow in less developed countries, "zero" investments (greenfield investments) act which are made in the form of new enterprises. A greenfield investment is a type of foreign direct investment where a company starts its operation in another countr as its subsidiary and invests in the construction of offices, plants, sites, building products, etc. hereby, it manag its operations and achieves the highest level of controls over its activities. In a greenfield project, a company's plant construction, for example, is done to its specifications, employees are trained to company standards and fabrication processes can be tightly controlled. New investments accelerate economic growth by increasing supply both nationally and in terms of the companies that are controllable by foreign proprietors under liberalised trade conditions in the country (Graham 2000). Based on the above, it is necessary to note that the growth of the international movement of capital is accompanied by the amplification of TNCs expansion in the countries of the CIS. The source of savings growth is FDI, borrowing from international organisations, with assistance from developed countries. The growth of domestic savings affects the inflow of FDI and stimulates the economic growth in the country. The levels of gross savings and savings rates vary from country to country. Scientists highlight connections between economic growth, incomes, and savings rates. In the short run, a growth rate of savings leads to a quantitative rise in production. In the long run, this process is accompanied by increases in capital intensity and the volume of produced output.

The development of privatisation and commercial activity opened and expanded access for foreign capital on the new markets and stimulated the creation of new manufacturing branches in countries that were recipients of foreign capital. In Table 7-1, data of the net annual FDI inflow/outflow in transition countries during the period from 2014 to 2019 is shown. It can be seen that the Russian Federation and Ukraine are falling behind the Central and East European countries, including European Union countries, on capital exports.

In bound FDI to economies in transition increased sharply in 2019 (by 59% to $55 billion), due to higher inflows in some large countries, especially the Russian Federation, Ukraine, and Uzbekistan. Flows to the rest of the region declined slightly (down 3% to $19 billion). In Ukraine, FDI flows rose by 30%, to $3.1 billion, after two years of decline. Finance, ICT, mining, real estate, and electricity and gas attracted the bulk of FDI (UNCTAD 2020b, 56).

Table 7-1. Net annual FDI flows (in million US dollars)

	2014	2015	2016	2017	2018	2019
Hungary	0.00	0.00	0.00		0.50	0.00
Poland	0.05	0.13	0.36	0.14	0.22	0.65
Slovakia	0.00	0.00	0.32		0.01	0.01
Slovenia	0.00	0.00	2.40		0.23	0.22
Czech Republic		0.09	10.09	0.11	0.07	0.11
Russian Federation	0.00	0.05	0.01	0.00		0.11
Ukraine	0.00	0.00	0.00	0.00	0.00	0.01

Source: Constructed using World Bank data, Net Foreign Direct Investment Flows (BPM 6) (2020), https://www.bsp.gov.ph/statistics/external/tab10_fdc.aspx

A significant share of FDI, at about one-third of the value in 2020, is estimated to be a round-tripping of the Ukrainian capital through offshore centers. FDI outflows from Ukraine reached $ 0.6 billion in 2019 (UNCTAD 2020 a, 57). Market-seeking projects will also suffer in that country and in others in the region as the economic downturn deepens. Foreign affiliates are facing exceptionally challenging operational, market and financial conditions. Their profits are expected to plummet in 2020 (UNCTAD 2020 a, 22).

Based on the above mentioned, we presume that international capital movement is accompanied by increasing international penetration and expansion of TNCs in transition countries. The internationalisation rate of companies from developing to transition economies increased by almost 2%, with foreign assets and sales growing faster (UNCTAD 2020 b, 24). There is comparison data of employment by foreign affiliates for the whole year in 1990 and 2019. It increased from 27,729 in 1990 to 82,360 in 2019 (UNCTAD 2020 b, 8). The pandemic and low oil prices have affected FDI flows.

Estimation of the pandemic's impact on global capital movements has drawn the attention of scientists towards the consequences resulting in recession in economies, production or supply chain disruption, a reduction in employment and an increase in unemployment, and an increase in inequality (UNCTAD 2020 b).

The relationship between foreign direct investment and labour productivity

The problem of interdependence between the quality and cost of labour has been a subject of many scientific works by economists in high income and transition countries. Labour productivity is the ratio of the volume of production in a specific time. The assessment of labour productivity is calculated as the volume of production per employee, the volume of net production, or the number of parts per hour worked.

In order to account the production takes into account the production and service sectors in labour productivity estimation requires deep theoretical research and its practical application. Restructuring processes affect labour markets and the study of labour market developments. The definition of labour productivity is based on its determination as a whole and at the level of branches, companies, individual workers, products, etc. Labour productivity could be defined as the rate of output per worker (or a group of workers) per unit of time, as compared with an established standard or expected rate of output.

Bulkley and Van Alstyne (2004, 5) differ the rate of growth of real product and the rate of growth of real factor input. The rates of growth of real product and real factor input are estimated, in turn, as weighted averages of the rates of growth of individual products and factors. Productivity increase is differentiated from the substitution of factors due to changes in the relative prices of inputs, which are identified when moving along the production function.

The main difference of labour productivity measurement in the USA from the dimension approach in East European countries is that the analysis includes both production and service spheres. The production value increase is created on three quarters by labour and on one quarter by capital. It means an increase is larger via labour than by capital in the process of product creation (Samuelson and Nordhouse 1995).

Comparison the narrow and broad definitions of labour productivity, there are two main approaches to its estimation. Sink (1995) suggests seven indices that affect a company's performance for labour productivity assessment. They include the following: efficiency, quality, labour environment, innovations and profit. The suggested approach is based on the measurement of specific indices for labour productivity efficiency. Little (1981) argues that labour productivity should be calculated through only one index. In this approach, labour productivity is defined as a broad category. The main motivation mechanism behind a company's good performance is considered to be profit maximisation. Labour productivity measurement depends on the internal technological organisation. Policies to improve labour productivity suggest *investment in physical capital: increasing the investment in capital goods; quality of education and training: offering opportunities, education, and training at an affordable cost; technological progress: developing new technologies.*

The neoclassical approach considers that efficient collective bargaining should occur at the company level, so that highly differentiated wages can be matched with highly differentiated labour productivities while price stability is maintained. Alcacer (2000, 12) asserts that wages have a negative and significant impact on FDI for countries with a high level of human capital.

Scientific discussions on the ratio of the quality and cost of labour confirm the relevance of FDI effects. Vahter (2004) asserts that different types of foreign direct investment can have different effects on the host country and that the existence of positive spillovers may depend on the level of economic development of the host country.

Measuring labour productivity depends on the company's internal technological organisation and market conditions. The proportion of all job changes that move workers from lowerproductivity firms to higherproductivity firms is only marginally higher than the proportion of those in the opposite direction. Almost half (49%) of all job changes move workers toward firms that have lower productivity levels than their previous employer (Albagli et al., 2021).

The main problem of the labour market in CIS countries is the low efficiency of workers. This determines the high share of wages in a commodity's value, which stimulates inflation. Scientific estimations confirm a significant share of spending on priority needs in the basket of consumer goods. In Ukraine, there is an inadequate growth rate of wages and productivity.

If we take the base as the first quarter of 2001, then real wages have tripled and labour productivity has increased 1.7 times (Shapovalov, 2007). It should be noted that if wages grow significantly at your own pace than labour productivity, then additional income is not earned by faster (efficient) work of individuals but workers receive wage in the process of redistribution.

Data analysis of the relationship between GDP and unemployment in Ukraine demonstrates inverse fluctuations (see Figure 7-1). After jumping to almost 10% in the second quarter of 2020, the unemployment rate will gradually return to neutral. The GDP growth does not demonstrate a significant value-added related to material production. Most of the GDP growth is provided by components that are not directly related to material production (net taxes, wholesale and retail trade) and, accordingly, the provision of adequate commodity coverage for the growing demand of the population. Sustainable development is associated with the improvement of the labor market and creation of the new jobs, professions, and personnel.

With the help of FDI, countries encourage the creation of jobs, expand local technical knowledge, and increase their overall economic standards. Shapovalov (2007) considers that domestic companies import technologies from MNCs through the purchase of production equipment, receive inputs from foreign-owned firms. The impact of outflows of FDI from transition countries on the host country's economic growth differs by distinguishing between the growth effects of horizontal (market-seeking) FDI and vertical (efficiency-seeking) FDI. Beugelsdijk et al. (2008) find that horizontal and vertical FDI have positive and significant growth effects in developed countries. The authors indicate a superior growth effect of horizontal FDI over vertical FDI and find no significant effects of horizontal or vertical FDI in developing countries.

The external effect of the interaction of foreign branches and domestic firms on the horizontal or vertical levels is accompanied by increased productivity in the country. Growing demand for intermediate products is forcing domestic firms to take advantage of economies of scale. FDI flows in transition economies in Southeast Europe and CIS declined by 27% in 2017, to $47 billion, the second-lowest level since 2005. Outflows from transition economies rose by 59% to $40 billion starting from 2016 to 2017 (UNCTAD 2018, 18).

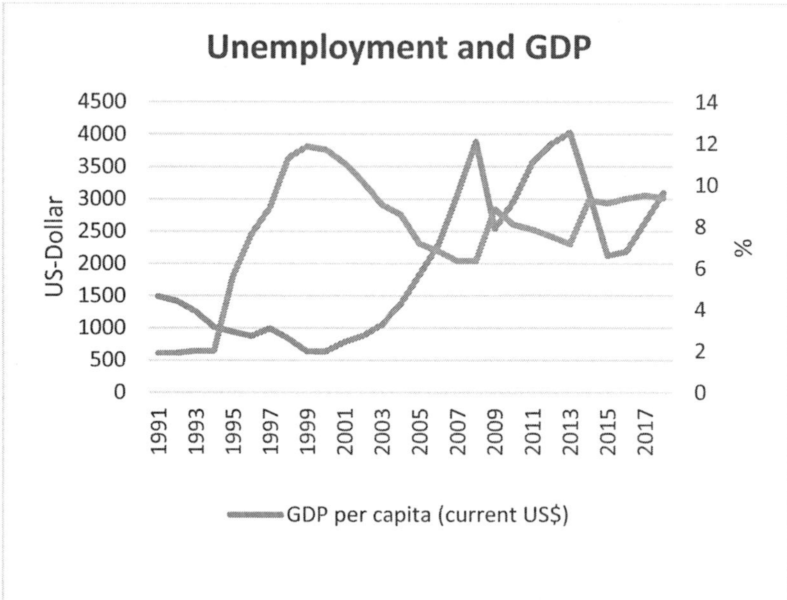

Figure 7-1. Gross domestic product and unemployment in Ukraine
Source: Constructed on data http://ukrstat.gov.ua.

To ensure the sustainable development of a country, it is necessary to ensure the growth of labour productivity. Trade policies can stimulate exports and imports, especially of intermediate and capital goods, which can lead to gains in productivity. In addition, encouraging firms to innovate and conduct research and development activities through fiscal incentives and financial benefits that are aimed at making industry (in particular, manufacturing) and services more efficient, technologically up to date and competitive can also lead to growth in productivity (Sharma, 2010).

Analysis by United Nations ESCAP (2015) revealed that, while the quality of the domestic business regulatory environment in the host country is generally the key determining factor in attracting FDI, high trade costs also have a significant impact on FDI. Indeed, a 10% reduction in comprehensive international trade costs (excluding tariffs) between source and host country leads to an 8% increase in FDI inflows on average (United Nations ESCAP 2015). Import tariffs of the host country are also found to have a significant but small negative impact on FDI inflows (United Nations Jude and Levieuge (2014, 27) show that FDI has a positive effect on growth only beyond a certain threshold of institutional quality. To benefit from FDI-led growth, institutional reforms should thus precede FDI attraction policies. Additionally, some reforms seem to promote faster marginal effects of FDI, while institutional complementarities may lead to an incremental effect on growth (United Nations ESCAP Published 2015. Accessed 16 June 2015).

Domestic companies import technologies from MNCs through the purchase of production equipment, industrial capacity, and differentiated products. Jude and Levieuge (2014, 27) show that FDI has a positive effect on growth only beyond a certain threshold of institutional quality. To benefit from FDI-led growth, institutional reforms should thus precede FDI attraction policies. Additionally, some reforms seem to promote faster marginal effects of FDI, while institutional complementarities may lead to an incremental effect on growth. Competition development among domestic firms, productivity increases, the construction of new organisational and production structures, and the introduction of new technologies all attract FDI inflow (Nosova 2016, 20).

Scientific debates on the relationship between the quality and cost of labour confirm that the impact of FDI on productivity can be either direct or indirect. Inward FDI is associated with the introduction of additional capital, and new products and managerial skills that have a direct effect on productive efficiency. FDI also provides indirect effects by knowledge diffusion (Blomström Kokko, 2001). Estrin et al. (2009, 711) identified 17 studies that examined the indirect effect of ownership on employment and found a marked tendency for privatised firms with foreign owners to increase employment relative to firms under state ownership. FDI via privatisation to foreign owners contributed to unemployment and enhanced competitiveness in the long run.

The effects of FDI on host countries' economies are mainly related to increasing labour productivity through technological transfers, and management and marketing proficiency that enables long-term technological progress and economic growth. Authors have shown that that the effect of privatization is mostly positive in Central Europe but quantitatively smaller than that to foreign owners and greater in the later than earlier transition period. In the Commonwealth of Independent States, privatization to foreign owners yields a positive or insignificant effect while privatization to domestic owners generates a negative or insignificant effect. Through technology transfer and technology spillovers FDI can facilitate international collaboration on R&D.

M&A is a widespread form of company penetration into national markets. Innovations in goods reduce future employment opportunities for unskilled labour. New technological industries require a high level of qualifications of employees.

MNCs try to place labor-intensive products in Eastern Europe and Asia, where wages and units of labour costs are cheaper than in Western Europe. Wage pressures are encouraged by increasing capital intensity and the need to increase the volume of R&D. These measures improve the quality of products and force companies to maintain higher prices in world markets. The introduction of new technologies requires skilled workers, as they cope better with technological change.

This is true for different types of firms and different levels of technological development. Technology transfers by multinational firms and the application of technology by local firms require the use of a minimum of human capital and the training of a skilled workforce. The use of new technologies usually requires significant organisational changes of companies. MNCs are accompanied better by the attraction of a skilled labour force. Lack of employees with higher education can be a more deterrent for firms in production and value-added services than for less complex production processes.

The lack of skilled workers is a common problem for firms in MNCs in developing countries. This is especially so for companies that plan to innovate and expand their scale of production. World Bank data (UNCTAD 2006, 136-137) shows that firms that consider the shortage of skilled workers to be a "major" or "very serious" constraint are those that improve their production processes. These firms are also more likely to invest in training their workforce. While large firms have the opportunity to organise internal training for their workforce, smaller firms often do not provide such functions.

A healthy investment climate increases the incentive for people to attain a higher level of education. This is the best indication of the large increase in income from education in the former centrally planned economies during their transition to market systems. Similar patterns have emerged in other countries. A high level of formal education is not required for all firms or activities. A lack of employees with higher education can be more of a deterrent for firms in manufacturing and value-added services than for less complex production processes.

The allocation of a large stock of MNC's foreign investment abroad may lead to its relocation in the event of real political and economic threats. The parent company will stimulate FDI outflows and capital transfers to new locations. Multinational firms use a model of negotiation abroad that they are familiar with in terms of international relations (IR) and international business (IB), and reconstituting intellectual boundaries.

Highlighting two approaches, Jarvis (2005, 220) suggests that the construction of new interdisciplinary rubrics jointly created from IR and IB offers a better means of appreciating the changing character of the global political economy, and some of its most important actors and emerging processes.

Increasing labour productivity can be ensured by minimising labour costs. Labour productivity is influenced by socio-economic factors, including: the level of qualifications and professional knowledge, skills, competence, responsibility, and professional suitability. Technological factors determine the level of technology. They are characterised by the modernisation of equipment, new technology, the level of modernisation, and the use of automatic equipment, new materials, and energy sources. Organisational factors determine the quality of labour and equipment, and include the improvement of the production system, new progressive labour forms, and the labour motivation system. Labour productivity can be estimated using indicators of the quality of labour, efficient equipment and technology, and the organisation of labour.

Effects of foreign direct investment and their impact on labour productivity

The objective of the study addresses FDI spillover effects leading to an increase in the productivity level of local firms and competition in Eastern Europe. The actual relationship between horizontal and vertical FDI spillover effects remains unclear, although the available research has identified some positive correlations. The use of the comparative analysis method for the practice of attracting foreign capital provides a sound policy and an appropriate analysis of crucial challenges to encourage FDI inflow.

Spillover effects comprise technology transfer, labour and management training, „supplier "results. Two indirect effects of the presence of foreign capital take place externally, to other firms in the host economy. Direct effects of foreign capital result in economic growth. Indirect effects of foreign capital within the host economy can take the form of horizontal or vertical spillovers of capital flows.

An evaluation of various empirical studies of FDI spillover effects on domestic firms reflecting various factors, conditions, technologies, products, and characteristics at the firm, industry, and national levels is summarised in Table 7.2.

Table 7.2. Technology spillovers from TNCs: empirical studies

	Author	Subject of research	Country	FDI spillover effects
1.	Acharya & Keller (2007)	Manufacturing industries	USA	Significant external effects for SMEs
2.	Boghean & State (2015)	High-tech sectors	European Union countries	Positive effects due to the technological effect
3.	Floyd (1996)	Manufacturing industries	Central and Eastern European countries	Positive and negative effects
4.	Estrin (2017)	FDI in regions	EU countries, former republics of the Soviet Union	Positive significant effects for EU countries. Positive insignificant effects for former republics of the Soviet Union.
5.	Kathuria (2000)	Indian manufacturing firms	India	Positive effect
6.	Clark et al. (2011)	Panel data of firms	USA	Positive effect
7.	Fillat & Woerz (2011)	Panel data in certain industries	35 OECD countries	Positive effect
8.	Lutz & Talavera (2005)	Individual Ukrainian firms	Ukraine	Positive and negative effects
9.	Haddad & Harrison (1993)	The Moroccan manufacturing sector	Morocco	The negative effect for domestic business
10.	Zhang et al. (2019)	Panel data	China	A positive effect with time lags of six years

In this case, domestic firms occupy adequate positions in the production chain with foreign affiliates, competing with them. They force less efficient firms to close. The average productivity of the industry in the host economy will rise.

Haddad and Harrison (1993) assessed the impact of FDI on the efficiency of firms by testing for such spillovers in the Moroccan manufacturing sector. The specific factors of firms were determined by the total productivity separately for each sector. Labour productivity is not uniformly distributed but tends to be localized over and above overall levels of labour productivity achieved by the most efficient firm. The presence of a foreign investor was defined as the share of foreign assets of an individual firm in the total assets and as the share of assets of foreign firms in the total assets of the sector. The results demonstrated that the dispersion of productivity was smaller in the sectors with more foreign firms. The outcomes obtained in determining the external effect allowed the authors to identify sectors with large volumes of FDI, in which the firms have a low variance in productivity. Thus, domestic firms are closer to the limit of efficient use of production capacity. The authors consider that the higher productivity of domestic firms could not be explained by the presence of the higher share of foreign capital in the Moroccan manufacturing sector. Foreign capital negatively correlates with productivity growth in domestic firms.

Estrin (2017, 2) believes that the inflow of FDI is associated with rising GDP and declining unemployment in general, as well as overtime in most regions. The effects were most noticeable and marked earlierin the EU's history, and least in the former Soviet republics and Russia. Direct investment affected natural resources in Russia and some Central Asian republics, and the impact on employment was less determined. The author zemphasizes that the indirect impact of FDI on the restructuring of a company, its productivity, and employment were very significant in the EU member states. Insufficient development of institutions and the gap between investment needs and domestic capabilities of companies hinder the attraction of foreign capital.

Kathuria (2000, 350) points out that domestic firms will not benefit from a foreign presence if it is measured by the share of sales at the same time they get access to foreign capital reserves. Additional research shows that domestic firms that belong to the R&D subgroup have a positive impact and ensure the transfer of new technical knowledge.

Access to foreign capital stocks helps increase the efficiency of domestic firms specialising in R&D. Firms that do not belong to the subgroup engaged in the creation of new knowledge do not benefit from the transfer of new technical information. The work of Acharya and Keller (2007) is devoted to determining the effects of technology transfers in the US manufacturing sector from attracting FDI and imports of finished products. The study aimed to determine the impact of FDI and import growth on productivity growth in domestic firms receiving investment. The foreign presence can be measured as the share of employment in foreign affiliates compare with total employment in the industry. The results of the study indicate that FDI creates conditions for obtaining significant production benefits for domestic firms. External effects were assessed on a large scale compared with other studies. External effects accounted for 8–19% of the production growth of American firms in the period from 1987 to 1996. Effects differ and depend on the size and productivity of the firm. Acharya and Keller (2007) hypothesized that a strong external effect is due to the influx of FDI into high-tech sectors. Small firms with low productivity receive a greater external effect of FDI compared with large firms with high productivity. The smaller external effect of imports of finished products compared with the effect of FDI can complement the positive feedback to sustain growth in the long run.

Boghean & State (2015, 276) estimate the relationship between FDI and labour productivity in the European Union and confirm the existence of a strong connection between the volume of FDI outflows and productivity zones. The impact of FDI on the economies of host countries is mainly due to increased productivity through technology transfer, and management and marketing skills, which allows for long-term technological progress and economic growth. The authors argue that FDI depends on additional factors to exert a significant effect on growth, i.e. a significant level of domestic investment or export orientation is necessary.

Fillat &Woerz (2011, 320) attempt to reconcile the often-inconclusive evidence on the role of FDI in the process of economic development. Using a comparable database at the industry level for 35 countries in the OECD and Eastern Europe from 1987 to 2002, the authors test for the influence of both the stage of development and sectoral FDI patterns in the relationship between FDI and productivity growth. The authors argue that a significant and positive relationship emerges when FDI coincides with high investment or the export orientation of a country. Lutz and Talavera (2005, 10) examine the effects of the presence of FDI on the performance of individual Ukrainian firms receiving it and prove that FDI may have not only positive but also negative economic effects for recipient countries. Clark et al. (2011) developed and substantiated an approach to determining the effect of FDI, which is associated with positive technological spillovers, economic growth, and increasing income inequality. Floyd (1996, 69) used firm-level data from manufacturing industries for the period of 2000–2005 in Central and Eastern European countries and found that vertical effects tend to be higher and thus economically more important than horizontal ones. In many cases, spillovers are negative and thus the foreign presence might also have some adverse impact on local firms' productivity. Zhang et al. (2019) applied a panel vector autoregressive model for the assessment of China's direct investments and obtained results that the investments directly affected economic growth with a time lag of six years.

The study of the above-mentioned approaches allows identification of the main factors stimulating economic growth and technology transfer through the placement of branches of foreign firms, the development of competition with domestic firms, and increasing productivity by attracting FDI (Nosova 2014, 124).

Empirical studies of FDI spillover effects on domestic firms across countries confirm the existence of direct and indirect effects and reflect various technologies, products, and characteristics at micro to macro levels. The reported results do not reproduce different effects of economic sectors, labour productivity, or undervalued labour costs per worker, and do not take into account the role of the shadow economy. Moreover, if internal and external effects act in the same direction, reducing labour costs per unit of output, they act as a factor stimulating the growth of productive efficiency, increasing output, increasing labour intensity, and improving a product's quality and competitiveness.

Conclusions

Analysis of the impact of FDI on labour productivity shows ambiguous trends that depend on the country's economic development, investment in R&D, and reduction of production costs. The inflow of FDI into the country considers different areas of investment, the short-term nature of the investment, and is influenced by the predominance of speculative motives.

If we take into account the total effects of FDI, it should be mentioned that they could act in different directions. The policy of attracting foreign capital inflows to a country for stimulating the internal and external effects of FDI on labour productivity will enhance economic growth. Improvement of the investment climate goes hand in hand with the enlargement and development of human capital. A skilled workforce is important for firms using new and productive technologies. A favourable investment climate increases returns on investment in human capital.

Governments need to take the initiative to enhance the development of education, to make it more comprehensive and responsive to the needs of the business.

The growth of the presence of foreign capital stimulates wage increases in foreign affiliates. Workers in industries with greater foreign participation experience faster wage growth in comparison with domestic firms. Creating an attractive investment climate, adjustment policies, and incentive programs to create new jobs are all aimed at increasing productivity and improving the living standards of the population in countries that are the recipients of foreign capital.

References

Acharya, R. and Keller, W. "Technology transfer through imports," 2007, *NBER working paper series*, *Working paper 13086,* accessed May 2007, http://www.nber.org/papers/w13086._DOI 10.3386/w13086

Alcacer, J. "The Role of Human Capital in Foreign Direct Investment." *Transition. The Newsletter about Reforming Economies, 2000,* World Bank/William Davidson Institute, May-July, 2000, vol. 11, no. 3-4.

Accessed July 2000. https://documents.worldbank.org/curated/en/883961468753006652/pdf /multi-page.pdf Albagli, E., Canales, M., Syverson, C., Tapia, N., Wlasul, J. Productivity Growth and Workers' Job Transitions: Evidence from Censal Microdata. April 2021- *Working paper*28657.

Beugelsdijk, S., Smeets, R., Zwinkels, R. The impact of horizontal and vertical FDI on host's country economic growth. International Business Review, 2008, vol. 17, issue 4, 452-472.

Blomström, M., Kokko, A. (2001). FDI and Human Capital: A Research Agenda. *OECD Development Centre*. December 2001. Available at https://www.oecd.org/dev/2699493.pdf

Boghean, C. and State, M. "The Relation between Foreign Direct Investments (FDI) and Labour Productivity in the European Union Countries." 2015, *Procedia Economics and Finance*, vol. 32: 278-285, accessed December 2015. DOI: 10.1016/S2212-5671(15)01392-1.

Bulkley, N. and Van Alstyne, M. *Why Information Should Influence Productivity*. A Research and Education Initiative at the MIT Sloan School of Management, 2004, Paper 202.

Cavalleru, M.C. and Cuasa, O. "How government can protect vulnerable workers." 2020. *VoxEU.org*, accessed 7 April 2020.

https://www.weforum.org/agenda/2020/07/how-non-standard-workers-are-affected-and-protected-during-the-covid-19-crisis-stylised-facts-and-policy-considerations/.

Clark, D., Highfill, J., Campino, J. and Rehman, S. "Income Inequality: A Selective Survey." *Global Economy Journal*, vol. 11, Issue 2, Article 1. 42. 2011. Accessed http://www.bepress.com/gej/vol11/iss2/1.

Dingel, J. and Neiman, B. "How many jobs can be done at home?". *VoxEU.org*, 2020, accessed 30 June 2020. https://voxeu.org/article/how-non-standard-workers-are-affected-and-protected-during-covid-19-crisis. 2020, https://doi.org/10.1787/dc2f7aec-en

Dohrn, R. and Heilemann, U. "The Chenery hypothesis and structural change in Eastern Europe." *Economics of Transition*, 1996, vol. 4: 411–425.

Estrin, S. "Foreign Direct Investment and Employment in Transition Economies." IZA World of Labor 2017: 330, accessed January 2017 doi: 10.15185/izawol.330

Estrin, S., Hanousek, J., Kocenda, E. and Svejnar, J. "The effects of privatisation and ownership in transition economies." *Journal of Economic Literature*, 2009, No. 47, 3: 699–728.

Fillat, C. and Woerz, J. "Good or Bad? The Influence of FDI On Productivity Growth: An Industry-Level Analysis." *The Journal of International Trade & Economic Development. An International and Comparative Review*. 2011. vol. 20, issue 3: 293-328.

Floyd, D. "Foreign Direct Investment in Poland: Is Low-Cost Labour Really the Sole Determinant?" *Economic Issues*. 1996. vol. 1, Part 2, September, 69.

Graham, E.M. *Fighting the wrong enemy. Antiglobal activists and multinational enterprises*. Institute for International Economics, Washington D.C, September. 2000.

Haddad, M. and Harrison, A.E. "Are there positive spillovers from direct foreign investment? Evidence from panel data for Morocco." *Journal of Development Economics*,1993, No. 42 (1): 51–74.

Jarvis, D.S.L. "Multinational enterprises, international relations and international business: reconstituting intellectual boundaries for the new millennium." *Australian Journal of International Affairs*, 2005, 59: 2, 201-223, DOI: 10.1080/10357710500134459.

Jude, C. and Levieuge, G. "Growth Effect of FDI in Developing Economies: the Role of Institutional Quality." *Working Papers*, 25 June 2014, https://halshs.archives-ouvertes.fr/halshs-01014404.

Kathuria, V. "Productivity Spillovers From Technology Transfer To Indian Manufacturing Firms." *Journal of International Development*, No. 12(3), April 2000, 343–369.

Krkoska, L. "Foreign direct investment financing of capital formation in central and eastern Europe." *European Bank for Reconstruction and Development. Working paper No. 67*, 2001.

Little, A.D. *Managing White Collar Productivity*, Inc., 1981.

Lutz, S. and Talavera, O. "Do Ukrainian Firms Benefit from FDI?" *Economics of Planning*. June 2005, vol. 37, issue 2, 77–98. (2004). Published 25 May 2005. https://doi.org/10.1007/s10644-004-4073-2

Net Foreign Direct Investment Flows (BPM 6), 2020. Accessed 2020. https://www.bsp.gov.ph/statistics/external/tab10_fdc.aspx

Nosova, O. *Investment Perspectives of Ukraine: Economic and Legal Model.* Monograph, LAPLAMBERT Academic Publishing, 2014.

Nosova, O. *Effect of Attracting FDI to Economic Growth of TNCs. Bulletin of the Research Center of Corporate Law*. Management and Venture Capital of Syktyvkar State University. 2016. No. 4: 13-23.

OECD. FDI in Figures. COVID-19 Disruptions Send Global FDI Plunging 50%. 2020. Accessed October 2020. http://www.oecd.org/investment/statistics.htm.

Paskeleva, M. Global Uncertainty During COVID 19 Pandemic and Its Effects On EU Member States With A Focus On Bulgaria. *International Conference Knowledge-Based Organization.* vol. XXVI no 2. 2020, 71-76, Accessed 20 July 2020 https://doi: 10.2478/kbo-2020-0055.

Samuelson, P.A. and Nordhaus, W.D. *Economics*, 15th ed., New York, McGraw Hill, 1995.

Shapovalov, A. "Behind the Scenes of the Monetary Phenomenon." *Mirror of the Week.* No. 39 (668), 20 October 2007, 7-8.

Sharma, C., 2010. Does productivity differ in domestic and foreign firms? Evidence from the Indian machinery industry. Indian economic review, 45 (1), 87–110.

Sink, D.S. *Productivity Management: Planning, Measurement, and Evaluation, Control and Improvement*, N.Y., John Wiley and Sons, 1995.

United Nations ESCAP. Reducing Trade Costs: Impact on Foreign Direct Investment. Published 2015. Accessed 16 June 2015. https://www.unescap.org/resources/reducing-trade-costs-impact-foreign-direct-investment#.

UNCTAD. 2001. World Investment Report: "Measures of the Transnationalization of Economic Activity." United Nations, New York and Geneva: UN, 2001 Accessed June 2001. https://digitallibrary.un.org/record/434373

UNCTAD. 2006. World Investment Report. «FDI from Developing and Transition Economies: Implications for Development," United Nations, New York and Geneva. Accessed 15 October 2006 https://unctad.org/system/files/official-document/wir2006_en.pdf.

UNCTAD. 2018. World Investment Report: "Investment and New Industrial Policies. Key Messages and Overview," United Nations, New York and Geneva, accessed June 2018 https://unctad.org/en/PublicationsLibrary/wir2018_en.pdf.

UNCTAD. 2020a. Investment Trends Monitor. Impact of the Coronavirus outbreak on global FDI. 2020, United Nations, New York and Geneva, accessed March 2020. https://unctad.org/system/files/information-document/diae_gitm34_coronavirus_8march2020.pdf.

UNCTAD. 2020b. World Investment Report: "International Production Beyond the Pandemic," United Nations, New York and Geneva, accessed June 2020. https://unctad.org/system/files/official-document/wir2020_en.pdf.

Vahter, P. 2004. "The Effect Of Foreign Direct Investment On Labour Productivity: Evidence From Estonia And Slovenia," University of Tartu - Faculty of Economics and Business Administration Working Paper Series 32.

Zhang, Y., Cheng, Z. and He, Q. 2019. "Time Lag Analysis of FDI Spillover Effect: Evidence from Belt and Road Developing Countries Introducing China's Direct Investment." *International Journal of Emerging Markets*, 1 November. dOI: 10.1108/IJOEM-03-2019-0225.

CHAPTER EIGHT

BANKS AND THEIR ROLE IN THE SYSTEM OF RESOURCE PROVISION FOR THE PRODUCTIVE CAPACITY OF COUNTRIES

SERGIY A. TSYGANOV,
NADIIA V. TSYGANOVA

Current developments in the world economy include the implementation of a logical chain of interrelated trends: deepening the division of labour and expansion of the boundaries of markets including geography, increasing globalisation and international competition, and accelerating innovation as a major competitive advantage. The increased transparency of the world's economic borders leaves no chance for a business to stay outside of innovation processes Previously, only the least expensive products were necessary for society but now society is willing to pay more for innovative products and services and so the economic meaning of the "efficiency" concept is changing. The development of the banking sector in this context is accompanied by significant quantitative and qualitative changes that significantly affect the sector's ability to finance the productive capacity of nations.

Deepening of the international division of labour increases the transparency of national borders for commodity, trade and financial flows. Foreign capital, the impact of which is ambiguous, has come to the national banking market. Foreign investment contributes to accelerating the development process, standards for providing traditional and innovative services to economic entities are being updated in financial markets, and competition and management in financial institutions is being enhanced, which is increasing their capitalisation and financial performance.

The banking system of Ukraine has passed the initial stage of its formation, but it now shows a significant backlog of the economy's needs: increased sensitivity to external shocks, structural imbalances and limited resource opportunities for real sector lending, especially of medium- and long-term credits.

The low level of customer and investor confidence, limited opportunities for equity growth and excessive risks that threaten the stability in both individual banks and the banking sector as a whole hinder the development of banks.

Therefore, the growth of banks and their consolidation are seen as real ways to solve many problems in the banking sector. The 2014–2015 crisis in the banking system of Ukraine has revealed the existence of a set of interrelated system problems that prevent the funding of sustainable economic development on innovative principles.

The escalation of the financial and economic crisis in Ukraine has exacerbated the imbalance between the credit sector and the manufacturing sector. Monetary measures aimed at curbing inflation did not contribute to business lending and economic growth. The restructuring of the banking sector, accompanied by the withdrawal from the market of a significant number of banks, did not contribute to restoring confidence and harmonising the relations of financial market actors.

Under these conditions, there is the need to stabilise the banking system. It is necessary to restore confidence in banks and to form a resource base in accordance with increases in countries' productive capacities, and to figure out the scientific basis of qualitative and quantitative parameters of banking.

Literature review

Scholars pay considerable attention to the research of the peculiarities of banking, and the place and role of banks in the system of resource provision for the productive capacity of countries. In particular, authors such as Schumpeter (1982), Campbell et al. (1988), Movsesyan (1997), Hubbard (2007), Lavrushin (2012), Yudina (2013), and Mishkin (2014) revealed in their works the formation of a theoretical basis of the development of financial intermediation and also determined the role of banks.

The works of Dzyublyuk and Malakhova (2008), Zveryakov and Zherdetska (2017), and others are devoted to theoretical and methodological aspects of banks' activity, regulation and supervision in Ukraine. The works of Panova (1997), Primostka (2012), Moiseev (2021), and others are devoted to the issues of the credit activity of banks, banking risks, assessment of capital adequacy and formation of the resource base.

The works of scientists including Miller and VanHoose (1993), Chub (2009), Fomishina (2017), Siskos and Rogach (2014), Rumyantsev (2018) and others are devoted to the study of international banking under global competition in financial markets.

However, given the achievements of fundamental and applied research, some theoretical, methodological and practical aspects of determining the role of banks in the system of resource provision of countries' productive capacity have receive insufficient attention.

The following issues remain controversial: clarifying the functional features of banks as major financial intermediaries, criteria for assessing their resource provision in accordance with changes in basic macroeconomic indicators, improving the parameters of banking regulation and supervision, and approaches to determining the stability of banks taking into account structural changes in the banking market.

Methodology

The main provisions of the expansionist theory of credit are the methodological basis for studying the role of banks in the system of resource provision for countries' productive capacity, according to which credit is the main driver of economic growth. Assessment of the banks' role in this system of resource provision is based primarily on determining their place in the financial market as the main intermediaries that accumulate and redistribute most of society's resources. This role is changing with increased competition in financial services and partial reorientation of cash flows to other market segments, increasing the FinTech share influenced by the concept of the financial supermarket. It is determined not only by the banks' lending capacity in the system's business resources, but also by the expansion of the range of banking transactions in the corporate securities market, which also promotes the role of banks in a set of measures for the resource productive capacity of countries.

The role of banks in the system of resource provision is also determined by the quantitative and qualitative parameters of their resources, according to the business needs and general macroeconomic parameters. The capacity of national financial markets determines the number of resources that are redistributed on the basis of their mechanisms.

This means that a change in the number of banks ambiguously affects their role in the resource provision system for the productive capacity of countries. Resource capabilities of individual banks depend on the number of banking institutions and the level of consolidation of the banking sector.

Therefore, to assess the formation of banks' capacity to finance the productive capacity, the following steps should be taken:

- analyse the impact of monetary conditions on the resource capacity and lending activities of banks;
- analyse the impact of a reduction in the number of banks on the size of their capital and liabilities, and the role of banking sector's consolidation in financing of the productive capacity of the banks.

The role of banks in resource provision for the productive capacity of countries

The system of resource provision for the productive capacity of countries, in addition to traditional investment channels, includes the redistribution of resources on the basis of fiscal and credit mechanisms. It is characterised by the growing role of lending by banks.

The role of banks is not limited to the redistribution of credit resources. Banks provide credit money creation and its movement as a means of payment. The role of banks is their ability to attract temporarily free funds and direct them to different sectors of the economy based on the criteria of the most efficient use. At the same time, banks provide a combination of their own business interests and the needs of economic entities to attract additional funds.

The redistribution of money resources takes place in the financial market, where they are transformed into loan capital, which moves from those who have a surplus of funds to those who need additional investment. In this case, loan capital is directed, as a rule, from those who have monetary resources but cannot use them effectively, to those who use them productively. This not only promotes an increase in the productivity and efficiency of the economy as a whole, but also improves the economic well-being of everyone in society (Miller and VanHoose 1993; Mishkin 2014).

By providing lending services, banking institutions redistribute financial resources in favour of economic entities that need them. Direct lending of free money capital by its owners to borrowers is difficult in economic practice.

In principle, cash can be transferred from the lender to the borrower without the mediation of banks but this increases the degree of risk, as the actors of credit relations do not have official information on each other's solvency, and the size and timing of cash supply might not match in terms of their needs.

Thus, the role of banks in the system of resource provision for the productive capacity of countries is implemented through their main functions:

- redistribution: banks ensure the accumulation and redistribution of most of the money market's resources;
- issuance: bank lending is a component of the modern issuance mechanism;
- settlement: banks play a key role in settlement systems and provide settlements between economic entities.

The number of banks as financial intermediaries and the variety of services they provide characterise the degree of development of the financial market.

Banks are involved in servicing almost all cash flows in the economy and create the basic preconditions for the development of production – namely, all stages of the process of social reproduction: distribution, exchange and consumption. Banks play a primary role in the market infrastructure, as they are an essential element of interaction in the field of monetary relations between market players and provide reproductive processes at micro and macro levels. Also, the bulk of financial resources moves through bank accounts, which determines the banks' decisive role in the system of financial market institutions.

Analysis of current trends in the functioning of banks and the formation of their resource provision

The deepening of the international division of labour causes the blurring of national economies and the formation of a world economic system. These processes are accompanied by banking internationalisation and the globalisation of financial markets. Isolated cases of international banking investments are replaced by a steadily growing cross-border movement of bank capital. In addition, there is not only an international movement of loan capital concentrated in the banking sector, but also the transfer of banks' equity (Dovgal and Cossack 2018; Fomishina 2017).

The movement of bank capital ensures not only the functioning of reproduction processes in the international financial environment, but also the international redistribution of financial resources using the tools of international investment mechanisms.

A steady trend of accelerated innovation of all components of economic systems has been observed at the present stage of development of the world economy (Rumyantsev 2018; Rogach 2019). Thus, banks are the engine of many changes and demonstrate significant innovations in the fields of digital banking, financial technologies, investment activities and more. They perform a dual role in these processes in generating and financing innovations. There is a direct link between financial globalisation, international competition and the acceleration of innovation.

The expansion of banks beyond national borders and the acceleration of the process of merging national banking systems occur under the influence of new technologies and financial innovations, and the rapid development of global financial market infrastructure, which provides increasingly powerful communications.

The priority for most developed countries is to try to subordinate the financial and banking activities to the tasks of ensuring sustainable economic development, enhancing the country's competitiveness through innovation growth. Under these conditions, banks are being transformed from financial intermediaries into powerful partners, integrating all components of the innovation process. However, the innovative development of Ukraine's economy is characterised by contradictions, and inconsistency of the banking system and financial markets with the needs of resource provision for the technological modernisation of the economy. Therefore, increasing bank capital using the resource potential of foreign capital in such a situation can help to solve this problem.

The main condition for general economic development is to increase efficiency on the basis of scientific and technological progress and increasing productivity. The mechanisms of market economy regulation are aimed at displacing from the market the economic entities whose products are low quality, high price, outdated, or do not meet the ever-growing needs of consumers.

That is why there are constant changes in the market of banking services: new services and banking products appear, customers' needs and demands change, and some banks are created while others leave the market as they are unable to compete. The formation of the banking industry was associated with the provision of a small number of basic banking services: credit and deposits, then settlement services, acceptance and discounting of bills, and placement of commercial and government securities.

Traditional banking services have been supplemented by leasing, factoring, forfeiting, trust, guarantee, consulting and other services. Modern banks can offer their customers about 500 different operations and services. Therefore, they are often compared to financial supermarkets.

With the development of information technologies, banking customer service is carried out using telecommunications, the Internet, ATMs, payment terminals and contactless technologies. The acceleration of economic growth is the result of the development of banking technologies, because the banking industry is able to influence the parameters of economic development in general. The banking system performs its functions and fosters the acceleration of other sectors of the economy more efficiently.

Technological development of the banking sector affects the state and functioning of the entire economic system. The growth of banks' resources and their ability to serve business on a qualitatively new basis, with the use of banking innovation, are the channels of such influence (see Figure 8-1).

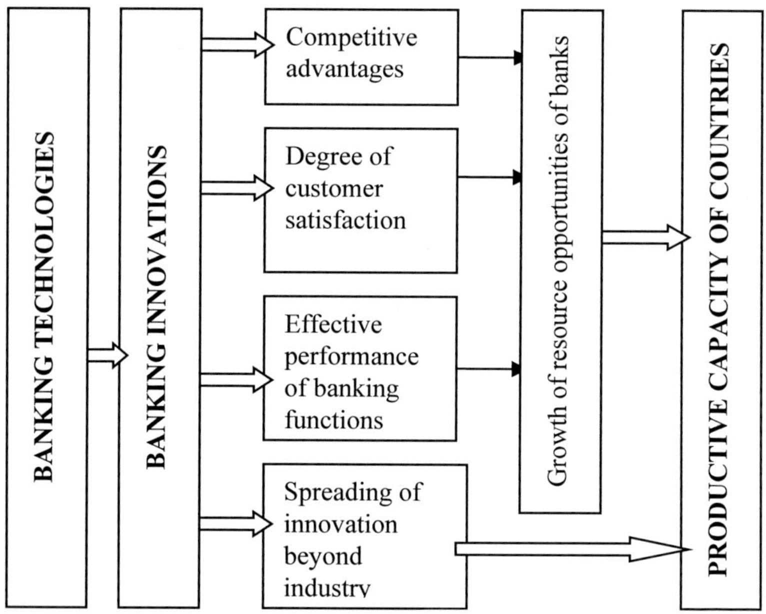

Figure 8-1. Channels of banking innovations' influence on economic development and productive capacity of countries

In modern conditions, the improvement of banking technologies is systematic and is an integral part of innovation processes in the economy.

The innovative financing needs of economic development, and the renewal of fixed assets, are causing the increased role of bank lending. However, a significant obstacle is the mismatch between the resource needs of business and the resource capabilities of banks. Banks should form the appropriate resources, which include banks' own and borrowed funds, accumulated in the money market not only in sufficient quantities, but also with certain characteristics (term, price, risk, currency, etc.), for successful financing of the economy. The increase of bank capital on the basis of internal sources and the further increase in the deposit base are limited to the indicators of bank profitability and confidence, the equity growth rate, and borrowed funds.

Undercapitalised banks are a significant obstacle for increasing business lending, especially under high-risk circumstances. The financial turmoil of 2014–2015 adversely affected bank confidence and the stability of the deposit base. But ensuring the productive capacity of countries is impossible without large-scale credit and financial support for business development from the banking system and government agencies.

First of all, it concerns small and medium enterprises (SMEs), which are the driving force of the economy and the basis of the middle class. The business of SMEs provides employment, as well as the receipt of taxes and other payments to the budget. It is a powerful factor in the development of scientific and technological progress, and creates a healthy competitive environment in the economy.

The economies of developed countries are largely based on SMEs. In particular, their share in the GDP of some European countries exceeds 50% – e.g. Italy (70%) and France (52%) – along with lower values seen elsewhere, such as Poland (47%), Russia (22%) and Belarus (23%) (Sych and Volos 2018). In Ukraine, small business is still in its formative stage (15% of GDP) and requires significant support (Sych and Volos 2018, 421).

Business structures cannot exist independently without the necessary credit receipts at the initial stage of their formation; they need constant financial support. However, the real economic situation in some countries with economies in transition, particularly in Ukraine, shows that banking relationships with business entities have not yet been properly developed; the legal basis for their interaction is imperfect. In countries with emerging markets, national socio-economic development programmes focus on the introduction of financial mechanisms to support entrepreneurship, the establishment of a credit guarantee funds system, tax benefits, subsidies and grants.

But still, the banking sector in many such countries is mainly interested in large projects with rapid payback; the cost of bank loans for SMEs is unattractive, while there is limited access to the resources of the banking system. It concerns not only the high rate of the central bank but also significant credit risks. The main reason for this is the lack of guarantees for banks in the form of collateral or highly liquid assets.

Central banks of countries with emerging markets support microcredit programmes not only within the credit lines of the European Bank for Reconstruction and Development. For example, in Ukraine, SMEs can apply for loans to the German–Ukrainian Fund (GUF) established by the National Bank, the Cabinet of Ministers of Ukraine and the German Reconstruction Credit Institute (KFW). In modern conditions, the German–Ukrainian Foundation has joined the Strategy for the Development of Small and Medium Business, developed by the Ministry of Economic Development and Trade.

For this purpose, the GUF both increases the volume of standard products to commercial partner banks (long-term credit lines in foreign currency) and develops new areas, such as long-term credit lines in Ukrainian hryvnias and a new mechanism for issuing credit guarantees. In particular, the GUF offers long-term lending in hryvnias due to currency risk hedging by the European Commission. The GUF financed 217 projects totalling UAH709 million, which helped to save 6217 jobs and create 587 more in 2017–2019 alone (Krupka and Yaremik 2018, 280). The influence of foreign capital on the accumulation of funds by business structures is significantly increased in the countries of Central and Eastern Europe due to the direct and indirect influences of multinational enterprises on this process by saving the funds of the population, state and business itself. In addition, there is a tendency to use mixed forms of lending, as well as loans from other foreign sources.

Such schemes are typical to EU PHARE programmes, the European Investment Fund, World Bank and EBRD terms of lending. Statistics show that the main external sources of financial assistance for foreign economic activity of enterprises in countries in transition are export/import, central banks' funds of foreign countries, specialised financial institutions, and consortia of leading banks in the world, as well as the support of insurance companies, and credit and guarantee institutions. The banks' resources are limited by the amount of their equity, which is the subject of increased attention of national regulators in accordance with the recommendations of the Basel Committee.

The main ways of increasing bank capital are the accumulation of banks' profits and their capitalisation, and the process of bank consolidation on a mergers and acquisitions (M&As) basis.

M&A transactions occur mainly on the domestic banking markets, but international M&As grow more rapidly, especially in emerging markets. For example, almost all such transactions in Ukraine in recent years have taken place with the participation of foreign banks. Consolidation processes differ in scale, forms, preconditions and consequences, depending on the level.

Thus, ensuring the effective functioning of the banking system at the national level requires comprehensive measures to improve the resource capacity of banks and increasing the adaptation of regulatory instruments to the requirements of international regulations, such as Basel III and Basel IV. Such work is carried out in developed countries in order to improve the functioning of financial markets, strengthening cooperation and transparency in the monitoring of sources of asset financing and the maturity of liabilities combating the shadowing of the financial sector, and assessing the effectiveness of macroprudential instruments. The Financial Stability Board (FSB) of the G-20 countries prioritises these areas to improve the regulation of the banking system (Siskos and Rogach 2020, 71-90; National Bank of Ukraine 2008).

The implementation of these and other measures of the banking system's regulation confirms that most countries have clear institutional activities for enhancing the reliability of credit and financial institutions under globalisation, namely:

- first, the use of stabilisation regulatory instruments that ensure the sustainable development of the banking system through a prudent policy of banking risk management;
- second, the use of a capital adequacy ratio, which will facilitate countercyclical policy;
- third, the introduction of structural standards aimed at eliminating imbalances in banking by limiting the use of borrowed funds, which reduces the bank debt risks or limitation of activity volume;
- fourth, increasing confidence in the banking system, attracting household funds to deposit accounts, regulating consumer lending by means of credit and payment cards, and expanding financial services and financial instruments for individual investors;
- fifth, stimulating the innovative development of the real sector of the economy, promoting the competitiveness of economic entities, and restructuring the relationship between the banking and real (production) sectors to ensure their adaptation to the requirements of globalisation.

Priorities for the development of the banking sector within the context of the financing of the productive capacity of countries

Banks are an important economic structure as the main channel of redistribution of financial resources in terms of transformational changes, which can attract funds for long-term investment and intensify the implementation of vital investment and innovation policies in priority areas. Banks are able to direct the accumulated funds to stimulate structural and technological changes that can meet basic social problems.

It is necessary to solve important strategic and tactical tasks for the normalisation of investment in banking security. This primarily refers to the formation by the central bank of favourable monetary conditions for business lending. Second, it involves the creation of a centralised investment trust fund to support commercial banks in lending their investments at lower interest rates to compensate for the latter's losses from such lending. Third, it includes a differentiated tax policy, in which the bank's income tax on speculative transactions should be much higher than the base tax, and investment loans should be stimulated by a significant decrease in the tax rate on income from them. Finally, the government provides guarantees for credit and investment projects, and encourages the creation of banking lending consortia for innovative projects.

The associated low profitability and high risks have a negative impact on bank lending to SMEs. This significantly affects interest rates and other lending terms. Credit relations of banks with businesses should be mutually beneficial and based on partnership. Thus, a bank loan should promote the production and sale of a company`s products, and allow it to strengthen its material and technical base, which, in turn, ensures the timely repayment of the loan.

Therefore, banks are economically interested in the rational use of the loan obtained by enterprises. Also, a company is interested in fulfilling its obligations to the bank because it may lead to the possibility of obtaining additional funds and other bank services. However, very often banks are guided only by their own interests when concluding loan agreements, without considering the efficiency of credit use and the financial capabilities of new businesses. In this regard, it is advisable to provide a system of state-level soft loans for SMEs at lower interest rates and an appropriate mechanism for compensation to commercial banks for these loans (Rogach 2020, 267-286).

Consolidation of banks and potential formation of financing for the productive capacity of countries

Analysis of current world banking practices and the peculiarities of the functioning of national banking systems shows that each country chooses its own mechanisms to improve the resource support of the banking sector, depending on the needs of the economy and the state of financial markets. Regulation of consolidation in the banking sector is of particular importance. Technological changes are a precondition for the consolidation of banks, which require financing of production processes in significant amounts.

Financial crises occupy a special place among the most important factors in the consolidation of banks, because they play a catalytic role in these processes. The procyclical nature of bank consolidation processes is the reason for this. Considering a crisis from the standpoint of the need for technological changes and to encourage innovative development in accordance with J. Schumpeter's (1982) theory, the growth of banks creates an economic basis for further technological renewal of the economy as a result of the crisis.

General development trends contribute to the increase in the activity of individual economic entities. The latter are able to increase their efficiency by so-called economies of scale and savings of certain common costs. Large enterprises also gain a number of significant competitive advantages – for example, they become virtually invulnerable to competitors after reaching a certain size. Also, for them it is easier to establish communications with clients, receive government orders, and form supply and sales channels. The effect of these advantages also extends to banks. In addition, for the successful operation of banks, their size must correspond to the scale of their clients.

A small bank will probably fail to serve a large business successfully: it will lack resources for lending, settlement services, etc. Therefore, the rapid business growth in some sectors of the economy has triggered a rapid consolidation in the banking sector. These trends are significantly intensified under the globalisation of financial and other markets. Consolidation is also accelerated by crises in the economy and financial markets. Requirements for the formation of banks' capital were increased according to the recommendations of the Basel Committee after the economic crisis in 2007–2009. Therefore, the scenario of forced mergers of small banks was implemented in some countries, and in particular in Ukraine, in order to form a structured banking system represented by large and medium-sized banks. It was believed that this would stabilise banks, increase their efficiency, improve their financial position and facilitate business lending. Thus, the consolidation of the Russian banking sector into 200 large banks would increase lending in the economy by 1% of GDP. According to experts, the forced consolidation of banks has both positive and negative consequences.

The positive aspects include reducing the cost of borrowed resources for the economy; increasing the money supply due to the credit multiplier; stimulating the consolidation of banks; improving the efficiency of the allocation of financial resources; and simplification and supervision of banking regulation and the reduction of its costs.

The negative effects of banking sector consolidation are as follows (Moiseev 2021):

- reduction of competition in key banking markets;
- market monopolisation and the need for antitrust regulation;
- deterioration of business financing conditions and reduction of lending volumes due to increased credit rationing;
- high costs associated with the reorganisation of systemically important banks;
- risks of systemic instability.

Similar processes are observed in Ukraine, where a sharp reduction in the number of banks boosted their resource capabilities but also increased the monopolisation of the banking market (see Figure 8-2).

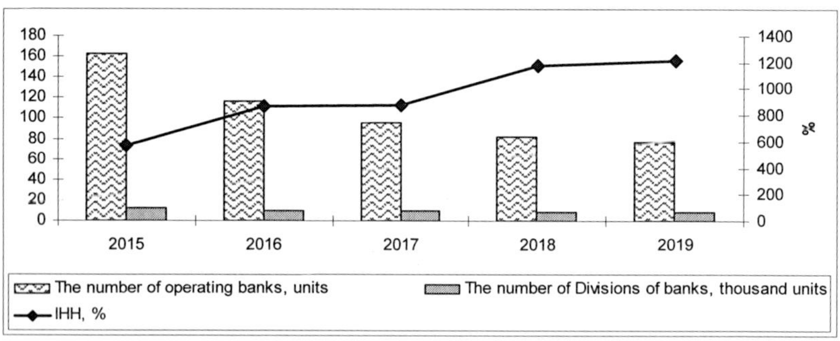

Figure 8-2. Changes in the number of operating banks and their divisions in Ukraine in 2015–2019 (IHH = Herfindahl-Hirschman index, %)
Source: based on data from the National Bank of Ukraine (2021).

As can be seen from Figure 8-2, the reduction in the number of banks and their branches is accompanied by an increase in the value of the

Herfindahl-Hirschman Index, which has exceeded 1000 since 2018 – hence, the Ukrainian banking market has moved to a state of monopolistic competition.

In today's world, emerging markets face the challenges of creating the conditions to support economic growth, making the progressive structural changes needed to reduce dependence on commodity markets, and integrating effectively into the world economy. The value of the banking system is difficult to overestimate in these conditions. These banks can and should provide uninterrupted payments and lending in the economy, expand investment, and promote economic growth.

Unlike approaches according to which the restructuring of the economy is associated with structural and institutional changes, in our opinion this process is due to the lack of balance in the formation of a new deficit economy.

Large-scale price liberalisation has led to a shift in emphasis onto the scarcity problem; namely, the trade deficit and normalised distribution gave way to oversupply in the investment and intermediate sectors. The alienation of banks from restructuring processes is evident in the limitation of credit support to the economy, which leads to a narrowing of the real money supply and recession. In fact, there is an excess of money supply over the effective demand of economic entities that proves the inconsistency over the course of stabilisation, developed on the basis of the liberal-monetarist interpretation of the national economy's restructuring.

The behaviour of enterprises in terms of financial constraints is a specific form of this expression: instead of curbing price increases and cost reduction, there is a sharp decline in output, loss of production capacity, rising defaults and falling liquidity. In this regard, it is timely to raise the issue of the mechanisms for the formation of financial resources in the economy. The sources of such mechanisms in developed countries are central banks, which regulate the processes of lending by the banking system to the real sector of the economy, the development of monetary instruments, and the formation of monetary policy on this basis.

In most emerging markets, financial resources are not generally replenished through the participation of central banks in intensifying lending processes, but on the basis of foreign exchange earnings. In most cases, this contributes to the export orientation of these countries, which ensures the inflow of foreign currency. In our view, such an approach may have negative consequences for the resource growth of the productive capacity of the national economies in these and other countries. The reason for this is that the unsustainable economy of emerging markets is becoming dependent on global and regional economic and political conditions. At the same time, there is no actual formation of the domestic national market, which narrows the opportunities for the banking system to participate in restructuring of the national economy. In addition, the work of financial instruments and mechanisms aimed at setting refinancing rates determining the price of financial resources is blocked under such conditions.

This significantly reduces the ability of government agencies to pursue active financial and monetary policies, and to influence the nature of economic development and the sectoral, technological and foreign economic structure. As a result, the negative trends in targeting the budget sources and GDP growth are preserved.

As an example, we can cite an expert assessment of technological structural changes in the economy of Ukraine: the sixth most promising technological level of innovation is not formed here at all. The share of the fifth technological level of innovation (military space equipment, communications) is up to 10%, the fourth is about 45%, the third is 30% and other levels are almost 15% (Siskos and Rogach 2014). Thus, Ukraine lags behind developed countries by a whole generation of technology. With a sharp reduction in the total production of the machine-building complex, this means a significant reduction in the investment potential of the economy to ensure the competitiveness of domestic products. In our opinion, the main reasons for the unfavourable changes in sectoral, technological and foreign economic structures are the inefficiency of the transfer mechanism of the capital resources between sectors of the economy and the low level of competition development (Siskos and Rogach 2014, 253-270).

It is obvious that the raw material orientation of the economies of such countries is preserved in this situation, as the main source of growth of the money supply is export-oriented industries, which are the suppliers of foreign currency. Other industries with the highest share of innovative enterprises have limited opportunities to obtain financial resources, which restrains positive structural changes in the economy and at the same time reduces the ability of the banking system to restructure the economy through lending and investing.

It is typical for countries with developed economies to use an interconnected systemic approach, according to which there is a steady growth of financial resources in both the economy and the banking sector. It is important that the process of restructuring the national economy and the normalisation of the financial situation in these countries solve the problem of bank capitalisation. Based on this, we can conclude that for countries with economies in transition it is inexpedient to conduct forced capitalisation of banks, and it is necessary to link this process with the restructuring of the national economy as a whole. Monetisation in emerging markets can have a significant impact on enhancing the banking system's ability to contribute to the resource capacity of national economies.

The limited access of SMEs to external sources of financing is becoming an important problem for most countries. In our opinion, in order to expand the access of SMEs to bank credits, it is necessary to:

- create a credit information service and a centre of movable property registration, similar to that which exists in EU countries;
- intensify the stimulating effect on the lending process by further regulation of creditors' rights (depositors in relation to banks and banks in relation to borrowers).

The latter point requires ensuring the preservation of movable property as collateral and the procedures of collateral seizure. It is also advisable to apply the restructuring of the banking sector by introducing a two- or three-tier banking licence (Mishchenko and Naumenkova 2016).

If Tier-1 licenced banks must comply with capital adequacy standards and create the necessary reserves to cover loan losses, then Tier-2 banks should offer higher interest rates on deposits to compensate the increased risk of depositors. Participation in financing and lending of innovative projects and the risky activity of small innovative enterprises that implement these projects may become attractive for second-tier banks. Such bank segmentation is well established in many countries. In particular, in the United States, according to the Glass–Steagall Act (1933), investment banks were separated from commercial ones, which improved both the deposit insurance system and the conditions of banks' participation in economic restructuring.

The formation of banks' resources at the expense of household deposits demonstrates problems of a more general nature and, in particular, they include the insufficient level of material well-being of the population and, therefore, limited opportunities for savings through the banking system. The problem of forming financial savings limits can be parameterised through indicators of social and subsistence levels. For most emerging markets, different living standards and dissimilar social protection systems in different countries play a significant role in the scale differences of material well-being. The possibilities for extensive development of banks in emerging markets are already exhausted in modern terms.

Thus, in Ukraine, reducing inflation and strengthening the national currency significantly reduces the possibility of obtaining a high bank margin due to the inflation redistribution of funds and operations on the foreign exchange market. The return on investments in government securities is also decreased. The ability of commercial banks to work with budget funds is becoming more limited; until recently, such funds were considered as one of the most stable liabilities. As a result, banks in emerging markets are currently faced with the need to substantially restructure their activities in line with the new macroeconomic conditions of relative financial stabilisation. The relationship between the process of consolidation of capital and the need to provide bank support to economic activity in the regions, primarily in those with a low level of business activity, is the problematic issue of restructuring the banking system.

As is well known, restructuring is manifested through the concentration of equity and assets, the opening of branches of large banks in the regions, the withdrawal of licences, and the liquidation of credit institutions. It is clear that this leads to strengthening of the positions of large banks, while the functioning of small and medium-sized banks becomes more complicated.

The case of Ukraine

The resource needs of the productive capacity of Ukraine's economy, overcoming the recession and the limited stock market are causing increased demand for bank loans, with a particularly acute problem of long-term resources, the demand for which is growing based on the need for investment as a necessary condition for enhanced production.

All this requires banks to pay special attention to the problems of formation of banking resources, namely the development and implementation of a resource policy that takes into account the peculiarities and interests of a particular banking institution, the banking system and the economy as a whole, while coordinating the needs and interests of depositors and shareholders.

The banking sector of Ukraine is characterised by a slow increase in the resource base of banks (see Figure 8-3), which, in combination with a rather tight monetary policy of the National Bank of Ukraine, does not contribute to the spread of bank lending.

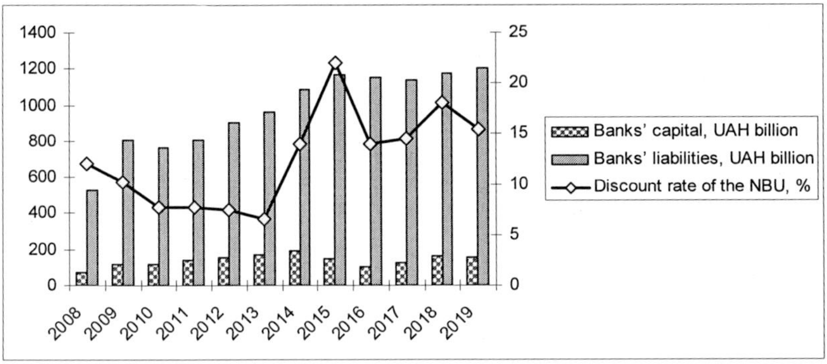

Figure 8-3. Dynamics of indicators of the resource provision of banks and changes in the discount rate of the NBU in 2008–2019
Source: based on data of the National Bank of Ukraine (2019).

The ratio of banks' capital to GDP characterises their ability for lending to the real sector and to provide resources for the productive capacity of countries.

This indicator also shows insufficient capitalisation and resource capabilities of the domestic banking sector (see Figure 8-4).

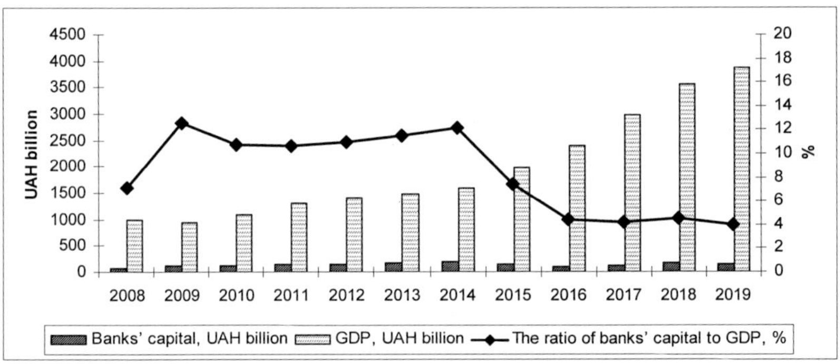

Figure 8-4. Dynamics of the capital of Ukrainian banks (UAH billion) and the ratio of its volume to Ukraine GDP (in %), data for 2019 is forecasted
Source: based on data of the National Bank of Ukraine (2019).

Before 2008 in Ukraine, the ratio of banks' capital to GDP was less than 4%, while the total capital of Russian banks reached almost 50% of monthly GDP and in the UK it was more than 100% of annual GDP.

After the crisis, in Ukraine this ratio increased slightly but then fell back to 10.7% in 2010 and to 10.6% in 2011. Over the next three years, this indicator improved slowly but steadily, so its dynamics can be considered positive with some reservations. Political and economic destabilisation in 2014 had a negative impact on this indicator: the figure decreased to 7.4% in 2015 and to 4.4% in 2016. The situation did not improve in the following years, which indicates the limited ability of banks to lend to the real sector of the economy.

The indicator of bank asset security has been steadily increasing in Ukraine and the most dynamic changes took place in the period 2015–2017. However, analysis of changes in other indicators of the banking sector shows that there are significant systemic problems, primarily related to ensuring the adequacy of bank capital. The absolute growth of banks' capital is not yet a sign of its adequacy given the needs of the economy, which is reflected in the limited lending to the real sector and the economic growth rate. The Ukrainian banking system lags far behind this indicator compared with the situation in other countries. An insufficiently formed capital base of the bank may impede the expansion of the range of banking operations. The reasons for this situation are hidden both in the specific situation in the banking sector of Ukraine and in the plane of general macroeconomic problems of the country's economy.

At the macro level, the financial situation of banks is affected significantly by: the dynamics of real GDP and worsening of business conditions; the crisis of confidence in banks, which causes problems of resource supply; the balance of payments position and depreciation of the national currency; inflation; high interest rates and reduced international reserves; and rising unemployment and impoverishment of the population. Thus, the general financial condition of banks is a reflection of the general economic problems of the state.

The sale of assets and thus reducing the parameters of balance sheets can be an important tool for bank recapitalisation. Some European and American banks have followed this path during the 2008 crisis. According to foreign experience, this is facilitated by the creation of reorganisation banks, an effective system of evaluation and the sale of assets. However, such a reduction has its limits at the level of the banking system, beyond which lending in the economy is suspended or significantly limited.

An effective asset valuation system has to answer the question of which of the assets should be sold immediately and which should be frozen for better times. Ukraine also needs to address the lack of an effective system for selling bank assets and the limited availability of effective buyers in this market segment.

The world partially solves these problems with the help of so-called Bad banks, which can accommodate bank assets and keep them for some time. Bad banks are created under significant destabilisation of the banking sector and the need for government intervention to stabilise it. The 2014–2015 crisis in the banking system of Ukraine revealed the existence of a set of interrelated systemic problems that prevent financing on an innovative basis for stable economic development.

This applies to all components of banking resources: own, raised and borrowed funds. The growth of equity is limited by the possibility of the share capital increasing, and decreasing profits in crisis and post-crisis situations. Unlike in developed countries, the possibility of public funds being used as a source of equity is not implemented enough. The weakening confidence in banks during the crisis led to an outflow of bank deposits and growth decreasing in the post-crisis period. The policy of the National Bank of Ukraine aimed at ensuring a tight money supply and bank liquidity also inhibits resource growth.

Conclusions

In the current context, consolidating the capital in the banking sector is essential for the formation of resource provision systems for the productive capacity of national economies, which are based on a number of objective and subjective factors, among them being technological changes in production that require large amounts of funding.

Therefore, prerequisites for the consolidation of the banking sector are formed on the basis of general economic trends. The basis of these processes is the contradiction between the need for banks' financing and servicing of economic entities and the available capabilities of banks. The financial limits of bank consolidation are determined by the parameters of the money market and its quantitative indicators specify the degree of banking systems' development. Consolidation of banks as an economic phenomenon, accompanied by a decrease in the number of banks and an increase in their size and market share, leads to increased control in the banking sector and changes in the competitive environment, accordingly.

Competition is a decisive factor in the development of the banking services market and it is the basis of market mechanisms for its self-regulation. Competitive mechanisms ensure the redistribution of resources between market participants in accordance with the efficiency and innovation of their activities. After all, combining relatively low cost and innovative characteristics of banking products and services forms the main competitive advantages in today's financial markets. Improving the overall performance of banks and the banking sector as a whole can be achieved by: focussing consolidation on expanding the market segment and obtaining competitive advantages such as increasing profits and growth of the customer base, using synergies and economies of scale, complying with regulatory capital requirements, and increasing stability parameters.

However, monopolistic pricing and the exclusion of competitors can only benefit individual consolidation entities and are inimical to the interests of other participants in the money market. Currently, the development of competition in the banking services market can be found in patterns such as banking universalisation and the entry of banks into new market segments, the liberalisation of government regulation, expansion of financial institutions (including territorial and functional aspects), and the desire of non-financial institutions to enter the financial services market. This has led to increased competition, changes in the strategic focus of financial institutions and the desire to obtain a competitive advantage using the effects of scale and financial innovation. The development of the credit system and the money market causes the expansion of the group of actors in the banking services market and, accordingly, the sphere of banking competition.

Competition between banks and other financial intermediaries, in attracting financial resources and opportunities to provide financial services, creates the preconditions for expanding consolidation processes beyond the banking sector. The consolidation process includes not only banks but also other financial intermediaries, including investment companies, insurers and pension funds. The spread of consolidation and competition beyond the banking industry necessitates changes in existing regulatory mechanisms. Rapid updates of banking technologies and innovations, whereby the banking system performs its functions more efficiently and stimulates the acceleration of economic development, are the driving force of modern development of the banking services market. This results not only in the expansion of the range of banking services, but also in the emergence of new types of intermediaries in the money market, changes in competitive conditions and expansion of the boundaries of consolidation processes.

References

Campbell, C.D., Campbell, R.G. and Dolan, E.G. 1988. *Money, Banking, and Monetary Policy.* Chicago: Dryden Press.

Chub, O.O. 2009. *Banks in the Global Economy: Monograph.* Kyiv: KNEU (Ukr.)

Dovgal, O.A. and Cossack, N.A. (eds.) 2018. *Globalization and regionalization as vectors of international economic relations development: a monograph*. Kharkiv: V. N. Karazin Kharkiv National University 3.5: 390-410. (Ukr.)

Dzyublyuk, O.V. and Malakhova, O.L. 2008. *Banks and enterprises: credit aspects of interaction under the market economy transformation: Monograph*. Ternopil: Vector. (Ukr.)

Fomishina, B.M. (ed.) 2017. *Modern tendencies of international economic relations and foreign economic relations of Ukraine: monograph.* Kherson: VKF STAR LTD 2.2.4: 180-193. (Ukr.)

Hubbard, R.G. 2007. *Money, the Financial System, and the Economy.* Publisher: Addison Wesley, 6th ed.

Krupka, M. and Yaremik, M. 2018. "Bank lending and its role in financing innovation processes in Ukraine." *Formation of a market economy in Ukraine*. 2018. Issue. 40, vol. 2, 277-284 (Ukr.)

Lavrushin, O.I. 2012. *The role of credit and the modernization of banks' lending activities*. Moscow: KNORUS. (Rus.)

Miller, R. LeR. and VanHoose, D.D. 1993. *Modern Money and Banking.* McGraw-Hill Education (ISE Editions); Internat.2r.e. ed.

Mishchenko, V.I. and Naumenkova, S.V. 2016. "The banking system of Ukraine: problems of formation and development." *Finance of Ukraine.* 2016. No. 5, 7-33. (Ukr.)

Mishkin, F. 2014. *Economics of Money, Banking and Financial Markets.* Publisher: Pearson, 11th ed.

Moiseev, S. 2021. "Consolidation of banks: pro at contra." Accessed 27 January 2021. https://republic.ru/posts/l/210781. (Rus.)

Movsesyan, A.G. 1997. *Integration of banking and industrial capital: current global trends and development problems in Russia.* Moscow: Finance and Statistics. (Rus.)

National Bank of Ukraine. 2008. "Regulations on the peculiarities of the bank's reorganization by the decision of its owners." *Resolution of the NBU Board.* 27 June 2008, No. 189. Accessed 27 January 2021. https://zakon.rada.gov.ua/laws/show/z0845-08#n16. (Ukr.)

National Bank of Ukraine. 2019. "Banking Sector Review, November 2019." Accessed 27 January 2021. https://bank.gov.ua/news/ all/ oglyad-bankivskogo-sektoru-listopad-2019-roku. (Ukr.)

National Bank of Ukraine. 2021a. "Supervisory Statistics." Accessed 27 January 2021. https://bank.gov.ua/control/uk/publish/article?art_id=34661442&cat_id =34798593. (Ukr.)

National Bank of Ukraine. 2021b. "Data of Supervisory Statistics." Accessed 27 January 2021. https://bank.gov.ua/statistic/supervision-statist/data-supervision#2. (Ukr.)
National Bank of Ukraine. 2021c. "Discount Rate of the National Bank." Accessed 27 January 2021. https://bank.gov.ua/monetary/stages/archive-rish. (Ukr.)
National Bank of Ukraine. 2021d. "Key performance indicators of the Ukrainian banks." Accessed 27 January 2021. https://bank.gov.ua/statistic/supervision-statist/data-supervision#2. (Ukr.)
Panova, G.S. 1997. *Commercial Bank Credit Policy.* Moscow: ICC "DIS". (Rus.)
Primostka, L.O. (ed.) 2012. *Regulation of Banks Under the Global Challenges: A monograph.* Kyiv: KNEU. (Ukr.)
Rogach, O. (ed.) 2019. *Modern Trends in International Capital Movements.* Kyiv: Center for Educational Literature. (Ukr.)
Rogach, O. (ed.) 2020. *Multinational Enterprises and the Global Economy: Monograph.* Kyiv: Center for Educational Literature 14: 267-286. (Ukr.)
Rumyantsev, A.P. (ed.) 2018. *Innovative Trends in World Trade Development: Monograph*. Kyiv: NAU. (Ukr.)
Schumpeter, J. 1982. *Theory of Economic Development (Study of entrepreneurial profits, capital, credit, interest and the business cycle).* Moscow: Progress. (Rus.)
Siskos, E. and Rogach, O. (eds.) 2014. *Global Economy: Issues and Challenges of Post-Crisis Development.* Kastoria: CHROMOTYP 16-17: 253-279.
Siskos, E. and Rogach, O. (eds.) 2020. *Internationalization of the World Economy: Current Trends.* Kastoria: EVKONOMIA Publisher 4: 71-90.
Sych, O. and Volos, I. 2018. "Current state and conditions of small and medium business lending in Ukraine." *A Young Scientist.* 2018. No. 2 (54).
Yudina, I.N. 2013. *The Banking System in Developing Economies: The experience of the formation and development of crises: a monograph.* Moscow: RIOR: INFRA. (Rus.)
Zveryakov, M.I. and Zherdetska, L.V. 2017. "Banking and real sectors of the Ukrainian economy: assessment of relationships and determinants of development." *Economy of Ukraine.* 2017. No. 10 (671). (Ukr.)

CHAPTER NINE

FOREIGN INVESTMENTS AND BUSINESS REGULATION IN SMALL AND LARGE ECONOMIES

OLEKSII A. CHUGAIEV

International investments are often considered to be an important factor of economic development because they can raise productivity and foster economic modernisation. This is why governments are interested in attracting foreign investments and retaining domestic capital inside the country. There is competition for investments between various types of countries, with various development levels, geographical locations and sizes of economies. Despite trade liberalisation and regulatory integration, large economies still have natural advantages in efficiency of investments. Therefore, countries have different strategies for establishing a favourable investment climate and reforming business regulation.

In this chapter, I review the results of research on the effects of the size of an economy on international investments. But it is necessary to verify the robustness of the previous findings by using more recent data. I applied analysis of variance (ANOVA) to the data in the post-crisis period (2009–2016) of global economic development. Also, unlike the traditional classification of countries into small and large economies, I distinguish medium-sized economies for several reasons:

- under the large variance of countries' GDP value, a dichotomic approach for classification results in the fact that the "small economies" group includes very different countries;
- there is a functional similarity of the medium-sized economies to either small or large economies in terms of various criteria;
- it provides better opportunities for finding non-linear relationships.

Previous research review

The effects on the financial openness of countries were analysed by Easterly and Kraay (1999), Martin and Rey (2000), and Pieretti et al. (2010). There are theoretical assumptions that it is necessary for small economies to be open to international movement of capital. A number of researchers have provided empirical evidence for this assumption using the data on foreign direct investments (FDI) per capita, current account deficit in % GDP, correlation between investments and savings, and the financial globalisation index (Özmen 2004; Anklesaria Aiyar 2008; AmirKhalkhali and Dar 2009; Docquier and Schiff 2009; Mozhovyi and Stukalo 2009; Herzog 2010). But economy size significantly affects financial openness only after reaching at least the average development level (Nyamtseren 2004).

Greater openness to foreign investments in small economies is caused by the lower amounts and less diversity of national capital and savings, opportunities for investment diversification, efficiency of regulation, possession of natural resources, and current account deficit. Large economies are less open because of the diversity of domestic financial assets, better resilience to shocks and the border effect due to the difference in regulatory environment.

But the findings about the relation between the size of economy and influx of capital are not supported by all the researchers (Commonwealth Secretariat et al. 2000; Fung et al. 2008; Laurent 2008; Gur et al. 2011). Sometimes, the research results depend on the analysed region or period of time; e.g. the opposite findings in the case of Central Europe can be explained by episodes of political instability in the smaller countries of the region in the 1990s. The effect of GDP on the correlation between savings and investments (the difference between them is offset by international movement of capital) is also controversial.

Also, the works cited above pay attention to incoming foreign capital but usually avoid considering outward investments; e.g. the explanation using the notion of the limited choice of assets for investments also provides a rationalisation for outward investments in small economies.

There is no consensus about the benefits of capital mobility for small economies. Jiránková (2009) stated that international financial markets affect them positively. Even a single large investment can substantially improve the economic performance of a small economy (Anklesaria Aiyar 2008). On the other hand, at least in theory, small economies face the risk of capital flight (especially of the most efficient companies) to large countries, where investors can benefit from economies of scale and stable sales (Brainard 1997; Ricci 1998; Gonzales 2001; Hummels 2006; Baldwin and Okubo 2012; Okubo et al. 2013), although trade liberalisation decreases that effect. There are also the risks of political influence of a foreign investor and volatility of incoming investments for small recipient countries (World Bank 2008; Ishise 2011).

The difference in risks considerably affects the difference in investment returns in small and large economies. The cost-to-benefit ratio is often worse in smaller economies due to: the fixed costs of checking a borrower and contract enforcement, underdeveloped institutions, and differences in regulation. Profitability of investments is more volatile in small economies. And finally, it is easier to move capital inside a large country than across a territory of a similar size that consists of several countries (Commonwealth Secretariat et al. 2000; Milner and Westaway 1993; Gonzales 2001; Wan 2005; Hassan 2009).

But there is the possibility of a net positive effect for the investor by benefitting from a monopoly rent (additional profit of a company under low competition) in a small economy. But the impact is positive only for the investor, while it is negative for consumers in a small economy. But we also should not overestimate this negative effect for a society, because foreign investors can limit the dominant position of domestic producers.

Demas (1965), Codrington (1989), Haufler and Wooton (1997), Anklesaria Aiyar (2008), Laurent (2008), Gnutzmann et al. (2008), Pieretti and Zanaj (2009), Pieretti et al. (2010), Ricka (2012), and Eldridge et al. (2012) analysed the differences in regulation of investments in small and large economies. They noted that small countries tried to offset the negative effect of economies of scale and the higher risks of openness by tax arbitrage, regulatory arbitrage and the quality of public services.

I also assume that the opportunity for income tax arbitrage in small economies is higher because they rely relatively more on taxes on international trade. A lower tax rate is not the only possible source of tax arbitrage. It may also appear in the case of a smaller number of taxes, which affects the simplicity of taxation procedures.

Researchers usually consider negative aspects of regulatory arbitrage in small economies. In the narrow sense, it is a liberal treatment of the origin of investments and the minimum required capital adequacy ratio etc., which can stimulate money laundering or risky operations. But I suppose that, in a broad sense, the notion of regulatory arbitrage can also include positive aspects of competition between countries in the area of the quality of governance. Moreover, since the capital adequacy ratio can be procyclical (Bukovynslyi et al. 2011), a lower level of the ratio in small economies can offset the volatility of economic growth.

In the previous works, an economy's size is measured either by GDP or population size. Therefore, the differences in methodology can partially explain the differences in research findings.

Methodology

I used the World Bank (2019) as the main source of statistical data. Unless otherwise specified, I used the average values for each country in the period 2009–2016. All the countries are classified into three groups according to their GDP in 2015 (the purchasing power parity (PPP) method of currency conversion is used in order to decrease the simultaneous effect of the development level affecting price level), as follows:

- 31 large economies (GDP is higher than the average value of $640 billion);
- 63 medium-sized economies (GDP is lower than the average value and higher than the median value of $70 billion);
- 95 small economies (GDP is lower than the median).

Such a classification is flexible in terms of the selected period of time, because both the average value and the median will change according to further developments in the GDP of countries. Also, the suggested classification fits the assumption about the distribution of data, which is that there are few large economies and many small economies in the world.

In order to estimate the effect of economy size, I used analysis of variance (ANOVA) with an F-test for the difference in means, Levene's test for the difference in variance, Fisher's least significant difference as a post-hoc criterion and normal probability plots for checking the normality of the distribution. The Kruskal–Wallis test and the median test were also used because the data were often not normally distributed. In addition, I calculated correlations between investment indicators and the log of GDP in two periods (2001–2008 and 2009–2016) to identify whether any changes in the effects took place.

The next step was to use a two-way ANOVA to estimate the effect on economic growth (real GDP per capita growth). I considered the main effect of an investment indicator (with grouping of countries according to two ranges divided by the mean value) and the interaction effect (between an investment indicator and the size of economy in their joint influence on economic growth). It allows the determination of the optimal range for an investment indicator for various types of economies and recommendations to be provided for their investment strategies.

Regression analysis was used for robustness checks. Real GDP per capita growth is also a dependent variable in this case. The independent variables include GDP per capita (to control for the effect of the development level), and indicators of international investments and business regulation with a significant effect on economic growth according to the ANOVA results. The ordinary least squares method was used to estimate regression coefficients. There were also additional checks for the absence of a substantial heteroscedasticity, normal distribution of residuals and absence of serial correlation. In small samples robustness was also checked by excluding outliers from a regression model.

Effect on international investments

Small economies are more dependent on FDI inflows (see Table 9-1). As for FDI outflows, non-parametric methods prove that they are less intensive in small economies, but the F-test does not support this conclusion because of outliers. In 2009–2016, the largest economies, the US and China, had outflows (inflows) of FDI equivalent to 2.2% (1.8%) and 1.1% (2.8%) of their GDP.

Again, only non-parametric methods show that there is a net inflow of portfolio investment in small economies (the median is 0.1% GDP) in comparison with medium-sized and large economies (–0.5% and –0.9%). Non-parametric methods also provide evidence that large economies tend to have more portfolio equity investments (median 0.4% GDP), unlike other economies (approximately 0%). Medium-sized and large economies receive more portfolio investments in bonds than small economies. When investments are analysed, including countries such as Luxemburg and Malta considerably affects the results of the ANOVA and therefore non-parametric methods are more reliable.

The greater dependence of small economies on foreign investments can be explained by a 60% lower level of gross domestic savings, which contrasts with the ratio of gross capital formation to GDP similar to other countries. The lower dependence of large economies on inflows of capital and higher outflows may be caused by the lower real interest rates.

Table 9-1. The effect of economy size on international investments in 2009–2016

Indicator	Mean values, types of economies			p-level (F-test/ K–W test/ median test)
	Small	Medium	Large	
Foreign direct investment, net outflows (% of GDP)	0.9	2.6	2.3	0.393/ 0.000/0.000
Foreign direct investment, net inflows (% of GDP)	6.9**	4.5	2.7	0.013/ 0.000/0.000
Portfolio investment, net (% GDP)	−0.1	0.4	−0.9	0.964/ 0.008/0.003
Portfolio equity, net inflows (% GDP)	0.2	1.2	0.6	0.496/ 0.000/0.000
Portfolio investment, bonds, net financial liabilities (% GDP)	0.4*	0.7	0.8	0.070/ 0.000/0.000
Gross capital formation (% of GDP)	25.2	24.2	23.9	0.671/ 0.759/0.606
Gross domestic savings (% of GDP)	10.6***	25.0	25.2	0.000/ 0.000/0.000
Real interest rate (%)	8.2*	6.3	3.6**	0.008/ 0.000/0.000

Note: The underlined p-levels indicate the most relevant tests considering the distribution of data. The means that are significantly different from the other groups are marked according to Fisher's least significant difference test:
*** = $p<0.01$, ** = $p<0.05$, * = $p<0.1$.
Source: Author's calculations based on data of the World Bank (2019).

The correlation analysis to check for robustness shows that several trends exist. In particular, a negative correlation between the real interest rate and the log of GDP appeared in 2009–2016 (−0.19) and virtually did not exist in 2001–2008. A positive correlation with portfolio investments in bonds also takes place only in 2009–2016 (0.25).

Differences in business regulation

The taxation burden does not differ much in countries with various sizes of economy (see Table 9-2). Nevertheless, one non-parametric test showed a marginal significance of the difference in medians (36% of commercial profits in small economies in comparison with 44% in large economies), but there is still too little evidence to prove the effect. There is also not enough evidence to consider that profit tax depends on the size of economy. However, smaller economies do have lower labour taxes.

Table 9-2. Tax regulation and the burden of corruption for business in various types of economies in 2009–2016

Indicator	Mean values, types of economies			p-level (F-test/ K–W test/ median test)
	Small	Medium	Large	
Total tax rate (% of commercial profits)	43.6	41.4	46.0	0.730/ 0.125/0.051
Profit tax (% of commercial profits)	16.5	15.4	17.3	0.657/ 0.500/0.062
Labour tax and contributions (% of commercial profits)	12.6***	19.2	21.8	0.000/ 0.000/0.001
Time to prepare and pay taxes (hours)	237	277	292	0.374/ 0.497/0.545
Tax payments (number)	33***	25**	17**	0.000/ 0.000/0.000
Firms expected to give gifts in meetings with tax officials (% of firms)	12.8	13.7	12.9	0.928/ 0.667/0.564
Bribery incidence (% of firms experiencing at least one bribe payment request)	18.6	18.3	17.0	0.925/ 0.949/0.821
Informal payments to public officials (% of firms)	22.1	22.1	22.0	1.000/ 0.679/0.477

Note: The underlined p-levels indicate the most relevant tests considering the distribution of data. The means that are significantly different from the other groups are marked according to Fisher's least significant difference test:
*** = p<0.01, ** = p<0.05, * = p<0.1.
Source: Author's calculations based on data of the World Bank (2019).

The ANOVA does not confirm the effect of economy size on the time to prepare and pay taxes. But small economies have a more complicated tax system due to the larger number of taxes. The correlation analysis shows that the effect only emerged in 2009–2016, when the correlation was −0.31 in comparison with −0.14 in 2001–2008. The advantages of small economies in terms of freedom from bribery can be traced only by median values, but even non-parametric tests do not show a significant difference.

Table 9-3 shows that the ease of doing business is worse in small economies, while the time spent dealing with the requirements of government regulations is not significantly different from the rest of the world. The relative (but not necessary absolute) cost and time of business start-up procedures are higher in small economies, but the same conclusion is not relevant in the case of the number of business start-up procedures. Small economies lag behind in terms of the time required to register property but not by the number of relevant procedures.

Table 9-3. Business regulation in small, medium-sized and large economies in 2009–2016

Indicator	Mean values, types of economies			p-level (F-test/ K-W test/ median test)
	Small	Medium	Large	
Ease of doing business index in 2017 (1 = most business-friendly regulations)	114***	81*	60*	0.000/ 0.000/0.000
Time spent dealing with the requirements of government regulations (% of senior management time)	9.1	11.0	9.3	0.365/ 0.764/0.867
Cost of business start-up procedures (% of GNI per capita)	50***	24	10	0.000/ 0.000/0.001
Start-up procedures to register a business (number)	7.7	7.8	8.1	0.322/ 0.846/0.955
Time required to start a business (days)	34*	22	20	0.063/ 0.067/0.291
Procedures to register property (number)	5.8	5.9	6.5	0.786/ 0.494/0.398
Time required to register property (days)	68**	45	33	0.010/ 0.006/0.041
Time required to obtain an operating licence (days)	21***	34	40	0.003/ 0.001/0.011

Time required to get electricity (days)	115	98	95	0.253/ 0.193/0.059
Time required to enforce a contract (days)	658	618	626	0.705/ 0.699/0.391
Time to resolve insolvency (years)	2.7	2.6	2.1*	0.042/ 0.029/0.057
Strength of legal rights (of lenders and borrowers) index (0 = weak to 12 = strong)	5.3	4.7	4.9	0.399/ 0.475/0.485
CPIA property rights and rule-based governance rating (1 = low to 6 = high)	2.9	2.8	-	0.866/ 0.756/0.784
CPIA transparency, accountability and corruption in the public sector rating (1 = low to 6 = high)	3.0	2.7	-	0.254/ 0.254/0.132
Bank capital to assets ratio (%)	12***	9.2	8.6	0.000/ 0.000/0.000

Note: The underlined p-levels indicate the most relevant tests considering the distribution of data. The means that are significantly different from the other groups are marked according to Fisher's least significant difference test:
*** = p<0.01, ** = p<0.05, * = p<0.1.
Source: Author's calculations based on data of the World Bank (2019).

There is no significant difference in the time required to get electricity, to enforce a contract, the strength of legal rights of lenders and borrowers, CPIA (Country policy and institutional assessment) indices of property rights and rule-based governance, and transparency, accountability and corruption in the public sector. Small economies have advantages in the time required to obtain an operating licence (this effect strengthened over time: the correlation in 2009–2016 was 0.33 compared with 0.21 in 2001–2008). Large economies are more attractive in terms of the time necessary to resolve insolvency (this effect only emerged recently: the correlation in 2009–2016 was −0.16 compared with −0.07 in 2001–2008). The actual bank capital to assets ratio turned out to be even higher in small economies (this effect strengthened over time: the correlation in 2009–2016 was −0.48 compared with −0.38 in 2001–2008).

All these findings prove that in reality most small economies in the 21st century do not posess an advantage of regulatory arbitrage. A more detailed view suggests that small economies are more attractive for investments due to lower labour taxes and less time required to obtain an operating licence. However, large economies outpace them in terms of the time to register property, and procedures to register business start-ups and to resolve insolvency.

Policy implications

Most of the analysed indicators do not have a proven optimal range of values in order to maximise economic growth, or at least the differences are not statistically significant (inflows of FDI, portfolio investments in bonds, real interest rate, tax rates, and corruption incidence; simplicity of registering business start-ups, obtaining electricity, enforcing contracts, and resolving insolvency; legal rights of borrowers and lenders, transparency in the public sector, and bank capital to assets ratio). But I have found several main and interaction effects in 2009–2016 according to the ANOVA results.

In all types of countries with FDI outflows lower than 1.7% GDP, the average annual GDP (per capita) growth rate was, on average, 1.6% (median 1.6%), while countries with more intensive outflows had on average GDP growth of 0.1% (0.5%). There is a marginal significance of the negative effect of inflows of portfolio investments in large economies: if the inflows were up to 1% GDP, the GDP growth was 2.1% (1.6%), otherwise the growth was 0.3% (0.3%).

Gross capital formation affects economic growth positively (at least in developing countries). Countries with such an indicator greater than 24.6% GDP had economic growth, on average, of 2.1% (2.0%). And if the gross capital formation was lower, the GDP growth was only 1.1% (1.0%). There is a marginal significance of the positive effect of gross domestic savings. Medium-sized developing economies with a ratio to GDP higher than 18.5% had, on average, economic growth of 3.3% (3.3%), otherwise it was 1.0% (1.7%).

In medium-sized economies with the time needed to prepare and pay taxes greater than 259 hours, the mean economic growth was 2.3% (2.2%), and if the time was shorter, the growth was 1.1% (1.0%). Medium-sized economies with a number of taxes greater than 28 had average economic growth of 2.6% (3.1%), otherwise it was 0.9% (1.0%). In large economies, a similar effect is marginally significant, i.e. under such conditions, a simplified tax system could be a disadvantage.

In medium-sized economies, if the time spent dealing with the requirements of government regulations is lower than 9.8% of senior management time, the economic growth is 2.6% (2.8%), otherwise it is

1.7% (1.5%). A similar marginally significant effect exists in large economies (at least in developing economies). There is also a marginally significant negative effect of the number of business start-up registering procedures in small developing economies. If the number is less than 7.8 procedures, the annual GDP growth rate is 2.1% (2.0%), and if the number is higher, the growth rate is 1.0% (1.2%). In large economies with the time required to register a business greater than 27.7 days, the GDP growth rate is 3.0% (2.9%), and if the time is shorter, the growth rate is only 1.0% (0.8%). However, this finding contradicts the theoretical assumption. Moreover, additional grouping of countries shows that in fact there is the effect of development level, which could distort the results in this case. A positive effect of decreasing the number of procedures to register property is not proved by the differences in median GDP growth rates.

In large economies (at least in developing economies) with the time to obtain an operating licence being less than 28 days, the GDP growth rate is 3.7% (1.1%), otherwise it is 2.8% (0.5%). In medium-sized developing economies with the CPIA property rights and rule-based governance index higher than 2.9, the GDP growth rate is 4.2% (4.6%), and if the index is lower, the growth rate is 2.4% (3.1%), but the difference is only marginally significant.

Table 9-4 summarises the recommendations for countries in the area of international investments and business regulation, according to the results of the ANOVA test.

I have also developed several regression models with the following general formula:

$$GDPgr = b_0 + b_1 GDPpc + b_2 Inv$$

where: GDPgr is the average annual GDP per capita growth rate in 2009–2016; GDPpc is the GDP per capita in thousand dollars; and Inv is an indicator of international investments or business regulation.

The regression analysis results partially proved the results of the ANOVA testing (see Table 9-5). The robustness check has failed to support the evidence in favour of the negative impact of FDI outflows and foreign portfolio equity investments, and the positive effect of the tax system complexity, property rights and rule-based governance. This can be partially explained by the correlation of the indicators with the development level, and a small number of cases or asymmetric influence of global business cycles in the analysed period of time.

Table 9-4. Optimal ranges for investment and business regulation indicators

Indicator	Small economies	Medium-sized economies	Large economies
Foreign direct investment, net outflows (% of GDP) – FDO	<1.7 (0.2)	<1.7 (0.2)	<1.7 (0.6)
Portfolio equity, net inflows (% GDP) – PEI			<1.0 (0.2)
Gross capital formation (% of GDP) – GCF	>24.6 (29.6)	>24.6 (28.0)	>24.6 (31.7)
Gross domestic savings (% of GDP) – GDS		>18.5 (25.9)	
Time to prepare and pay taxes (hours) – TPPT		>259 (317)	
Tax payments (number) – TPN		>28 (42)	>28 (44)
Time spent dealing with the requirements of government regulations (% of senior management time) – TRR		<9.8 (5.1)	<9.8 (3.5)
Start-up procedures to register a business (number) – SRB	<7.8 (6.0)		
Time required to obtain an operating licence (days) – TOL			<28 (14.3)
CPIA property rights and rule-based governance rating (1 = low to 6 = high) – PRG		>2.9 (3.4)	

Note: The table shows the lower (>) or upper (<) bound for the optimal ranges for indicators that provide faster economic growth. The medians within the optimal ranges are in brackets. Empty cells mean that no significant effect on economic growth has been found.
Source: Author's calculations based on data of the World Bank (2019).

Table 9-5. Regression models for the effects of investment and business regulation indicators on economic growth

Variable	Coefficients				
Type of economy	All	Medium	Large	Small	Large
b_0 (Intercept)	−0.335 (0.552)	0.993 (0.601)	1.287** (0.469)	3.617*** (0.658)	3.669*** (0.642)
b_1 (GDPpc)	−0.030*** (0.009)	−0.054*** (0.015)		−0.053*** (0.019)	
b_2 (Inv = GCF)	0.0967*** (0.020)				
b_2 (Inv = GDS)		0.0680*** (0.023)			
b_2 (Inv = 1/TRR)			5.367*** (1.189)		
b_2 (Inv = SRB)				−0.236*** (0.078)	
b_2 (Inv = TOL)					−0.0248** (0.011)
R^2	0.19***	0.22***	0.59***	0.15***	0.27**
F-stat	18.09	8.19	20.36	7.79	5.13
N	159	60	16	88	16

Note: Standard errors are in brackets. F- and t-tests for statistical significance: *** = $p<0.01$, ** = $p<0.05$, * = $p<0.1$.
Source: Author's calculations based on data of the World Bank (2019).

The modelling provided proof of the positive effects of gross capital formation in all types of economies and of gross domestic savings in medium-sized economies; e.g. increasing the gross capital formation by 10% of GDP results in an additional 1% of economic growth. This positive effect is stronger in medium-sized and large economies (1.5%) than in small economies (0.6%). The negative effect of time spent dealing with the requirements of government regulations was confirmed only in the case of large economies and the relationship is non-linear. Large economies should also try to decrease the time it takes to obtain an operating licence. Small economies can accelerate economic growth by making procedures to register business start-ups easier.

By comparing the actual and optimal values of the indicators in tables 9-1 to 9-5, it can be presumed that most medium-sized economies already benefit from a sufficient ratio of gross domestic savings to GDP and large economies are often weakened by the time that is required to obtain an operating licence.

The case of Ukraine

The size of the economy is one of the most important factors of Ukraine's participation in the international movement of capital. The International Monetary Fund (2018) has provided data about the GDP of 182 countries. The share of Ukraine in the total GDP of these countries was 0.34%. Meanwhile, the average share in the total GDP in this sample was 0.55%, the median was 0.066% and the upper quartile was 0.36% – this shows that Ukraine is a medium-sized economy. I extrapolated the above-mentioned research results by comparing the data for Ukraine with the average values for small, medium-sized and large economies in order to assess the peculiarities of international investments and business regulation in Ukraine. Data of the World Bank (2019) was used. My findings can be applied during elaboration and implementation of the foreign economic strategy of Ukraine.

In 2018, FDI outflows from Ukraine were 0.09% GDP, the value was typical to small economies. The FDI inflows (1.9% GDP) were also very small, even compared to typical large economies. The data about the net portfolio and portfolio equity investments are less informative due to the high volatility and controversial relationship to the size of economy. The net portfolio investments in bonds were −1.5% GDP.

In 2018, the gross capital formation was 18.9% GDP, which was below the mean of all 182 countries. The gross domestic savings were even lower (10.2% GDP), which was a typical value for small economies. Both of these indicators are below the estimated optimal level for maximisation of economic growth (>24.6% and >18.5%, respectively). The real interest rate was low (3.1%), which was lower than the mean even in large economies. But this indicator was quite volatile (1.8% in 2016, −4.7% in 2017 and 2.9% on average in 2009–2016).

In recent years, the attractiveness of Ukraine for foreign investments was negatively affected by the existing economic dynamics, while at the same time being positively affected by the low value of assets. Also, despite Ukraine having a wide range of industries, its economy is not large enough to provide efficiency for some of the industries. This is also related to the limited investment options due to other criteria (riskiness, payback period, shadow economy, etc.), i.e. the economy does not possess all types of assets in order to satisfy the needs of some types of investors (those who prefer specific industries, long-term investments, or to avoid risks or corruption). High volatility of production in Ukraine also makes it similar to small economies and curbs foreign investment.

The Ukrainian market is too small for some industries, although opening up foreign markets for Ukrainian products under free trade agreements can provide some compensation for this. Foreign companies would be unlikely to enter the market in the form of FDI for the production of equipment and other capital goods, since domestic demand for equipment in Ukraine is limited. But in the case of the consumer goods, the many millions of potential buyers in Ukraine are a stimulus to establishing manufacturing in the country instead of exporting to it.

As for the risks of political influence, the economy in Ukraine is too large to allow domination by one foreign corporation, but it is still small enough to be vulnerable to domination by several large investors from a large economy. Instead, the existence of large national capital in Ukraine restrains the risk of excessive dependence on foreign investors. In fact, the opposite effect is more possible – the presence of foreign capital can limit domination by the large national capital, which ensures competition.

According to the calculations based on the data of the International Monetary Fund (2018), economic growth in Ukraine correlates with trends in large economies such as the EU and Russia. But it is possible to also motivate investors from countries with a business cycle that is less synchronised with Ukraine (e.g. Greece, Egypt, India, Ireland, New Zealand, Oman, etc.) by offering them opportunities for investment portfolio diversification.

Therefore, Ukraine lacks investments (both national and foreign) and especially domestic savings to ensure fast economic growth. The low level of gross domestic savings can be partially explained by the low real interest rate. Restoring sufficient capital formation is important for Ukraine, but it is not that important whether it is provided by foreign or national investors.

In 2018, the main taxes were equivalent to 41.7% of commercial profit (i.e. the value was typical for medium-sized economies). Although Ukraine previously suffered from the problem of negative tax arbitrage, nowadays it is actually settled and there are only structural disproportions. The profit tax is 11%, which is lower than the average value in all 182 countries. The labour tax and contributions are 29.6% (although previously they were equal to 43% for a long period of time), which is higher even in comparison with large economies.

The time to prepare and pay taxes was 328 hours, which is above the mean in all 182 countries, but in this respect there has been major progress since 2007 (2085 hours). The number of tax payments (according to the

World Bank's statistical methodology) was 5, which is a very low value (a substantial reduction took place in 2012–2014 in comparison with 135 in 2011). However, it should be noted that simplification of the taxation system does not provide a statistically significant effect on economic growth (see Table 9-4). The latest comparable data about bribery (in 2013) is too obsolete for analysis.

In 2018, Ukraine ranked 71th in terms of the index for ease of doing business, which is a relatively good position for a medium-sized economy. The cost of business start-up procedures was 0.6% of GNI per capita, which is lower than the lower quartile even in large economies (1.7%). The number of procedures to register a business start-up was 6, which is equivalent to the lower quartile in all 182 countries. Also, the time taken up by these procedures was very low (6.5 days), i.e. lower than the lower quartile in large economies (7.6%). Therefore, the ease of registering start-ups is already similar to the level in the leading large economies.

The number of procedures required to register property in Ukraine is equal to the upper quartile in all 182 countries (7). But the time needed for these procedures is 17 days, which is lower than the median in medium-sized economies (29 days) and even in large economies (20 days). There has been major progress since 2007 (117 days) in terms of this criterion.

The time required to get electricity was relatively long (281 days) in comparison with even the upper quartile in all 182 countries (132 days). The time required to enforce a contract was 378 days, which was lower than the lower quartile in all 182 countries (446 days). The time necessary to resolve insolvency (2.9 years) was close to the means in small and medium-sized economies. The strength of legal rights of lenders and borrowers was scored as 8 points, which is better than the upper quartile in all 182 countries (7 points). In 2017, the bank capital to assets ratio was 11.9%, which was higher than in typical medium-sized economies and was close to the mean in small economies.

Thus, Ukraine has overcome the problem of negative tax arbitrage, but traditionally it has faced the problem of corruption. Ukraine has considerably improved its business regulation in the recent years. It is quite easy to register business start-ups and property, and to obtain an operating licence. There is still a problem of lengthy delays when trying to connect to the electricity networks.

As for further improvements, the economy of Ukraine is too large to efficiently use tax and regulatory arbitrage. It is not enough to slightly decrease taxes in order to attract capital from large economies – in many cases, it does not offset the effect of the smaller home market. Moreover, under a high level of corruption, formally cutting taxes can just lead to an increase in the corruption payments to officials. Thus, the total tax and corruption burden may even remain constant. It is also not easy to decrease taxes under the substantial accumulated public debt and the risk of political instability in the case of a radical cutting of social benefits.

Liberal treatment for the origin of money is restrained by international obligations, a small per capita effect (under the large population), and the need to fight corruption and decrease the share of the shadow economy, of which the latter are two of the most important problems. Meanwhile, public services are often poor quality, which means that reforms should be continued and this is the main option to consider. It is also still possible to compete with small economies that benefit from tax and regulatory arbitrage – for example, in the case of the production of goods for mass consumption, where the home market effect already allows the arbitrage to be offset, or in the case of geographically oriented industries (some sellable natural resources or, subject to the improvement of the geopolitical situation, international transit through the territory of Ukraine).

Conclusions

Small economies often face a trade balance deficit and lack domestic savings, and therefore they are more dependent on the inflows of FDI. Larger economies are likely to export more capital (which is stimulated by the lower real interest rate as a result of overaccumulation of capital under the better competitiveness and trade surpluses) and are more involved in portfolio investments (because of better developed and more liquid financial markets). Small economies have to pay a higher price for attracting capital under conditions of higher risks and insufficient savings.

Some small economies have tried to offset the disadvantages of economies of scale through lower taxes and liberal business regulation. But nowadays, these advantages largely disappear as a result of reforms in larger economies, and fighting tax evasion and money laundering. Nevertheless, small economies usually have lower labour taxes and grant operating licences faster. Conversely, large economies outpace smaller economies in terms of the speed of registering business start-ups and property, and resolving insolvency.

A high level of capital formation is preferable in all types of economies. Small economies are recommended to simplify business start-up procedures. It is preferable for medium-sized economies to have a higher level of domestic savings. It is suggested that large economies should simplify business regulation. At the same time, I have found no significant advantages for economic growth in the analysed period of post-crisis recovery (2009–2016) in terms of the preference for foreign investments over national investments, influencing real interest rates, cutting taxes and simplifying their payment, elimination of corruption, and several other indicators of business regulation. Nevertheless, some of the criteria (e.g. freedom from bribery) are an element of freedom and should be protected regardless of the findings.

Ukraine is a medium-sized economy in terms of GDP, which affects its foreign economic relations. Gross domestic savings in Ukraine are below the optimal level under low real interest rates and the existing risks. Inflows of capital are limited by the relatively small size of the domestic market, volatility of production and other factors. Nevertheless, the medium-size of its economy allows Ukraine to be an attractive proposition to enterprises for the production of mass consumption goods and in geographically oriented industries (natural resources, international transit).

By many criteria, Ukraine experienced a substantial improvement of the regulatory component of its investment climate. It has simple procedures for business start-ups and registering property, like in large economies, and offers only a short delay when issuing an operating licence, like in small economies. Still, it lags behind in terms of speed of access to the electricity supply and the workload for management to conform to the requirements of government regulations. Considering the size of its population and public debt, it is not easy for Ukraine to apply tax arbitrage, especially if a tax cut is offset by corruption payments. Therefore, the main efforts should be made in the areas of improving the quality of public services and procedures in business regulation, especially considering ongoing reforms in other countries.

References

AmirKhalkhali, S. and A. Dar. 2009. "Capital Mobility, Intertemporal Budget Constraint, Government Policy and Country Size." Accessed 16 March 2015. http://ecomod.net/sites/default/files/document-conference/ecomod2009/878.pdf.

Anklesaria Aiyar, S.S. 2008. "Small States: Not Handicapped and Under-Aided, but Advantaged and Over-Aided." *Cato Journal* 28, 3: 449-478.

Baldwin, R. and T. Okubo. 2012. "International Trade, Offshoring and Heterogeneous Firms." Discussion Paper DP2012-014. Tokyo, Kyoto: KEIO / Kyoto Joint Global Center of Excellence.

Brainard, S.L. 1997. "An Empirical Assessment of the Proximity-Concentration Trade-off between Multinational Sales and Trade." *The American Economic Review* 87, 4: 520-544.

Bukovynslyi, S.A., T.Y. Unkovska and O.L. Yaremenko. 2011. "The Lessons of the Global Economic Crisis: Methodological Problems of Reforming the International Standards of Banking Regulation and Oversight." *Economic Theory* 1: 79-89. (Ukr.)

Codrington, H. 1989. "Country Size and Taxation in Developing Countries." *The Journal of Development Studies* 25, 4: 508-520.

Commonwealth Secretariat, World Bank, Joint Task Force on Small States. 2000. *Small States: Meeting Challenges in the Global Economy*. London, Washington, D. C.

Demas, W.G. 1965. *The Economics of Development in Small Countries: With Special Reference to the Caribbean*. Montreal: McGill University Press.

Docquier, F. and M. Schiff. 2009. "Measuring Skilled Migration Rates. The Case of Small States." Policy Research Working Paper 4827. Washington DC: The World Bank, Development Research Group, Trade Team.

Easterly, W. and A. Kraay. 1999. "Small States, Small Problems? Income, Growth, and Volatility in Small States. World Bank." Accessed 20 April 2016.
http://siteresources.worldbank.org/DEC/Resources/SmallStatesSmallProblems.pdf.

Eldridge, D.S., H.H. Ryoo and A. Wieneke. 2012. "Bank Capital Regulation with Asymmetric Countries." Working Paper 8. Melbourne: La Trobe University, School of Economics.

Fung, K.C., I. Korhonen, K. Li and F. Ng. 2008. "China and Central and Eastern European Countries: Regional Networks, Global Supply Chain, or International Competitors?" Policy Research Working Paper 4689. Washington D. C.: The World Bank, Development Research Group, Trade Team.

Gnutzmann, H., K. McCarthy and B. Unger. 2008. "Dancing with the Devil: A Study of Country Size and the Incentive to Tolerate Money Laundering." Discussion Paper 08-18. Utrecht: Tjalling C. Koopmans Research Institute, Utrecht School of Economics, Utrecht University.

Gonzales, A.P. 2001. *Trade and Integration Dialogue: Trade Liberalization and Small Economies*. Washington D. C.: Inter-American Development Bank.

Gur, T. H., L. Erden and I. Ozkan. 2011. "An Empirical Investigation on the Determinants of the Saving-Investment Interaction." *Panoeconomicus* 3: 343-353.

Hassan, T.A. 2009. "Country Size, Currency Unions, and International Asset Returns." Working Paper 154. Wien: Oesterreichische Nationalbank.

Haufler, A. and I. Wooton. 1997. "Country Size and Tax Competition for Foreign Direct Investment." Accessed 24 April 2016. http://www.gla.-ac.uk/media/media_219038_en.pdf.

Herzog, R.W. 2010. "Explaining the Saving-Investment Relationship with Threshold Effects." Paper 32087. Munich Personal RePEc Archive. Accessed 16 March 2015. https://mpra.ub.uni-muenchen.de/32087/1/MPRA_paper_32087.pdf.

Hummels, D. 2006. "The Role of Geography and Size." Occasional Paper No. 35. Buenos Aires: American Development Bank, Integration and Regional Programs Department, Institute for the Integration of Latin America and the Caribbean IDB-INTAL, Integration Trade, and Hemispheric Issues Department.

Ishise, H. 2011. "The World Has More Than Two Countries: Implications of Multi-Country International Real Business Cycle Models." IMES Discussion Paper 2011-E-11. Tokyo: Institute for Monetary and Economic Studies, Bank of Japan.

International Monetary Fund. 2018. "World Economic Outlook Databases." Accessed 16 January 2018. https://www.imf.org/en/Publications/SPROLLS/world-economic-outlook-databases.

Jiránková, M. 2009. "The Opportunities for a Small Economy in Globalization [Příležitosti malé ekonomiky v globalizaci]." *Acta Oeconomica Pragensia* 3: 25-43.

Laurent, É. 2008. "Economic Consequences of the Size of Nations, 50 Years on." Document de Travail 2008-26. Paris: Observatoire Français des Conjonctures Économiques.

Martin, P. and H. Rey. 2000. *Financial Super-Markets: Size Matters for Asset Trade*. London: Centre for Economic Performance, London School of Economics and Political Science.

Milner, C. and T. Westaway. 1993. "Country Size and the Medium-Term Growth Process: Some Cross-Country Evidence." *World Development* 21, 2: 203-211.

Mozhovyi, O. and N. Stukalo. 2009. "Integrative Index Method for Estimation of Financial Globalization Level of Countries of the World." *International Economic Policy* 1-2: 5-32. (Ukr.)

Nyamtseren, L. 2004. "Challenges and Opportunities of Small Countries for Integration into the Global Economy, as a Case of Mongolia." Dresden discussion paper in economics 13/04. Dresden: Dresden University of Technology.
Okubo, T., P. Picard and J.-F. Thisse. 2013. "On the Impact of Competition on Trade and Firm Location." CREA Discussion Paper 2014-05. Luxemburg: Center for Research in Economic Analysis, University of Luxembourg.
Özmen, E. 2004. "Current Account Deficits, Macroeconomic Policy Stance and Governance: An Empirical Investigation." ERC Working Paper in Economics 04/14. Ankara: Economic Research Center, Middle East Technical University.
Pieretti, P. and S. Zanaj. 2009. "On Tax Competition, Public Goods Provision and Jurisdictions' Size." Discussion paper No. 2009/12. Louvain-la-Neuve: CORE.
Pieretti, P., S. Zanaj and B. Zou. 2010. "The Long Run Survival of Small Nations: A Dynamic View." Working paper 437. Bielefeld: Bielefeld University.
Ricci, L.A. 1998. "Uncertainty, Flexible Exchange Rates, and Agglomeration." Working paper WP/98/9. Washington D. C.: International Monetary Fund.
Ricka, F. 2012. "The Right-Wing Power of Small Countries." Working paper 153. London: European Bank for Reconstruction and Development.
World Bank. 2008. "The Growth Report – Highlights on Small States." Accessed 25 August 2015. http://siteresources.worldbank.org/EXTPREMNET/Resources/489960-1338997241035/Growth_Commission_Final_Report_Regional_Highlights_Small_States.pdf.
World Bank. 2019. "World Development Indicators." Accessed 28 June 2019. http://data.worldbank.org/data-catalog/world-development-indicators.
Wan, H. Jr. 2005. "Chinese Trade Expansion and Development and Growth in Today's World." Paper presented at DEGIT X Conference, Mexico City, June 2005. Accessed 9 July 2015. http://degit.sam.sdu.dk/papers/degit_10/C010_004.pdf.

CHAPTER TEN

PRODUCTIVE EFFICIENCY AND ECONOMIC GROWTH IN THE COUNTRIES OF CENTRAL AND EASTERN EUROPE

YURIY I. BILENKO

Introduction

More than 30 years of experience in the economic development in a market economy of post-socialist countries allows us to conduct research on the models of productive efficiency and the economic growth along with their correspondence with classical exogenous and new endogenous theories of economic growth, to determine the dominant factors of the trajectory of development of countries in different institutional environments.

The command and administration system in Central and Eastern Europe has led to a decrease in the efficiency of centralised economic management. Overloading of central management bodies to solve current problems, the need to eliminate individual imbalances, a constant shortage of different types of resources, distortion of economic information – all these objectively limited the ability to formulate and implement effective structural policies. The socialist economy was unable to meet the ordinary needs of the average consumer. The absence of a market regulator led to a large number of non-selling products being produced; at the same time, there was an acute shortage of many types of other products. Industry became increasingly material and energy intensive. The return on investment in fixed assets was falling, labour productivity was declining and the rate of growth of national income was falling.

Gradually, in the 1980s, the crisis of the economic system of socialism became more acute and apparent not only to economists. Major macroeconomic indicators began to decline rapidly, causing all countries in the communist camp to face the objective need to radically change the entire economic system. It was necessary to carry out deep economic reforms that would bring changes in the system of the economy, organisation of production and management of the economy, which would affect monetary, credit, social and environmental spheres. These reforms had to change the relationships between different forms of ownership, between state regulation and market self-regulation, and between liberalisation and protectionism.

Correspondingly, in the early 1990s, transformational processes were initiated in the countries of Central and Eastern Europe and the former Soviet republics, which were intended to change the socio-economic environment. In fact, it was necessary to make the transition from a centrally planned economy to a market economy. As a result of these changes, the so-called camp of socialist countries disappeared and a group of countries with economies in transition emerged. This group of countries includes states that are in the process of reforming their political and socio-economic structures, and transforming their previously administrative-command economic systems into a market economy. These include countries of the so-called second world; that is, the totality of post-socialist states of Central and Eastern Europe and the former Soviet republics.

Mostly radical methods of reforming the economy were chosen by Poland (the "Balcerowicz Plan" of 1989), to a lesser extent by the Czech Republic (the "Klaus Plan" of 1990) and in part by Estonia. However, most countries in Central and Eastern Europe, such as Hungary (the "Kupy Plan" of 1990), Romania (the "Summary of the Strategy for the Transition to a Market Economy of 1990") and the entire CIS region, have favoured the evolutionary nature of market transformations (Campos and Coricelli 2002).

The transformation of transition economies is, first and foremost, a transition from an old system embodied with a totalitarian society and a socialist primary economy to a new system – a pluralistic democracy and a capitalist market economy.

According to the definition of the well-known German economist Hans-Jürgen Wagener (1999), transformation is a certain type of institutional change that differs from the categories of evolution, reform and revolution. Accordingly, the transformation process involves the replacement of the old political, economic and social system with the new system.

Any transformation can only happen when there is the will, collective action and cooperation of society. The cohesion of these actions and, accordingly, the success of the transformation depends on the fairness of the distribution of wealth in the state.

Transformation is concerned mainly with systemic changes that relate to the basic economic paradigm. The transition from socialist planning to capitalist competition is a change in the integral paradigm. The main elements of such a transformation are price liberalisation, foreign sector liberalisation, macroeconomic stabilisation, financial sector reform and enterprise restructuring. These elements make it possible to create an economic order that is consistent with the capitalist market economy.

John Williamson (1997) summarised the main steps of the Washington Consensus that provide the transition from stabilisation to economic growth. The most important of these are:

- fiscal discipline and the absence of inflationary taxes, with significant budget deficits;
- government spending is channelled into high-income industries, not politically oriented ones;
- tax reform by broadening the tax base;
- financial liberalisation through market setting of interest rates;
- unified exchange rates;
- liberalisation of foreign trade through reduction of customs tariffs;
- facilitating the access of foreign firms to markets;
- state-owned enterprises should be privatised;
- deregulation of public administration by prohibiting any restrictions on the access of new firms to the market and the process of their competition;
- all regulatory actions should focus on compliance with security,
- environmental protection and legal control of the functioning of financial institutions;
- ensuring the protection of property rights.

A number of authors have criticised this approach as being limited and effective only in the short term, and incapable of leading to sustainable economic growth (Schadler et al. 2006). If the process of formal institutionalisation is neglected or spontaneous, informal institutionalisation is possible and the proceeds flow into the shadow economy.

The two basic mechanisms of transition, according to O. Blanchard (1997), are reallocation and restructuring. The first means the reallocation of capital and labour to the production of goods of higher quality. With regard to state-owned firms, the capital intensity was high and there was considerable hoarding of inputs, including labour.

The main instrument for achieving better reallocation of resources is changing the form of the ownership (Aghion et al. 1994), privatisation of the state-owned firms, and corporatisation of large enterprises to make a more efficient incentive structure.

Successful restructuring should result in higher levels of technology and management skills, and optimal combination of inputs for higher productivity.

My study aims to measure the efficiency of the economic performance of countries in Central and Eastern Europe during a period of economic reforms and transition to a market economy, and to explain which factors play an important role in their performance either increasing or decreasing.

Methodology

Estimation of the level of efficiency of different countries was mainly performed by non-parametric methods (Färe et al. 1994; Kumar and Russell 2002; Jerzmanowski 2007) and parametric stochastic frontier analysis (SFA), especially for CEE (Central and Eastern Europe) countries (Deliktas and Balcilar 2005).

For estimation of the technical efficiency of a country, I have used the parametric technique of stochastic frontier production function, first proposed by Aigner et al. (1977), Schmidt and Lovell (1979), and Meeusen and van den Broeck (1977), as follows:

$$Y_i = f(x_i;\beta) + \varepsilon_i, i = 1,\ldots,N, \quad (1)$$

where Y_i is the maximum output obtainable from x_i, a vector of (non-stochastic) inputs, β is an unknown parameter vector to be estimated, and ε_i is an error term, which comprises two components:

$$\varepsilon_i = v_i + u_i,\ i = 1,\ldots,N \quad (2)$$

where the error component v_i represents the symmetric disturbance as N(0, σ_v^2), the error component u_i is assumed to be distributed independently of v_i and to satisfy $u_i \leq 0$, which represents technical inefficiency of the production unit and is independently half-normally N(0; σ_u^2) distributed.

SFA is not sensitive to outliers and the measurement problems of inputs and output. Along with the fact that standard errors can be obtained and hypotheses tested, these are the main advantages of SFA over non-parametric frontier methods. Moreover, SFA also provides a framework to analyse the sources of production inefficiency or variations of productivity levels, which can give important insights into how to reduce the inefficiency (Kumbhakar et al. 2017).

The maximum likelihood estimation of this stochastic frontier model is programmed within the statistical program STATA. The technical efficiency of the *i*th country in time *t* is:

$$TE_{it} = \exp\left(-u_{it}\right) \tag{3}$$

To specify the functional form for empirical estimation of frontier models, the Cobb–Douglas function (Efficiency1) has been chosen, which better fits the data and provides a statistically significant effect of explainable variables instead of a translog or quadratic log production function, which I also tested. Therefore, the estimation model is specified as follows:

$$Ln\mathrm{Y}_{it} = \alpha_0 + \alpha_1 Ln\mathrm{K}_{it} + \alpha_2 LnL_{it} + v_{it} - u_{it} \tag{4}$$

where Y is the value added, K is the capital stock, L is the number of employees and u_{it} is the technical inefficiency.

In world economic thought since the 1960s, in connection with the latest scientific and technological revolution, the construction of the information society led to the introduction of a new category of "human capital", based on the theory of human capital founded by T. Schultz (1961) and G. Becker (1964) who examined the impacts of investment in education, health, professional knowledge and people's motivation (their human capital) on income. The basic unit of measurement in the theory of human capital is the flow of wages during life, which can be regarded as dividends on the funds invested by people. This makes it possible to economically analyse the intellectual component of the production process using discounting methods.

The evolution of human capital is an alternative explanation for technological progress and, accordingly, economic growth. Individuals acquire human capital through general and special education, work experience, and the like. Its accumulation is extremely similar to the accumulation of physical capital.

The models of R. Lucas (1988; 1990) are related to the external effects of the use of human capital, and show that the overall productivity of workers, even those who have not received a sufficient formal education, increases as the overall skill level increases. Concentration and localisation of a particular professional branch in a certain territory, or the formation of a particular professional cluster, enhances productivity through the ability to exchange professional ideas experience, both explicitly and implicitly. Endogenous growth will be observed if the external additional effects are significant enough to offset the declining profitability of the factors of production and also because the motivation to invest in human capital will not decline if the human capital stock increases (Romer 1986). Therefore, human capital will accumulate without any restrictions. However, citizens will invest in human capital less than the socially optimal level because they do not take into account the additional benefits that society can derive from such investments. The Lucas model (1990) predicts that the well-being of society will increase if there are mechanisms to encourage workers to improve their education and professional skills. Therefore, it is proposed to analyse the efficiency of a country (Efficiency2) using a new model with human capital:

$$Lngdpemp_{it} = \alpha_0 + \alpha_1 Lnkempl_{it} + \alpha_2 Lnhcinc_{it} + v_{it} - u_{it} \quad (5)$$

where u_{it} is the technical inefficiency, *gdpemp* is GDP per employee, *kempl* is capital per employee, and *hcinc* is human capital per employee; all variables are in natural logs.

Data analysis and results

For the analysis, I selected a group of 15 countries of Central and Eastern Europe that have joined the European Union: Bulgaria, Romania, Poland, Hungary, Czech Republic, Slovakia, Slovenia, Estonia, Lithuania and Latvia, as well as post-Soviet European countries: Ukraine, Belarus, Russia and Moldova and Albania. For efficiency estimation, the most productive countries in the world, USA and Germany, were also included. Research was performed for the period 1991–2013 (390 observations).

Physical capital was calculated based on the PIM (perpetual inventory method) method, with a level of depreciation of capital of 5%, and for the period from 1990 until 2013 in USD PPP (purchasing power parity) at constant 2005 prices. The quantity of capital for 1990 was estimated according to a ratio of capital to GDP equal to 3. Efficiency1 was estimated according to model (4) and Efficiency2 was estimated according to model (5).

Human capital, *hinc*, was estimated according to the income method, where the function φ(E) reflects the efficiency of a unit of labour with E years of schooling, as follows:

$$hinc = e^{\varphi(E)} \qquad (6)$$

relative to a unit of labour with no schooling (φ (0) = 0). The derivative φ'(E) is the return from schooling estimated in a Mincerian wage regression, where an additional year of schooling raises a worker's efficiency. The average number of years of schooling of an employed person were taken from the Barro-Lee (2014) database of educational attainment. Returns on investment were from Psacharopoulos (1994): the first four years of education produce a rate of return of 13.4%, the next four years produce a rate of 10.1% and for education beyond the eighth year the rate is 6.8%.

Table 10-1. Stochastic production frontier estimation results (Efficiency1)

Stochastic, frontier normal/half-normal model	Coefficient	Std. err.	z	P>|z|
Lgdptotal (dependent variable)				
Lkapital	1.060	0.027	38.740	0.000
Llabour	−0.092	0.032	−2.930	0.003
Cons	−0.236	0.186	−1.270	0.205
$\ln \sigma_v^2$	−3.784	0.375	−10.100	0.000
$\ln \sigma_u^2$	−2.030	0.239	−8.500	0.000
σ_v	0.151	0.028		
σ_u	0.362	0.043		
σ_s^2	0.154	0.024		
λ	2.404	0.069		

Log likelihood = −25,77149 Likelihood-ratio test of sigma_u = 0: chibar2(01) = 11,93 Prob >chi2 = 0.0000 Wald chi2(2) = 16488.33 Number of obs = 390	

Source: Author's calculations

The output from frontier modelling includes estimates of the standard deviations of the two error components, σ_v and σ_u, which in the log likelihood are parameterised as as Lnσ_v^2 and Lnσ_u^2. The estimate of the total error variance is $\sigma_u^2 + \sigma_v^2 = \sigma_S^2$ and the estimate of the ratio of the standard deviation of the inefficiency component to the standard deviation of the idiosyncratic component, $\lambda = \sigma_u/\sigma_v$, is labelled lambda. At the bottom of the output of stochastic frontier I report the results of a test that there is no technical inefficiency component in the model. This is a test of the null hypothesis H_0 : σ_u^2 =0 against the alternative hypotheses H_1 : σ_u^2>0.

If the null hypothesis is true, the stochastic frontier model reduces to an OLS (ordinary least squares) model with normal errors. In Table 10-1, the output shows LR (Likelihood ratio test) = 11.93 with a p-value of 0.00 for the half-normal model and the large value of λ=2.404 means that the inefficiency function is significant in explaining the economic performance of the country in our case; hence, the model is well specified and statistically significant.

Table 10-2. Stochastic production frontier estimation results (Efficiency2)

Stochastic, frontier normal/half-normal model	Coefficient	Std. err.	z	P>|z|
lgdpempl (dependent variable)				
Lkl	0.953	0.031	31.090	0.000
Lhkinc	0.720	0.174	4.140	0.000
Cons	−1.140	0.317	−3.590	0.000
$\ln \sigma_v^2$	−3.867	0.353	−10.960	0.000
$\ln \sigma_u^2$	−1.992	0.209	−9.520	0.000
σ_v	0.145	0.026		
σ_u	0.369	0.039		
σ_s^2	0.157	0.023		
λ	2.554	0.062		
Log likelihood = −24.46 Likelihood-ratio test of sigma_u = 0: chibar2(01) = 13.87 Prob >chi2 = 0.0000 Wald chi2(2) = 1501.28 Number of obs = 390				

Source: Author's calculations

The estimation of model (5), including human capital, is presented in Table 10-2. Here, the output shows LR = 13.87 with a p-value of 0.00 for the half-normal model and the large value of λ=2.554 means that the inefficiency function is significant in explaining the economic performance of the country in our case; hence, the model is well specified and statistically significant. Coefficients behind physical capital per worker and human capital are statistically significant at 1%.

Results of the estimation of average efficiency using models (4) and (5) are presented in Table 10-3.

Table 10-3. Efficiency and economic growth in CEE

Countries	Variables		
	Average annual growth (1990–2013), %	Efficiency1	Efficiency2
Albania	4.84	0.834	0.837
Belarus	4.80	0.719	0.691
Bulgaria	2.64	0.834	0.852
Czech Republic	1.91	0.696	0.688
Estonia	3.93	0.918	0.918
Hungary	1.42	0.757	0.776
Latvia	3.95	0.579	0.615
Lithuania	2.62	0.709	0.751
Moldova	−1.29	0.638	0.625
Poland	5.59	0.887	0.892
Romania	1.98	0.798	0.783
Russian Federation	0.98	0.735	0.682
Slovak Republic	2.95	0.689	0.688
Slovenia	1.98	0.870	0.889
Ukraine	−0.82	0.590	0.541
USA	3.56	0.879	0.838
Germany	1.55	0.868	0.878

Source: Author's calculations

This study finds that the level of difference of efficiency between CEE countries and USA and Germany in both models – (4) and (5) – is not very large.

In this sample, there are several very efficient countries ("stars"): Estonia (efficiency level of 91%), Poland (89%) and Slovenia (88%). These countries are more efficient than USA and Germany. Estonia (annual rate of growth of 3,9%) and Poland (5,5%) have highest levels of economic growth.

Some countries are outliers with relatively low levels of economic efficiency. Among them are Ukraine (59%), Moldova (63%) and Latvia

(61%), the first two of which have negative rates of growth (−0,8% and −1,2%, respectively).

A preliminary analysis of capital per worker, which may be the main cause of the above situation, indicates that it has doubled in the new EU member states of Poland, Slovakia and the Baltic states. In the post-Soviet European countries, growth of the capital per worker does not exceed 20–30% and, given the significant fall in employment in these countries, the total amount of capital in the economy has only changed very slightly.

The dynamic analysis of efficiency behaviour during the period of 1991–2013 (see figures 10-1 and 10-2) shows that there are two periods of declining efficiency: the first half of the 1990s and after the world financial crisis in 2008. Efficiency increased significantly from 1994 to 2007, except in post-Soviet republics which demonstrated efficiency growth only from 2002 until the 2008 crisis.

Volatility of the efficiency level measured by the coefficient of variation (sd/mean) differs more than the mean of efficiency. The highest level of volatility was in Ukraine (0,207), and the lowest levels were in Estonia (0,027), Poland (0,029) and Germany (0,017). High levels of volatility were also found in Latvia (0,179), Moldova (0,172), Russia (0,160) and Belarus (0,125). These estimations were performed for Efficiency1. The main trend that can be observed from this analysis is that a lower level of average efficiency led to a higher level of volatility.

The coefficient of correlation between efficiency and economic growth on an annual basis is 0,25–0,27 with the highest level of probability. If averages of efficiency and the rate of growth for the whole period are used, the coefficient of correlation increases to 0,55 (level of probability = 95%). So, efficiency is a very important factor of long-term and sustainable growth; in the short-term, the influence is less.

The next step in this analysis is to consider the main structural, macroeconomic and institutional factors that determine the economic efficiency of a country.

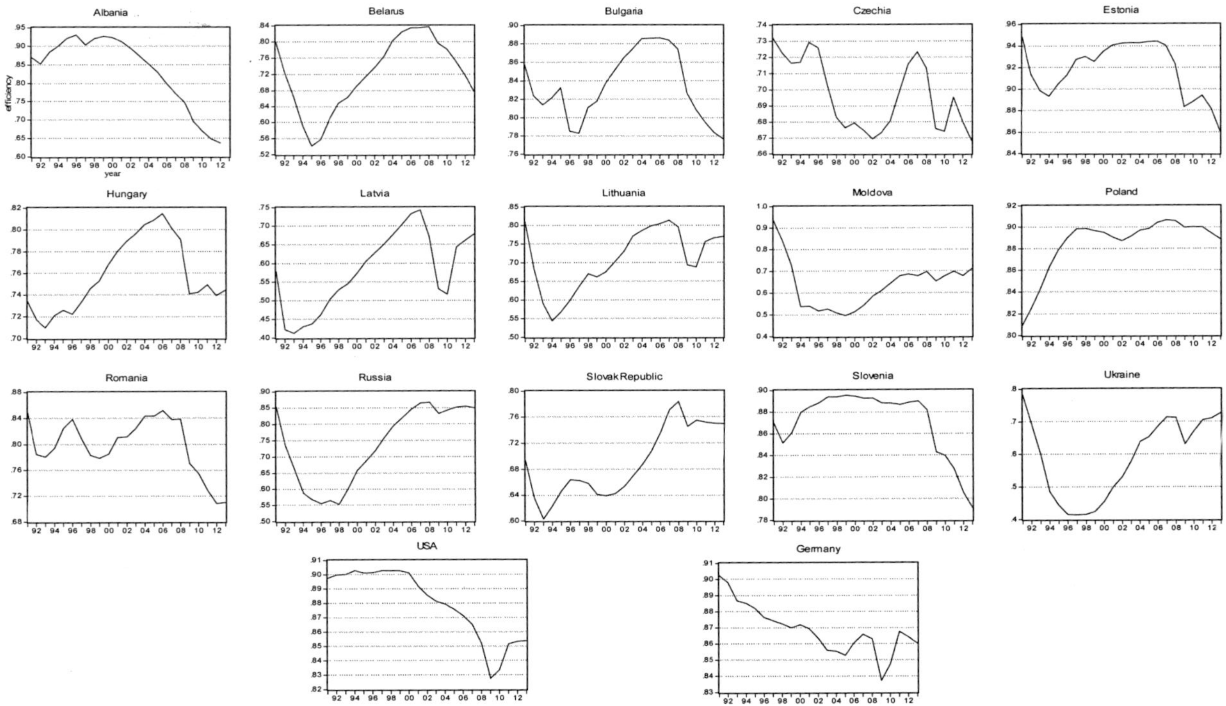

Figure 10-1. Efficiency1 in CEE countries, USA and Germany, estimated by Cobb–Douglas model

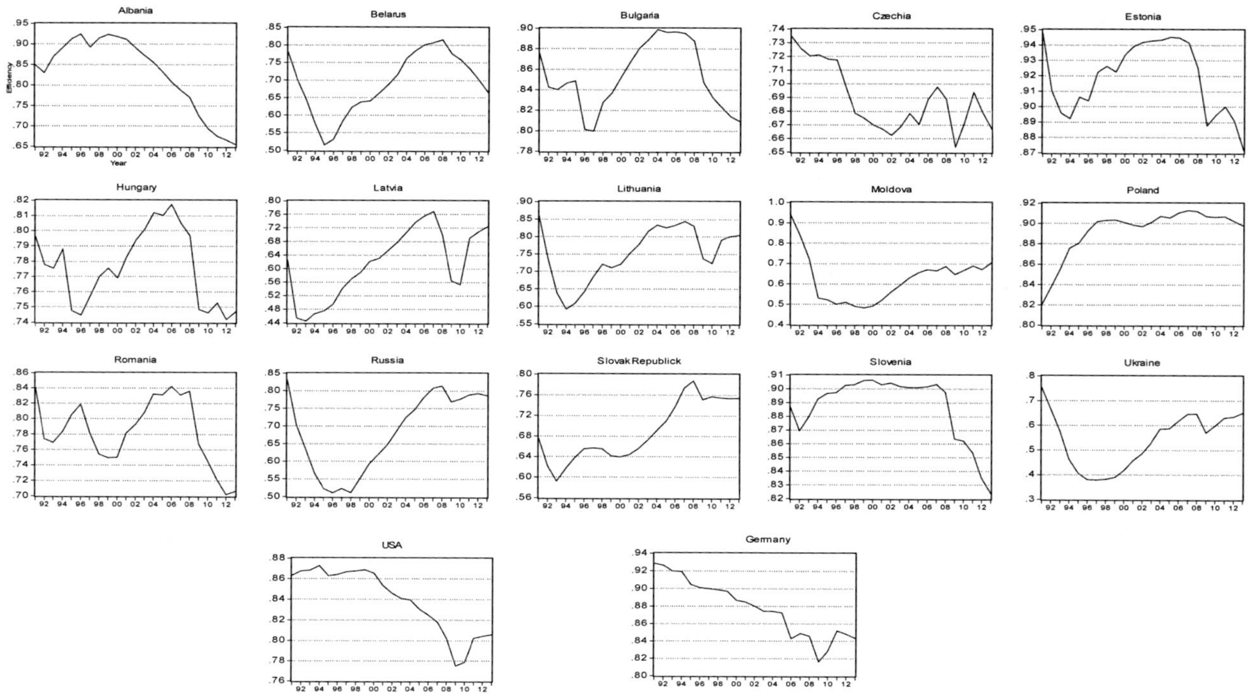

Figure 10-2. Efficiency2 in CEE countries, USA and Germany, estimated by R. Lucas model

A very large set of economic and social indicators were used, as well as some institutional indicators (more than 100 variables), mainly from the World Bank (2019b) WDI database. Structural and macroeconomic variables with the highest level of correlation (probability greater than 99%) were chosen.

The list includes the following structural and macroeconomic indicators:

- domestic credit to the private sector (% of GDP);
- percentage of workers employed in industry, %;
- share of workers employed in services, %;
- energy use in oil equivalent per $1,000 of GDP (at constant 2011 PPP prices);
- central government debt, total (% of GDP);
- export value index (2000 = 100);
- share of food exports in total exports;
- growth rates of consumption expenditures, %;
- FDI inflow (in % to GDP);
- FDI stock (in % to GDP);
- GDP growth rate, %;
- GDP per capita growth rate, %;
- GDP per capita in US dollars (at constant 2011 PPP prices);
- capital investment growth rate, %;
- share of capital investment (% to GDP);
- general government final consumption expenditure (annual % growth);
- total capital of economy (annual % growth);
- interest rate on loans, %;
- life expectancy (in years);
- consumer price inflation, %;
- value-added growth in industry, %;
- share of value-added services, %;
- market capitalisation of listed companies (% of GDP);
- manufacturing, value added (% of GDP);
- manufacturing, value added (annual % growth);
- PPP ratio to market rate (PPP conversion factor);
- share of broad money to GDP, %;
- broad money growth, %;
- interest rate spread (difference between deposit and loan interest rates);

- wages per month (USD).

The main results were presented in Table 10-4 for Efficiency1 and Efficiency2. The strongest relationship with efficiency shows annual growth of the total capital of the economy (0, 51) and energy use (kg of oil equivalent) per $1,000 GDP (constant 2011 PPP) (−0, 57). To summarise, the most positive influences on efficiency are the following indicators:

- GDP per capita, PPP (constant 2011 international $);
- PPP ratio to market rate (PPP conversion factor);
- share broad money to GDP, %;
- wages per month (USD);
- GDP growth (annual %);
- FDI stock (% to GDP);
- gross capital formation (annual % growth);
- manufacturing, value added (annual % growth);
- market capitalisation of listed companies (% of GDP).

Conversely, the indicators that had the most negative influence are:

- general government final consumption expenditure (annual % growth);
- inflation;
- consumer prices (annual %);
- central government debt, total (% of GDP);
- interest rate spread (lending rate minus deposit rate, %).

Analysis of the list of positive factors allows the conclusion to be drawn that annual growth of capital, growth of fixed capital, foreign capital, money capital and domestic credits – or, simply, investment in the economy – are the main factors for increasing the efficiency of an economy.

Table 10-4. Structural and macroeconomic indicators and level of efficiency

Variables	Coefficient of correlation with Efficiency2	Coefficient of correlation with Efficiency1
GDP growth (annual %)	0.246	0.268
GDP per capita, PPP (constant 2011 international $)	0.380	0.364
GDP per unit of energy use (PPP $ per kg of oil equivalent)	0.374	0.364
Employment in industry (% of total employment)	0.200	0.181
Energy use (kg of oil equivalent) per $1,000 GDP (constant 2011 PPP)	−0.577	−0.495
FDI stock (% to GDP)	0.267	0.182
Foreign direct investment, net inflows (% of GDP)	0.182	0.166
Food exports (% of merchandise exports)	−0.351	−0.399
Domestic credit to private sector (% of GDP)	0.265	0.231
Final consumption expenditure, etc. (annual % growth)	0.147	0.189
General government final consumption expenditure (annual % growth)	−0.206	−0.236
Gross capital formation (annual % growth)	0.242	0.254

Inflation, consumer prices (annual %)	−0.163	−0.151
Industry, value added (annual % growth)	0.216	0.232
Market capitalisation of listed companies (% of GDP)	0.217	0.321
Manufacturing, value added (% of GDP)	−0.211	−0.183
Manufacturing, value added (annual % growth)	0.244	0.259
PPP conversion factor (GDP) to market exchange rate ratio	0.356	0.304
Broad money (% of GDP)	0.338	0.302
Interest rate spread (lending rate minus deposit rate, %)	−0.196	−0.187
Central government debt, total (% of GDP)	−0.241	−0.275
Wages per month (USD)	0.343	0.302

Source: Author's calculations

In fact, the idea of capital accumulation was dominant in ensuring successful economic development and the transition to higher levels of economic well-being in the twentieth century, and remains relevant in the modern era, especially for post-socialist countries in Europe and Asia. The accumulation of capital, which implies the launch of technological progress, and technological changes that are incorporated into machinery and equipment, and accompanied by an intensification of the learning process, have yielded positive results in Germany and Japan. To this can be added the stimulation of export of manufactured goods, which contributed to the high economic growth in the countries of South-east Asia.

This paradigm in the late 1980s and early 1990s was complemented by a policy of facilitating market forces, strengthening market institutions, improving the allocation of resources, reducing the transaction costs of doing business, generating quality human capital to deepen technological capabilities, and structural change.

Today's fastest growing economies in the world, India and China which have been growing for over 20 years, maintain an investment rate of 40–50% of GDP. In the fast-growing East Asian economies, the share of investment in GDP reaches 30% and above. This suggests that high and increasing rates of capital accumulation are still just as important as 30 or 50 years ago. Such processes help to increase production capacity, allow industry to realise economies of scale, diversify production, and promote the construction of infrastructure and the development of urbanisation, which stimulates the efficiency of the economy (Yusuf 2009).

Economic science has not yet revealed the mystery of which economic policy instruments are suitable to stimulate investment (Yusuf 2009). Ordinary fiscal and financial instruments, as well as the exchange rate, have a very limited impact on resource mobilisation, especially investment, according to Easterly (2005).

Ineffective macroeconomic policy can last much longer than expected because it generates large incomes, dividends and privileges for small influential groups, and losses are scattered in relatively small quantities per capita, but the well-known economist A. Dixit (1996) concludes that if institutional reforms and free-market institutions do not stimulate the mobilisation of resources and economic growth, the state can take the lead in mobilising and increasing investment. Although government-owned investments and direct lending to government-owned or -controlled financial institutions can be risky and a waste of financial resources, in China, Malaysia and Singapore, the lion's share of government investment has been successful enough. In South Korea, direct loans from state or quasi-state banks have mainly financed the industrialisation process. The expected difficulty of influencing investment by market incentives through interest rates leads to the need to take into account the institutional environment in which the economic processes take place, that is, to speak of a visible hand of government that would determine profitable investments in new industries, that is, to ensure balanced economic growth, investment flows are emphasised by D. Rodrik (2004).

Investments are weak or not productive due to the fact that market and non-market institutions that stimulate entrepreneurship, as well as effectively place private investments, are missing or slowly evolving. Financial systems remain weak, and extremely scarce resources are mobilised and invested in the most profitable sectors of the economy. Market signals are missing or distorted. Investor risks exceed the acceptable level. Low levels of income on capital and high risks contribute to capital flight. If the state has low solvency of the population, low production efficiency, low national income, no savings of the population and no accumulation of profits of enterprises, there will accordingly be no investment process or formation of capital. Capital is a precondition for crisis-free economic development.

If you create certain institutional conditions (honest, responsible, do not organise criminal schemes while conducting business), which means reducing taxes, and having a fair, professional and high-paying bureaucratic apparatus that fully performs public (and not private criminal) functions, in addition to the conditions to create social, transport and industrial infrastructure, then investments will go to industry and physical capital will start to make a profit. It is a mechanism of success, where the cost of creating high-quality institutions is greater than simply the material costs. Honesty is much more expensive than money, which may be partially absent.

I assessed the influence of certain institutional variables on the levels of efficiency in countries of Central and Eastern Europe. The list of institutional variables includes: dummy variables: European Union membership (Membership in EU), post-Soviet states (Ukraine, Belarus, Russia, Moldova) (Post-Soviet European states), WTO membership (Membership in WTO); and capital account openness (kaopen) measured according to the methodology of Chinn and Ito (2008) (Capital mobility(kaopen)); also I included indices of structural reforms of European Bank of Reconstruction and Development EBRD (EBRD 2014): large privatisation index (Large-scale privatisation), small privatisation index (Small-scale privatisation), governance reform and restructuring index (Governance and enterprise restructuring), reform in trade and monetary system index (Trade & Forex system).

The most complete list of elements of the institutional environment is provided by the World Bank (Kaufman, Kraay and Mastruzzi 2010), which forms the basis of worldwide governance indicators. This list also refers to the traditions and institutions by which the government in a country uses its power – in particular, the processes of selecting, monitoring and replacing the government – and effectively formulates and implements the right policies. In addition, the list describes the traditions that define the respect of the people and the state for the institutions that govern economic and social interactions among them.

The first group of indicators includes political freedom and political stability; the second includes the efficiency and quality of government regulatory activity; and the third includes the rule of law (which evaluates the quality of human rights, property and the quality of justice), law enforcement, and control of corruption, covering evaluation of how the state power is used for private gain. Estimations of governance performance range from approximately −2.5 (weak) to 2.5 (strong).

Table 10-5. Institutional indicators and level of efficiency

Variables	Coefficient of correlation with Efficiency2	Coefficient of correlation with Efficiency1
Membership in EU	0.270	0.140
Membership in WTO	0.357	0.283
Post-Soviet European states	−0.524	−0.381
Capital mobility (kaopen)	0.272	0.181
Large-scale privatisation	0.163	0.115
Small-scale privatisation	0.164	0.131
Governance and enterprise restructuring	0.314	0.242
Trade & Forex system	0.281	0.213
Control of Corruption: Estimate	0.514	0.397
Government Effectiveness: Estimate	0.389	0.261
Regulatory Quality: Estimate	0.377	0.233
Rule of Law: Estimate	0.381	0.245
Life expectancy at birth, total (years)	0.494	0.421

Source: Author's calculations based on data of the World Bank (2019a).

Efficiency is more sensitive to institutional variables, especially the indicator of Efficiency2 which includes human capital. Control of corruption, government effectiveness, rule of law and regulatory quality have more powerful influences on efficiency than structural reform indices, which describe the transition to a market economy. EU membership positively relates to efficiency level (see Table 10-5).

Life expectancy and other welfare indicators (GDP per capita, PPP at constant 2011 international $) explain a high level of economy efficiency.

My results confirm Parente and Prescott's (2000; 2005) theory of country-specific TFP, which they refer to as a *theory of relative efficiency* based on policy differences. More specifically, they show how various policies that constrain choices of technology and work practices at the level of the production unit determine the aggregate efficiency at which a country uses its resources in production These policies and practices take the form of regulations and bribes for factor providers (i.e. suppliers of capital, labour, etc) whose services are eliminated or diminished as they move to more productive technology. In some cases, the policy is in the form of a law that specifically prohibits the use of certain technology.

Conclusions

The economic results of political transformation based on shock therapy are greater in the countries of Central and Eastern Europe that joined the European Union when the post-Soviet states opted for gradualism. This gradualism came to an end with partial reforms, formation of financial oligarchies, significant uneven distribution of income and dissatisfaction of people with the results of economic reform.

Joseph Stiglitz (1999) points out that the poor performance of economic reforms in some transition economies is associated with an underestimation of the importance of social, organisational and information capital, and the consideration of political obstacles to the formation of new business; also, voucher privatisation creates weakness in corporate governance.

Stiglitz (1999) also notes that the transition from a planned administrative system to a market one has more to do with institutional transformation than with day-to-day economic management. Social transformation involves collective action that can take place within or outside government at the national and local levels. Centrality certainly plays a significant role but it is more effective when the institutional environment is evolving, including experimentation at the local level.

Expansion of production and its efficiency in connection with accession to the European Union, which is conditioned by the expansion of the market and access to the external demand generated in all countries of the integrated association, will accelerate the process of capital accumulation and stimulate investment-oriented economic growth. Although, it should be noted here that the effect of the law of diminishing returns on capital may, over time when reaching a stable position, reduce the rate of return on capital. Such a reduction may be halted by the economies of scale that can be successfully obtained within the common market.

The financial crisis of 1998 led to retrograde changes in the political economy of the post-Soviet state countries, the revival of authoritarianism and dictatorship, and a shift from a liberal economy model to an oligarchic clan administrative economic model while maintaining monetary and fiscal policies of the neoclassical type.

This has happened to the post-Soviet countries through the introduction of partial institutional reforms and the maintenance of policies of soft budget constraints. The result of such processes was a significant level of budget deficit, as well as the collapse of the financial and banking system with a major devaluation of the national currency.

In my view, the delays in the process of restructuring large enterprises, streamlining their management and introducing an effective incentive system have resulted in constant waste of public resources, very low efficiency and a constant depression of the economy.

For a better understanding of the differences in efficiency levels between economies of Central and Eastern Europe, I have used a very wide set of economic and institutional variables. The control of corruption, government effectiveness and EU membership coupled with growth of capital sourcing by FDI flow, fixed capital investment, and foreign and domestic credits explain the level of efficiency of post-socialist countries.

References

Aghion, P., O. Blanchard and R. Burgess. 1994. "The Behavior of State Firms in Eastern Europe Pre-Privatization." *European Economic Review* 38: 132-49.

Aigner, D., C. Lovell and P. Schmidt. 1977. "Formulation and estimation of stochastic frontier production function models." *Journal of Econometrics* 6: 21-37.

Barro, R.J. and J-W. Lee. 2000. "International Data on Educational Attainment: Updates and Implications." NBER Working Papers 7911, Cambridge, MA: NBER.

Barro-Lee. Data Set. 2014, http://www.barrolee.com.

Becker, G. 1964. *Human Capital: A Theoretical and Empirical Analysis, with Special Reference to Education.* New York: National Bureau of Economic Research.

Blanchard, O. 1997. *The Economics of Post-Communist Transition.* Oxford: Clarendon Press.

Campos, N. and F. Coricelli. 2002. "Growth in Transition: What We Know, What We Don't, and What We Should." *Journal of Economic Literature* 40, 3: 793-836.

Chinn, M.D. and H. Ito. 2008. "A New Measure of Financial Openness." *Journal of Comparative Policy Analysis* 10, 3: 309-322. http://web.pdx.edu/~ito/Chinn-Ito_website.htm.

Deliktas, E. and M. Balcilar. 2005. "A Comparative Analysis of Productivity Growth, Catch-Up, and Convergence in Transition

Economies." *Emerging Markets Finance and Trade* 41, 1: 6-28.
Dixit, A. 1996. *The Making of Economic Policy*. Cambridge, MA: MIT Press.
Easterly, W. 2005. "National Policies and Economic Growth: A Reappraisal." In: *Handbook of Economic Growth*, edited by P. Aghion and S.N. Durlauf, 1015-1059. Amsterdam: Elsevier.
EBRD. 2014. *Transition Report 2014*. London: EBRD
Färe, R., S. Grosskopf, M. Norris and Z. Zhang. 1994. "Productivity Growth, Technical Progress, and Efficiency Change in Industrialized Countries." *American Economic Review*, vol. 84: 66-83.
Jerzmanowski, M. 2007. "Total Factor productivity differences: Appropriate technology vs. efficiency." *European Economic Review* 51, 8: 2080-2110.
Kaufmann, D., A. Kraay and M. Mastruzzi. 2010. "The Worldwide Governance Indicators: Methodology and Analytical Issues Governance," Draft Policy Research Working Paper. Washington, DC: World Bank.
Kumar, S. and R. Russell. 2002. "Technological Change, Technological Catch-up, and Capital Deepening: Relative Contributions to Growth and Convergence." *American Economic Review* 92. 3: 527-548.
Kumbhakar, S., C. Parmeter and V. Zelenyuk. 2017. "Stochastic Frontier Analysis: Foundations and Advantages." Working Papers, 2017-10. University of Miami, Department of Economics.
Meeusen, W. and J. van den Broeck. 1977. "Efficiency estimation from Cobb-Douglas Production functions with composed error." *International Economic Review* 18: 435-444.
Lucas, R. 1988. "On the Mechanics of Economic Development." *Journal of Monetary Economics*, 22: 3-42.
Lucas, R. 1990. "Why Doesn't Capital Flow from Rich to Poor Countries?" *American Economic Review, Papers and Proceedings*. 80: 92-96.
Parente, S.L. and E.C. Prescott. 2000. *Barriers to Riches*. Cambridge, MA. MIT Press.
Parente, S.L. and E.C. Prescott. 2005. "A Unified Theory of the Evolution of International Income Levels." In: *Handbook of Economic Growth*, edited by P. Aghion and S.N. Durlauf, 1371-1416. Amsterdam: Elsevier.
Psacharopoulos, G. 1994. "Returns to Investment in Education: A Global Update." *World Development* 22, 9: 1325-1340.
Rodrik, D. 2004. "Industrial Policy for the Twenty-First Century." CEPR Discussion Paper 4767. London: Centre for Economic Policy Research.

Romer, P. 1986. "Increasing Returns and Long-Run Growth." *Journal of Political Economy*, 94: 1002-1038.

Schadler, S., A. Mody, A. Abiad and D. Leigh. 2006. *Growth in the Central and Eastern European countries of the European Union*. Washington, D.C.: International Monetary Fund.

Schmidt, P. and C.A. Lovell. 1979. "Estimating Technical and Allocative Inefficiency Relative to Stochastic Production and Cost Frontiers." *Journal of Econometrics* 9: 343-366.

Schultz, T. 1961. "Investment in Human Capital". *American Economic Review*, vol. 51.1: 1-17.

Stiglitz, J. 1999. *Whither Reform? Ten years of transition*. Washington: World Bank.

Wagener H.-J. 1999. "Social Security – A Second Phase Transformation Phenomenon." In: *Transformation of Social Security: Pensions in Central-Eastern Europe.* Heidelberg: Physica-Verlag.

Williamson J. 1997. "The Washington Consensus Revisited." In: *Economic and Social Development in XXI Century.* Washington: Inter-American Development Bank.

World Bank. 2019a. "The Worldwide Governance Indicators." Accessed 20 September 2019. http://www.govindicators.org.

World Bank. 2019b. "World Development Indicators." Accessed 8 September 2019.
http://data.worldbank.org/data-catalog/world-development-indicators.

Yusuf, S. 2009. *Development economics through the decades: a critical look at thirty years of the world development report.* Washington: The World Bank.

SELECTED BIBLIOGRAPHY

Acemoglu, D. and J.A. Robinson. 2013. *Why Nations Fail: The Origins of Power, Prosperity, and Poverty*. New York: Crown Business.

Ackoff, R.L. and F. Emery. 2005. *On Purposeful Systems. An Interdisciplinary Analysis of Individual and Social Behavior as a System of Purposeful Events.* New Brunswick: Aldine Transaction.

Agrell, P.J. and J. Wikner. 1996. "A coherent methodology for productivity analysis employing integrated partial efficiency." *International Journal of Production Economics* 46-47: 401-411.

Aigner, D., C. Lovell and P. Schmidt. 1977. "Formulation and estimation of stochastic frontier production function models." *Journal of Econometrics* 6: 21-37.

Albert, M. 1993. *Capitalism Vs. Capitalism*. New York: Four Wall Eight Windows.

Amable, B. 2000. "Institutional Complementarity and Diversity of Social Systems of Innovation and Production." *Review of International Political Economy* 7, no. 4, April: 645-687.

Amable, B. 2003 *The Diversity of Modern Capitalism*. Oxford: Oxford Press.

Amable, B. 2016. "Institutional complementarities in the dynamic comparative analysis of capitalism." *Journal of Institutional Economics* 12, no. 1: 79-103.

Arrow, K. J. 1972. Gifts and Exchanges. *Philosophy and Public Affairs,* vol. 1, no. 4, pp. 343-362.

Bachtler, J. et al. 2019. "Towards cohesion policy 4.0. Structural transformation and inclusive growth." *Regional studies policy impact books* 1, 1: 17-28.

Badiou, A. 2003. *Manifesto of Philosophy.* Saint Petersburg: Machina.

Barath, L. and I. Ferto. 2016. "Productivity and Convergence in European Agriculture." *Discussion papers MT-DT*26: 3-34.

Baudrillard, J. 1981. *For a Critique of the Political Economy of the Sign.* St. Louis: Telos Press.

Blommaert, T., S, Van den Broek and E. Kolthof. 2017. *Management in Singularity: From Linear to Exponential Management*. Kindle Edition.

Breque, M., De Nul, L. and Petridis, A. 2021. "Industry 5.0. Towards a sustainable, human-centric and resilient European industry." Policy brief January 2021. Directorate-General for Research and Innovation.

Carr, N. 2005. *Does IT Matter? Information Technology and the Corrosion of Competitive Advantage.* Moscow: Secret Firmy.

Castels, M. et al. 2017. *Another economy is possible. Culture and economy in a time of crisis.* Malden: Polity.

Campbell, C.D., R.G. Campbell and E.G. Dolan. 1988. *Money, banking, and monetary policy.* Chicago: Dryden Press.

Chandler, D. 2007. *Semiotics: The Basics.* New York: Routledge.

Chub, O.O. 2009. *Banks in the Global Economy: Monograph.* Kyiv: KNEU. (Ukr.)

Colemann, J. 1990. *Foundations of Social Theory.* Cambridge: Mass, Harvard University Press.

Collin, C. and K. Tarron. 2018. "Geography, Economic Structures and Institutions: A Synthesis." Working Papers in Technology Governance and Economic Dynamics no. 80. Oslo/Tallin; Other Canon Foundation / Tallinn University of Technology. 47 p.

Crouch, C. and W. Streeck. 1997. *Political Economy of Modern Capitalism: Mapping Convergence and Diversity*. London: Sage.

Deliktas, E. and M. Balcilar. 2005. "A Comparative Analysis of Productivity Growth, Catch-Up, and Convergence in Transition Economies". *Emerging Markets Finance and Trade* 41, 1: 6-28.

Derrida, J. 1997. *Of Grammatology.* Baltimore: The Johns Hopkins University Press.

Dieppe, A. (ed.) 2020. *Global Productivity. Trends, Drivers, and Policies.* Washington DC: World Bank.

Dixit, A. 1996. *The Making of Economic Policy*. Cambridge, MA: MIT Press.

Doellgast, V. and D. Marsden. 2018. "Institutions as constraints and resources: Explaining crossnational divergence in performance management. Human Resource." *Management Journal* 29, no. 2 August: 199-216.

Drexler, K.E. 2013. *Radical Abundance: How a Revolution in Nanotechnology Will Change Civilization*. Perseus: Public Affairs.

Dubrovskyi, D.I. and S.M. Klimova (eds.). 2014. *Global future 2045: Anthropological crisis. Convergent technologies. Transhumanistic projects: Materials of the First All-Russian Conference, Belgorod, April 11-12, 2013*. Moscow: Kanon+ Regional Society of Disabled People "Rehabilitation".

Easterly, W. 2005. "National Policies and Economic Growth: A Reappraisal." In: *Handbook of Economic Growth*, edited by P. Aghion and S.N. Durlauf, 1015-1059. Amsterdam: Elsevier.

Faundez, J. 2016. "Douglass North's Theory of Institutions: Lessons for Law and Development," *Hague J Rule Law* 8: 373-419, https://doi.org/10.1007/s40803-016-0028-8.

Filipenko, A. 2019. *International Economics: History, Theory, Policy.* Kyiv: Lybid.

Floridi, L. 2003. *The Blackwell Guide to the Philosophy of Computing and Information.* New Jersey: Wiley-Blackwell.

Fukuyama, F. 1995. *Trust: The Social Virtues and the Creation of Prosperity*. New York: Free Press.

Giddens, A. 2000. *Runaway World: How Globalization Is Reshaping Our Lives*. Routledge.

Greif, A. 2006. *Institutions and the Path to the Modern Economy. Lessons from Medieval Trade*. Cambridge: Cambridge University Press,.

Gumiliev, L.N. 1993. *Ethnic sphere. History of people and history of nature*. Moscow: Express.

Hardin, R. 1993. "The Street–level Epistemology of Trust." *Polities and Society*, vol. 21, no. 4, pp. 505-529.

Hodgson, G. 2003. *Economics and Institutions: A Manifesto for a Modern Institutional Economics*. Moscow: Delo. Huateng, M., M. Zhaoli, Y. Delhi and W. Huali. 2019. *Digital transformation of China. Experience in transforming the infrastructure of the national economy*. Translated from Chinese. M.: Intellectual Literature.

Ilyin, V.V. 2003. *Philosophy of History.* Moscow: Moscow University Publishing House.

Jerzmanowski, M. 2007. "Total Factor productivity differences: Appropriate technology vs. efficiency." *European Economic Review* 51, 8: 2080-2110.

Jorgenson, D.W. (ed.) 2009. *The Economics of Productivity.* Cheltenham: Edward Elgar Publishing Limited.

Kogut, B. 2010. "Qualitative Comparative Analysis of Social Science Data." In: *The Oxford Handbook of Comparative Institutional Analysis*, edited by G. Morgan, J. Campbell, C. Crouch, O. Pedersen and R. Whitley, 139-179. Oxford: Oxford University Press.

Kolot, A., S. Kozmenko, O. Herasymenko and D. Štreimikienė. 2020. "Development of a Decent Work Institute as a Social Quality Imperative: Lessons for Ukraine." *Economics and Sociology*. vol. 13. no. 2.P. 70-85.

Lucas, R.E. Jr. 2013. *Lectures on Economic Growth*. (Rus.)

Luhmann, N. 1979. *Trust and Power*. New York: Wiley.

Lukyanenko, D., V. Chuzhykov and M.G. Wozniak (eds.). 2018. *Convergence of economic models of Poland and Ukraine*. Kyiv: KNEU. (Ukr.)

Marshall, A. 1993. *Principles of Economics*. vol. 1, Moskva: Progress.

Mason, P. 2016. "PostCapitalism: A Guide to Our Future." URL: http://pinguet.free.fr/mason2015.pdf.

Miller, R.L. and D.D. VanHoose. 1993. *Modern Money and Banking*. McGraw-Hill Education (ISE Editions); Internat.2r.e. ed.

Milton, F. 1994. "The Methodology of Positive Economics." *THESIS*, 4:43.

Mishkin, F. 2014. *Economics of Money, Banking and Financial Markets*. Publisher: Pearson; 11th ed.

Moiseev, S. 2021. "Consolidation of banks: pro at contra." Accessed 27 January 2021. https://republic.ru/posts/l/210781. (Rus.)

Moskalenko, O. 2014. *Theory and model of advanced economic development in the system of social strategic needs*. Kyiv: KNEU Publishing House. (Ukr.)

North, D.C. 1990. *Institutions, institutional change, and economic performance*. Cambridge: Cambridge University Press.

Nosova, O. 2016. "Effect of Attracting FDI to Economic Growth of TNCs. Bulletin of the Research Center of Corporate Law." Management and Venture Capital of Syktyvkar State University. No. 4: 13-23.

OECD. 2019. *Productivity Growth in the Digital Age*. Paris: OECD. Accessed 30 October 2020. www.oecd.org/going-digital.

Paskeleva, M. 2020. "Global Uncertainty During COVID 19 Pandemic and Its Effects On EU Member States With A Focus On Bulgaria." *International Conference Knowledge-Based Organization*. vol. XXVI no 2, 71-76. https://doi: 10.2478/kbo-2020-0055.

Podkaminer, L. 2003. "Transition Countries Resist Global Slowdown: Productivity Gains Offset Effects of Appreciation." *WIIW Research Reports*. No. 293, February.

Reinert, E.S. 2020. "Industrial policy: A long-term perspective and overview of theoretical arguments." *UCL Institute for Innovation and Public Purpose: Working Paper*. 04. URL: https://www.ucl.ac.uk/bartlett/public-purpose/sites/public-purpose/files/final_industrial_policy_reinert_16_jun.pdf.

Rodrik, D. 2004. "Industrial Policy for the Twenty-First Century." CEPR Discussion Paper 4767. London: Centre for Economic Policy Research.

Rodrik, D. 2016. *Economics Rules: The Rights and Wrongs of the Dismal Science*. New York. London: W.W. Norton Company. URL: https://www.economicas.uba.ar/wp-content/uploads/2016/03/Economics-Rules-Dani-Rodrik.pdf.

Romer, P. 1986. "Increasing Returns and Long-Run Growth." *Journal of Political Economy* 94: 1002-1038.

Schmidt, V. 2000. "Comparative institutional analysis." In: *Handbook of Comparative Politics,* edited by T. Landman and N. Robinson, 125-143. London: Sage.

Schnitzer, M. 1994. *Comparative Economic System.* Nashville: South-Western Pub. Co.

Schumpeter, J.A. 1995. *Capitalism, Socialism and Democracy*. Translated from English. Kyiv: Basics.

Schwab, K. 2016. *The Fourth Industrial Revolution*. Geneva: World Economic Forum.

Stiglitz, J. 1999. *Whither Reform? Ten years of transition*. Washington: World Bank.

Strick, W. 2019. *Purchased time. Delayed crisis of democratic capitalism. A series of lectures within the framework of the Frankfurt readings in memory of Adorno.* Translation from German I. Zhenin, Ed. M. Dobryakova. Moscow: Pub. House of Higher School of Economics. (Rus.)

Tarscott, D. and A. Tarscott. 2018. *Blockchain revolution. How the Technology behind bitcoin and other cryptocurrencies is changing the World.* New York: Portfolio/Penguin.

Tinbergen, J. 1956. *Economic policies: principles and design*. Amsterdam: North Holland.

Tyrol, J. 2020. *Economy for the common good.* Moscow: Gaidar Institute Publishing House. (Rus.)

Thaler, R.H. 2015. *Misbehaving: The Making of Behavioral Economics*. New York: W.W. Norton.

Theil, H. 1956. "On the theory of economic policy." *American Economic Review* 46: 360-366.

Toffler, A. 1981. *The Third Wave*. London: Pan Books Ltd.

UNCTAD. 2020. World Investment Report: "International Production Beyond the Pandemic." United Nations, New York and Geneva. Accessed June 2020. https://unctad.org/system/files/official-document/wir2020_en.pdf.

Vernadsky, V. 1988. *Works on the History of Science*. Moscow: Science. (Rus.)

Vernadsky, V. 2004. *The Biosphere and the Noosphere*. Moscow: Ajris-press. (Rus.)

Wiener, N. 1961. *Cybernetics: Or Control and Communication in the Animal and the Machine*. Paris: Hermann & Cie, Camb. Mass. (MIT Press).

Wilson, T. 2002. "The Nonsense of 'Knowledge Management'." *Information Research* 8, 1. Accessed 25 August 2020. http://informationr.net/ir/8-1/paper144.html.

Wolff, E.N. 2014. *Productive Convergence. Theory and evidence*. Cambridge: Cambridge University Press.

Yemelin, V.A. 2017. *Identity in the Information Space.* Moscow: Kanon+ Publishing House Regional Society of Disabled People "Rehabilitation".

Zaitsev, Y.K. and O.M. Moskalenko. 2020. *Contemporary political economy as a theoretical foundation for social economic development*: in two books. Book2. *Contemporary political economy as a methodological paradigm of economic development policy in a globalized society*. Kyiv: KNEU. (Ukr.)

Zhang, Y., Z. Cheng and Q. He. 2019. "Time Lag Analysis of FDI Spillover Effect: Evidence from Belt and Road Developing Countries Introducing China's Direct Investment." *International Journal of Emerging Markets*, 1 November.

CONTRIBUTORS

Anton S. Filipenko, Professor, Doctor of Science in Economics, Professor of the Department of the World Economy and International Economic Relations, Institute of International Relations, Taras Shevchenko National University of Kyiv, Ukraine, e-mail: anton_filipenko@ukr.net.

Oleksandra M. Moskalenko, Professor, Doctor of Science in Economics, Professor of the Department of Economic Theory, Kyiv National Economic University named after Vadym Hetman, Ukraine, e-mail: oleksandra.moskalenko@kneu.edu.ua.

Yurii K. Zaitsev, Professor, Doctor of Science in Economics, Professor of the Management and Economics Department, International European University, Ukraine, Kyiv, e-mail: zyk3000@ukr.net.

Anatolii M. Kolot, Professor, Doctor of of Science in Economics, Vice-Rector of Scientific and Pedagogical Work, Professor of the Personnel Management and Labour Economics Department, Kyiv National Economic University named after Vadym Hetman, Ukraine, Kyiv, e-mail: kolot@kneu.edu.ua.

Oksana O. Herasymenko, Associate Professor, PhD in Economics, Associate Professor of the Department of Innovation and Investment Management, Taras Shevchenko National University of Kyiv, Ukraine, Kyiv, e-mail: gerasimenko_o_o@ukr.net.

Igor G. Khanin, Professor, Doctor of Science in Economics, National University of Water Management and Nature Resources Use, Ukraine, Rivne, e-mail: khanin.ig@gmail.com.

Volodymyr V. Lypov, Professor, Doctor of Science in Economics, Leading Researcher at the Institute for Economics and Forecasting, National Academy of Science of Ukraine, Kyiv, Ukraine, e-mail: lypov_vl@ukr.net.

Olga V. Nosova, Doctor of Science in Economics, Professor of the Department of Marketing, Management and Entrepreneurship, V. N. Karazin Kharkiv National University, Ukraine, e-mail: olgano59@gmail.com.

Sergiy A. Tsyganov, Professor, Doctor of Science in Economics, Professor of the Department of International Finance of Institute of International Relations, Taras Shevchenko National University of Kyiv, Ukraine, e-mail: S_Tsyganov@ukr.net.

Nadiia V. Tsyganova, Associate Professor, Doctor of Science in Economics, Professor of the Banking Department, Kyiv National Economic University named after Vadym Hetman, Ukraine, e-mail: N_Tsyganova@ukr.net.

Oleksii A. Chugaiev, Professor, Doctor of Science in Economics, Institute of International Relations, Taras Shevchenko National University of Kyiv, Ukraine, e-mail: alxcv@ukr.net.

Yuriy I. Bilenko, Associate Professor, PhD in Economics, Head of the Department of International Economic Analysis and Finance, Ivan Franko National University of Lviv, Ukraine, e-mail: yuriy.bilenko@lnu.edu.ua.